SOVIET SOCIAL REALITY
IN THE MIRROR OF GLASNOST

Also by Jim Riordan

DEAR COMRADE EDITOR: Letters to the Editor under Perestroika
  (*with Sue Bridger*)
SOVIET EDUCATION: The Gifted and the Handicapped
SOVIET SPORT: Background to the Olympics
THE SOVIET UNION: Land and Peoples
SOVIET YOUTH CULTURE
SPORT IN SOVIET SOCIETY
SPORT, POLITICS AND COMMUNISM
SPORT UNDER COMMUNISM
SEX AND SOVIET SOCIETY (*with Igor Kon*)

Soviet Social Reality in the Mirror of Glasnost

Edited by

Jim Riordan
*Head of the Department of Linguistic and International Studies
and Professor of Russian Studies
University of Surrey*

St. Martin's Press

First published in Great Britain 1992 by
THE MACMILLAN PRESS LTD
Houndmills, Basingstoke, Hampshire RG21 2XS
and London
Companies and representatives
throughout the world

A catalogue record for this book is available
from the British Library.

ISBN 0–333–56966–0

Printed in Great Britain by
Billing and Sons Ltd
Worcester

First published in the United States of America 1992 by
Scholarly and Reference Division,
ST. MARTIN'S PRESS, INC.,
175 Fifth Avenue,
New York, N.Y. 10010

ISBN 0–312–07901–X

Library of Congress Cataloging-in-Publication Data
Soviet social reality in the mirror of glasnost / edited by Jim
Riordan.
p.   cm.
Includes index.
ISBN 0–312–07901–X
1. Soviet Union—Social conditions—1970–   2. Glasnost.   3. Soviet
Union—Social policy.   4. Soviet Union—Economic conditions—1985–
I. Riordan, James, 1936–
HN523.5.S6655   1992
306'.0947—dc20   91–44871
                                                              CIP

To the memory of Andrei Dmitrievich Sakharov,
who cared, fought and died

Contents

Preface

Glasnost means telling the truth. Since Mikhail Gorbachov launched his glasnost policy in late 1986, a year after perestroika, a whole torrent of truths has poured forth. They have illuminated Soviet reality as never before, shining light into the darkest corners, confirming the assurances of some and appalling others caught in the duplicity of their own past – how was it they (we) did not see the truth even when it was staring them (us) in the face?

It is not an easy question to answer, especially in the absence of genuine sociological studies and data. So inaccessible was Soviet society to objective study and so seductive the ideology to some that many scholars were persuaded to accept the ideal for the actual. This lack of objectivity was reinforced by the vilification of detractors and the repression of institutions like political parties, independent youth groups and research centres which might have presented an alternative picture.

Glasnost is now enabling scholars from East and West to work together, to pool their knowledge and experience, to use the same methodology, to share a common academic curiosity to discover the truth. The major aim of this book is to bring together scholars from the Soviet Union, United States and United Kingdom so that together they may shed light on social issues against the background of the revelations of the late 1980s and early 1990s.

Three contributors are Soviet sociologists engaged in the longitudinal study *Paths of a Generation* under the stewardship of the Estonian sociologist Professor Mikk Titma. These valuable research data and conclusions, as well as acknowledgement of past mistakes, are supplemented by material from investigatory journalists in such periodicals as *Sotsialnaya zashchita* (*Social Protection*), *Moscow News*, *Molodoi kommunist* (*Young Communist*) and *Argumenty i fakty* (*Arguments and Facts*). The conclusions are often surprising and disturbing, particularly on the passivity and conservatism of modern youth. At least, for the first time in some sixty years, they are based on genuine sociological research.

The Western team includes two US scholars – Ian Bremmer of the Political Science Department and Raymond Taras of the Hoover Institution of Stanford University. Their painstaking and sometimes risky research into the Soviet black market is presented for the first time. Since today the black market controls most retail trade, this work is of special significance. Mervyn Matthews has long campaigned for objectivity and honesty in the study of Soviet affairs; here he brings up to date his study of elites and privileges. Other issues dealt with are prostitution, the churches and charity, and ecology. It was the ecological issue more than any other that paved the way for openness; it was, after all, the terrible Chernobyl disaster of April 1986 which first drew aside the veil of secrecy from the Soviet media. The material here on Chernobyl, the Aral Sea and other ecological tragedies gives cause for everyone to stop, think and act.

The book covers six major issues of paramount importance to Soviet people today: the family, young people, certain social groups, social care, deviance and leisure. Together they present a coherent picture of Soviet social reality at the conclusion of its communist experiment.

JIM RIORDAN

Notes on the Contributors

Jim Riordan is Head of the Department of Linguistic and International Studies and Professor of Russian Studies at the University of Surrey. He studied and worked for five years in the Soviet Union before returning to academic life in Britain in 1965. His works include *Sport in Soviet Society*, *Sport under Communism*, *The Soviet Union. Land and People*, *Soviet Education: the Gifted and the Handicapped*, *Soviet Youth Culture*, *Dear Soviet Editor. Letters to the Editor during Perestroika* (with Sue Bridger) and *Sport, Politics and Communism*.

Ian Bremmer is George Holopigian Memorial Fellow in the doctoral programme of the Department of Political Science at Stanford University. A specialist on the second economy and the Soviet periphery, he has written several articles and edited *Soviet Nationalities Problems*. He is presently completing a second volume, *Fraternal Illusions: Nations and Politics in the USSR*.

Olga Bridges was born in Krasnodar, USSR. After coming to England she worked at Aston University and Trinity College Dublin before moving to Surrey in 1979. Early research studies were on factors affecting bilingualism in the Soviet Union. More recently her research emphasis has moved to environmental issues in Eastern Europe.

Igor Ilynsky is Director of the Youth Research Centre at the Institute for Youth Studies (formerly the Higher Komsomol School) in Moscow. A onetime Komsomol official, he has written extensively on youth problems and the Komsomol; he is the main architect of the new Youth Law recently ratified by the USSR Parliament and intended to provide guarantees and protection for young people in the transition to market conditions. Professor Ilynsky is a member of the USSR Academy of Pedagogical Sciences.

Ludmilla Koklyagina is Head of the Socio-Economic Research Laboratory at the USSR Institute for Youth Studies in Moscow. She is currently Chairperson of the Research Committee on Sociology of Youth Education attached to the USSR Sociology Association. Born in the southern Urals, she took a first degree in History and English in Kurgan followed by a Candidate of Philosophy at the USSR Institute of Sociology. Since 1983 she has been involved in the longitudinal survey 'Paths of a Generation' – a study of youth behaviour in various parts of the USSR. Her publications include *Nachalo puti: pokolenie so srednim obrazovaniem* (co-editor with Mikk Titma); *Zhiznennie puti odnovo pokoleniya* (co-editor with Mikk Titma).

Marina Malysheva is a Research Fellow at the USSR Institute of Sociology in Moscow, and Associate Member of the newly-established Centre for Gender Studies attached to the Institute. She has written a number of works on the professional and social status of women and the family, and on the demographic behaviour of young people. Her publications include 'The professional activity of women in production: analysis of regional differences,' *Sotsiologicheskie issledovaniya*, No. 1, 1983; 'Women's employment and demographic differences,' *Sotsiologicheskie issledovaniya* No. 4, 1984; 'Prospects for the young family' in *Youth Preparation for Married Life*.

Mervyn Matthews graduated in Russian at the University of Manchester in 1955, and took a D. Phil at the University of Oxford. He subsequently lived in Russia for three years until expelled by the KGB. The policies of Mikhail Gorbachov permitted various visits from 1988, but the future is now again unclear. Dr Matthews has been employed at the University of Surrey since 1966, and has written a number of books on Soviet social issues, including *Party, State and Citizen in the Soviet Union* and *Patterns of Deprivation in the Soviet Union under Brezhnev and Gorbachev*.

Suzanne Oliver read French and Russian at Lady Margaret Hall, Oxford, and graduated with honours in 1988. She subsequently worked as research assistant to Michael Bourdeaux at Keston College (Centre for the Study of Religion and Communism) in England. She cooperated on a book on Gorbachov's reforms and religious policy in the Soviet Union, which was completed in 1990. She spent the academic year 1990/91 reading for an MA in Soviet and East European Studies at SSEES, London.

Victoria Semyonova is Senior Research Fellow at the USSR Institute of Sociology in Moscow. She is currently responsible for coordinating the project 'Paths of a Generation' for the Russian Republic. Author of several articles on youth subculture, her major publications are 'The social activity of young people' in *The Younger Generation Leaving School*; and *Informal Youth Groups: Yesterday, Today and Tomorrow*. She was Visiting Research Fellow at the University of Cambridge in 1991.

Raymond Taras completed his graduate work at the University of Essex and the University of Warsaw. He has taught at a number of universities in England, Canada and the United States and is presently National Fellow at the Hoover Institution, Stanford University. He has written numerous articles on Soviet and East European politics and authored and edited books, including *The Road to Disillusion: From Critical Marxism to Post-Communism*.

Elizabeth Waters lived and worked for a number of years in Moscow; she now teaches Russian and Soviet History at the Australian National University. She has written widely on women, the family and social problems in the contemporary USSR and in the post-revolutionary period. Her *Women in a Bolshevik World: Work Marriage and Motherhood in Urban Russia, 1917–1928* will shortly be published by Macmillan. She is currently working on a book about gender and Soviet society for Cambridge University Press and on a social history of prostitution in the 1920s and early 1930s.

Part One
The Family

1 Some Thoughts on the Soviet Family

Marina Malysheva

The extreme over-ideologisation of all forms of social life because of the totalitarian regime and utter destruction of civil society created a unique historical situation in the USSR. People's private lives, organised within the family, began to perform functions that civil society should have performed. In terms of human evolution this period in the history of people inhabiting the Soviet Union may only be compared with primitive society when role taboos and prescriptions, first formulated in people's daily lives, enabled them to survive. The shift from universal human values to class ideology, which caused fierce conflict over the decades, left no room for social structures which could form in people feelings of human worth and respect for individuals irrespective of social origin. The concept of civic duty similarly changed so that it became normal to denounce anyone who thought differently, especially those who held different beliefs. The same happened in respect of the law. Laws were interpreted freely to fit the interests of the ruling elite. The family actually became the only institution in which a person could express ideas and ways of resistance to society's spiritual vacuum.

Yet the whole paradox of what happened lies mainly in the mystical embodiment of those tragic premonitions clearly foreseen by progressive Russian intellectuals in the late nineteenth century. Where the class ideology might lead was described by V.Y. Stoyunin in 1884:

> What is Russian reality? It is generals, officials, landlords, artists, scholars and merchants. They all have their class interests. The development of those interests has hampered an awareness of human dignity and respect for the individual; it produced a separation that weakened everyone and encouraged hostile relations. Until now education has separated us from our own people, rather than bringing us together. They stopped understanding us a long time ago and we stopped taking their interests into consideration. Could we really have developed an awareness of civil and humane interests?[1]

3

A correct answer to that question existed even then, yet an awareness of it came to us only a century later. The government has only now started those reforms, the need for which was clear even in the late nineteenth century.

The change from tsarist government to worker government ruling in the name of the people (yet seeing the people merely as a class-structured mass necessary to meet the interests of the ruling class) actually changed nothing.

Social progress was replaced by regress. History has shown clearly that unlimited acquisition of power, whether by the aristocracy or the working class through dictatorship, leads to totalitarianism and demoralisation. Stoyunin wrote of such a society:

> It is not people morally connected to one another by common interests or civil aspirations, it is people united by *forms of life*. It is a regiment dressed in the same uniform and moving in a line by command. The form of life was all-powerful, but what was the content of that life and what was its moral foundation? What lay behind the forms of life dressed in uniform were bribery, theft, servile attitudes to everyone who do not belong to that society.[2]

Lawlessness, corruption and the merging of the state apparatus with criminal elements – all that is typical of Soviet society today. The picture drawn by Stoyunin a century ago is as relevant as ever. Its logical conclusion is a description of the situation which was initially laid as the foundation of educational institutions, concerned as they were to educate people unable to oppose the ruling regime, fully subordinate and attached to it. Evidently social reformers dreamed of refining the old methods of such education (used by the tsarist regime) by adding a new progressive ideology and bringing positive results. Practice exceeded all expectations. Stoyunin wrote:

> You cannot require schools to produce young people with ready ideals. Moral, living ideals develop and penetrate the heart only through real social life. Schools must prepare a young person's spiritual powers to create the ideals; they must awaken unselfish love for truth, justice, kindness and beauty, and an aspiration for them. But schools must not impose any theory for life or any exclusive idea to which one's life should be dedicated, as Jesuit schools do. Without these fetters a young person must enter life with full freedom to choose his or her own way of life. The only condition is that the person must have intelligence, a sense of justice, honesty and a desire to link his or her own well-being to the common good.[3]

How far we are from such an understanding of the role of educational institutions is clear from the fact that private schools are said to be incompatible with the socialist system. Officials see in them a threat to society. The possibility of dissidents appearing frightens them more than the stereotypes and monosyllabic thinking, the forcing of everything into the framework of uniform theories and notions throughout the country.

The family became the only sphere of human life where the autonomy of will and awareness of the individual was preserved. This does not mean that the author is blind to the great influence of the totalitarian system upon private lives. The demoralisation of society is bound inevitably to lead to demoralisation of the family. Just look at the official statistics on the growth of crime among children and teenagers, of alcoholism and drug addition among children and adults, of prostitution and rape, of abandoned and runaway children, and of divorce. Apart from purely demographic destruction, the deformity of moral values reproduced in the family is also great. Nevertheless, an analysis of the contemporary family as a social institution shows that degradation did not go so far as to prevent any reviving of civil and patriotic awareness.

Some years ago such an approach to the family in the context of interaction between state and civil society was impossible. Research into the family normally focused on relations between its members, covering the following themes:

(a) a breakdown in marital roles;
(b) the structure of power within the family;
(c) divorce and conflict;
(d) motives for marriage and its dissolution;
(e) hierarchy of family and non-family values;
(f) family problems after divorce.

They relied mainly on theories of a middle- and micro-level. In other words, they adhered to the small-group notion, where the family was considered as one such small group. The major methods of analysis were taken from various psychological schools.

In recent years some works have appeared on the family's economic status. To go beyond the framework of a study of interpersonal relations within the family has to be done by studying its changing structure from the viewpoint of the functioning and development of the demographic system. Only demographers have worked on such a high level of generalisation that demands sociological and psychological methods. Sociology has lagged behind the social and political situation and it could not as a science perform any of its functions, either descriptive, explanatory or forecasting.

This 'flat empiricism' for which we so fiercely criticised 'bourgeois' scholars has become firmly entrenched in that field of investigation. It is all the clearer today, the further democratisation goes and the more the ideological fetters on the family are laid bare.

The author considers her main task here is to transfer the focus from the family as a marital institution to the family as an institution of civil society playing a primary and fundamental role in reproducing human and all democratic values. If that is true of any civilised state, it is doubly true of the Soviet Union, bearing in mind its historical conditions of development. Alienation from the state that acquired enormous scope has led to the privatisation of people's lives and a complete withdrawal from society into the family.

A great deal of sociological research and the longitudinal study *Paths of a Generation* undertaken under the guidance of Professor Mikk Titma serve to confirm that. According to the survey carried out in 1988 in several regions of the country, even in such urban–industrial areas such as Estonia, the family was shown to be of fundamental value for young people, surpassing all others in importance – social work, study, personal contacts, contacts with a loved one, employment, and so on. Moreover, the importance of the family was ten times greater than that of social work. Only communion with a loved one and friends had a comparable value for young people. Work, study, sport and literature did not comprise a vital need at all.

As the principal component in young people's lives, the family determines the relationship between them and society. Judging by the answers of respondents in Estonia, for example, young people in their everyday lives largely follow the rules adopted by their families or by themselves. There are three times fewer who follow the rules adopted by society. In general, only a tenth of respondents fully follow rules adopted in society and a third follow rules adopted by their families. The family therefore has indisputable authority over society. That means that society is supported by the family and not vice versa, for no social system can function if the activity of its members is not regulated by universal rules and prescriptions. These rules come from the family.

According to the same investigation, young people feel better in their parents' home than where they live or work. But the situation is not everywhere the same. There is a difference in degree of closeness to the house of their parents, depending on the social origin of the parents. Among school-leavers whose parents have higher status and qualifications, only one in seven young persons live partly on suffrance with parents; among graduates from technical schools one in six; and among those from junior technical colleges (most such children are from families of low-skilled workers) one in four.

We may conclude that it is in the environment of the least educated workers that children grow up deprived of fundamental social values and moral guidance. They perceive society as something alien to them and do not find the necessary support in the family. So they lose the last chance they have to retain a positive stimulus for arranging relations with people on a humane footing, which means that they are deprived of being able to organise civil society.

The study was not intended to determine exactly what values the contemporary family espouses, what traditions are maintained within it, or what moral guidelines dominate. The major question remains unanswered: what is the greatest difference between the rules of the family and those of society?

Bearing in mind Soviet conditions with over a hundred different ethnic groups sharing entirely different cultures both in content and in level of development, we cannot possibly construct a general typology of values for the present-day family. Any attempt to construct a hierarchy in order to answer this question is doomed to failure. Only as applied to each separate region of the country can we seek the dominants of people's spiritual activity at the level of the family and of society. For example, various elements of archaic social and economic structures – vestiges of feudal and clan relationships – have come to life and acquired unprecedented power in the Central Asian areas of the country and in some parts of Transcaucasia.[4] The administrative-command method of running society was the perfect soil for this. Furthermore, the effect of tribal/clan groupings enabled leaders to transform the abstract idealist values of socialism into that primitive form which has flourished in the USSR for several decades.

Clan relations have put their fetters on all forms of production, distribution and power. What is more, because of the extreme authoritarianism and conservative traditions of relationships, the population of Central Asia did not experience on such a sweeping scale the gulf between family and social values. The preservation of the *shariat*, the Muslim code of ethics requiring total subordination of power of junior to elder family members, as well as women to men, presupposed total subordination to the authorities even beyond the framework of the family, and the low status of women in society. In other words, the family acted as the repository of society's traditional values, while society in the form of its new authorities did everything possible to safeguard the family supports.

Young people did not become separated from the general mass of the population as a social demographic group; they contain all the failings of society, its patriarchal norms and traditions. Youth demonstrations in Tadzhikistan, Uzbekistan and Azerbaidzhan did not take the form of social protest against the old system of repression of personal interests. As previously, there is no widespread understanding of the erosion of their way of life, which is of much greater concern to the people of those areas than the power of the centre and the fancied domination by Russians. Everyone is still searching for an enemy, but not within themselves. For many people this enemy has now moved from the West to their own country in the form of other ethnic groups. There is a spontaneous expression of dissatisfaction with the conditions in which they live without any obvious comprehension of the means of resolving the accumulated problems. It is difficult to hope for any democratic transformation in the Eastern regions in the absence of a conscious protest by the younger generation against the tyranny of their elders, against the organised clan relationships that fetter all spheres of life and the interests of each individual personality which have dissolved into the requirements of the oriental system.

In the Russian 'interior' the principles of constructing relations between generations differ little from those of Central Asia. Their internal essence remains the same, while their form of expression does not take such an inflexible form. The findings of a survey the author conducted in the Tula Region of the Russian Federation showed that the conservative nature of erstwhile traditions continues and is reproduced in the new generations. That is clear from a special supplementary survey for the *Paths of a Generation* longitudinal study. Together with Dr Victoria Semyonova, the author compiled a 'Parents' Questionnaire'. This enabled us to shift from an intra-generational analysis of the survey group to an inter-generational analysis. The respondents' children became the object of investigation.

With the help of this questionnaire, we supplemented the social characteristics of the 'longitudinals' with those of their ideas on the education of children. Of the 140 people surveyed between the ages of 21 and 23, the great bulk (127) invariably admitted that each child born is an individual personality. Only nine people said that it cannot become a personality until it grows up, while four persons had no opinion at all.

It would seem that such results must testify to the dominant idea among young parents of developing the child's personality qualities. However, further analysis showed that a substantial number of respondents saw the main objective of education as the formation of respect for their elders, for their mother and father, in the children (64 persons).

Just as numerous was the group of parents who regarded the main purpose for the life of their children as having good health and material well-being (73). Those people who actually recognised their child as an individual personality, and regarded the most important factor in education to be the development of the child's capabilities, numbered only 26.

True, when responding to questions on paramount values in bringing up children, the parents frequently found it hard to single out one particular value and tended to opt for health or respect for elders (or vice versa). Only exceptionally did we come across situations when the parents wished to bring out in their children both respect for elders and development of their own capabilities. An obvious contradiction of values was revealed. These two latter values correlated very poorly, yet health and respect displayed a very close correlation.

We may conclude that the present younger generation brings up its children by taking on the traditions of its parents' family which are based mainly on an authoritarian relationship. Despite an awareness of the fact that each child is an independent being, parents continue to strive to set respect and deference for elders as the cornerstones of upbringing. What is more, the chief means of shaping such virtues in the child's behaviour is not their natural stimulation through any desire to develop the children's individual capabilities; they resort to what from our viewpoint are the least effective means – moralising, sermonising, punishing, materially rewarding or prohibiting.

Parents' attitudes to their children are built on analogy with their attitudes to society. In such circumstances as an authoritarian-bureaucratic means of running society, the ruling regime is least of all interested in bringing out the individual capabilities of the population. The whole repressive apparatus is superbly tuned to moralising and sermonising, thus manifesting a given ideology. Material rewards or prohibition depend on each person's toleration of and ability to subordinate themselves to the authorities and the bosses, not on the results of their labour.

In Eisenstadt's terms, Soviet society may be justly classed as 'primitive'. The values that fill the lives of children in the family are identical with those which organise their adult life, while a change in the child's status as it grows into an adult does not pose any particular problem. Parents need physically healthy and obedient children, while society needs physically fit and obedient servants. All other values are of secondary, subordinate importance. The skills and knowledge of adults are acquired 'naturally', as part of the experience of growing up, and the moment of transition to adulthood is a ritual action associated with gaining a degree, a passport or Party membership. It is as if the period of youth does not exist.

The structural gap between the family in which children grow up and the economic and social system where they have to take their place has only been noticed recently in large urbanised centres. The change in status from child to adult, like the need to fulfil other ideas and ways of life, starts to acquire shades of generation confrontation. A struggle is beginning against

Stalinism, the militant ideology of communism, the halo about the notion of eternal self-denial and sacrifice. Youth has become an important structural position for young people, although its right to existence is being constantly challenged by a substantial part of the adult population and continues to be internalised within traditional ritual frameworks of the 'natural' transition from parents to children. Society's evolution is looked upon as a process of adaptation to what had been worked out by previous generations. Only a small part of intellectuals realises that evolution is moving in the direction indicated by the law of variety. In particular, some social scientists have taken up the theory of the botanist and evolutionist S. Meyen who accords great importance to the period of childhood in his evolutionary studies. Only now is the idea becoming popular that the adult organism hardly takes part or takes no part at all in the evolution of the species.[5]

Evolution consists in altering the paths of development of the offspring and sometimes other immature forms. This is a crucial premise for sociology, in so far as the social sciences have taken and are taking the evolutionary element from biology. In both biology and sociology evolution depends little on adults, inasmuch as their ability to change is so small. That is why any social shock ultimately brings young people into the limelight. What is now happening in the Soviet Union may also be called a great social shock. The main consequence of the political transformations has been a growth in people's awareness freed of ideological propaganda. There has come into being a multitude of informal institutions in which the most educated and innovative part of young people is passing through new stages of socialisation, relating to the revival of values of civil society. We are seeing the beginning of the end of the family as a paramount and sole intermediary making contact with society.

Eisenstadt singles out two aspects of the emergence of youth culture relating to the estrangement of young people from the family and their transition to a wider social system of developed democratic society: first, the marginalisation of social status and, second, the marginalisation of the power structure. As applied to the USSR, bearing in mind the uniqueness of its historical experience in creating a new species of human being (*homo soveticus*), completely deprived of its social roots, the marginalisation had reached the bounds beyond which a person unconnected with his or her parents' family would simply fall into a historical void. That person is deprived of those moral guidelines that enable the person to latch on to any social community.[6]

The family ideology, withdrawing from under the influence of class ideology, has become so transformed today that it has begun to represent a set of situational rules and purely functional prescriptions relating to a pragmatic assessment of real conditions of vital activity. As the situation changes, so does family ideology. As the family departs from the scene there occurs a wearing away of the already mobile fundamental norms and values. Youth identification with certain groups is taking place by temporary and unstable attributes: a student of a technical college or institute, a worker of a particular skill, or a form of skilled enterprise.

All this is taking place against the background of mass migration of young people from the village to the town because of the very low level of the rural infrastructure, and the priority location of educational institutions in the cities and large district centres. We therefore have a standard model of a marginal whose norms of village subculture have been undermined and who has not yet mastered the urban subculture. Having adapted at some time to the new conditions of life, for many years young people cannot assimilate in the new milieu. They are bearers of social and spiritual marginalisation passed on by inheritance to the children. According to the Titma research project, three-quarters of people up to the age of 30 live and work in a different place to where they were born. A relative stabilisation of a person's socio-skill status, and of his or her place in the social structure, occurs about the age of 27.[7] That means that the whole socialisation process, which is already extremely complex for young people today, becomes exceedingly tortuous, not infrequently leading to destructive consequences for personality development. According to the latest census, 47 per cent of the Soviet population, and 57 per cent of town-dwellers, live in a different place from where they were born.[8] Each fresh generation has had to commence life without having the most elementary material and everyday conditions. All the naturally arising contacts have been broken up and continue to be broken up. The pendulum of movement from the village to the town has shown such a high swing that young people are simply being faced with a demographic catastrophe.

The earlier difficulty of creating a family was due to the sharp rise in numbers of women in the population. Now the balance has been restored, but there is inequality of distribution of men and women throughout the country. Young men substantially outnumber young women in villages of the European areas. In Central Asia, the opposite is the case: the rural composition in all Central Asian republics shows a much greater preponderance of women over men. In Uzbekistan, for example, there are 55,600 more rural women, in Azerbaidzhan some 40,700 more women, in Tadzhikistan 24,300 more women, and in Turkmenia 11,500 more women.[9] Evidently, the male population of those areas will be forced to migrate to the countryside in order to form a family. Yet the lack of opportunity to buy land prevents many of them doing so. That means that thousands of women will remain unwed, which will lead in turn to polygamy, to a reinforcement of the old ways, to a strengthening of despotic rules of Asiatic living, the degradation of women and children to the status of slaves. Many of the democratic gains of recent years that have been won with such difficulty will not find the needed response and will be buried under the weight of conservative family traditions.

The sexual disproportion in the European parts of the country is even greater. It runs into hundreds of thousands of people in some republics. Thus, in the Russian Federation there are 500,000 fewer women between 16 and 30 in the countryside than men; in the Ukraine it is almost 200,000 more, and in Belorussia some 65,000 more. A very difficult situation has developed in this respect in Kazakhstan where men outnumber women in the countryside by as many as 107,000.

So we can expect a large migration of young people with the objective of forming a family. Young men in the most economically active age group will once more quit the village and go to the town. Hundreds of villages and hamlets in Russia, Belorussia and the Ukraine are evidently doomed to extinction. Many young men will remain without a family and without children. Our society is totally unprepared for tackling problems of this nature. The lack of such a precedent has caught the authorities totally unawares in spite of the innumerable warnings from demographers and sociologists. The principal worry of social scientists is backed up by numerous foreign and Soviet investigations: an unmarried man is more prone to alcoholism and anti-social behaviour, to neurotic problems and suicide. He is less concerned for his own health and therefore is more frequently sick and liable to all manner of accidents. Finally, no marriage – no family. Apparently, the falling birth-rate is already programmed for the European parts of the country because of the above-mentioned sex imbalance. For urban women this situation is fraught with a growth in extra-marital relations through lack of a sex partner, the birth of illegitimate children and prostitution.

Already today the loss of contact with the parent family, the lack of opportunity to create one's own family through migration and unsettled living conditions have led to a situation where children's homes annually receive virtually two-thirds of the children from living parents, of whom about half are from single mothers. The main reason for this state of affairs is the marginalisation of young people, their economic insolvency, particularly of single mothers who receive as child benefit only 20 roubles a month or 14 times less than the average industrial pay and four times less than the minimum wage.

The government has recognised the need for urgent measures to improve the position of women and to strengthen the family. In April 1990 the USSR Supreme Soviet adopted a special decree to raise social protection allowances for young families with children and for single mothers. The size of the state allowance paid to single mothers for bringing up and maintaining children was increased to the level of the minimum wage.[10]

Nonetheless, it is evident that no allowances and decrees can substantially change destruction of family relations. The demoralisation of society and of the family is an indissoluble process. In the number of divorces (per 100 marriages) the USSR is second only to Sweden. Marriage began to disintegrate particularly intensively in the late 1950s and early 1960s. It is from these families that the youth of today has come. It has witnessed very poor lessons in family life. Family squabbles and conflicts, and the absence of a father, have been the first stages of many young people's entry into life. They will work out models of their own personal lives at their own risk and trepidation, inevitably repeating the mistakes of their parents. The lack of family protection in an anti-humane, unjust society has become the ultimate tragic link in the chain of marginalisation.

Our young people are:

(a) marginals by social origin;
(b) marginals by social status;
(c) marginals by place of residence;
(d) marginals in family relationships.

Effectively all channels of socialisation are blocked. We have witnessed a rupture in social relationships, and consequently a transformation in social values and interests into biological requirements.[11] A moral vacuum has formed; it can be filled only through a rebirth of the family. As the primary and paramount element in personality socialisation the family cannot be replaced by any other social institution. When a person departs from the bosom of his or her parents' family and begins actively to interact with other social institutions, the formation of the value structure of that person and the moral regulators of behaviour are already completed. Young people must, finally, stop being a marginal mass which the state manipulates for its economic and ideological interests. They must become rooted in social space through stable family relationships. Otherwise, the renaissance of civil society is impossible, just as the social protection of young people is impossible outside state policy.

NOTES

1. 'V. Y. Stoyunin kak pedagog i chelovek', *Rech F. A. Vitberga* (Sankt Peterburg: Znanie, 1899), p. 25.
2. V. M. Chulitsky, *Pedagogicheskie sovety V. Y. Stoyunina russkomu obshchestvu* (Sankt Peterburg: Znanie, 1909), p. 66.
3. 'V. Y. Stoyunin kak pedagog i chelovek', pp. 13–14.
4. G. V. Starovoitova, 'E Pluribus unum,' in *V chelovecheskom izmerenii* (Moscow, 1989), p. 91.
5. Y. V. Chaikovsky, 'Molodyozh v raznoobraznom mire', *Sotsiologicheskie issledovaniya*, No. 1, 1988, p. 81.
6. S. N. Eisenstadt, *From Generation to Generation* (Chicago: Free Press, 1956), p. 11.
7. M. H. Titma and E. L. Saar, *Molodoe pokolenie* (Moscow: Molodaya gvardia, 1986), pp. 225–9.
8. V. I. Perevedentsev, 'Propiska i demokratiya', *Moskovskie novosti*, No. 20, 1968, p. 3.
9. *Molodyozh SSSR. Statistichesky sbornik* (Moscow: Finansy i statistika, 1989), pp. 4–35.
10. 'Postanovlenie Verkhovnovo Soveta SSSR "O neotlozhnykh merakh po uluchsheniyu polozheniya zhenshchin, okhrane materinstva i detstva, ukrepleniyu semi"', *Izvestiya*, 13 January 1990, p. 1.
11. Y. N. Starikov, 'Marginaly', in *V chelovecheskom izmerenii*, p. 199.

2 Soviet Women: Lives and Destinies*

Soviet Women: Lives and Destinies
Tamara Sidorova

Women comprise half the Soviet population: 52.9 per cent or 151.1 million. Over 59 million women are employed, of whom some 55 per cent work in material production. Another 5.3 million work on collective and state farms.

* * *

I recall someone proposing at the first congress of Soviet deputies that we should raise the pay of nurses at all kindergartens and improve the quality of work in day nurseries. Nothing more was heard.

Only a short time passed and the country was facing the threat of a general strike whose consequences for the economy would have been incalculable should tens of millions of women stop work. Only then, under pressure from below, did the authorities start to get to grips with the grave problems of children's pre-school institutions: the miserly pay levels, the dreadful overcrowding, the inequitable food allocations to different categories of nurseries ... Some measures have now been taken and the heat has for the moment gone out of the situation.

Now we can expect an even stronger social explosion. Women are being faced with the loss of guarantees for their constitutional human rights – first and foremost, the right to work.

Unemployment among women is likely to burgeon disastrously with a market economy. It is already severe in the republics of Central Asia. Women make up 94 per cent of the jobless in Tadzhikistan, 98 per cent in Turkmenia and well over 50 per cent in Kirgizia. These statistics explode the myth of women's overemployment in production. It is precisely those republics that are lowest in provision of pre-school institutions. That makes women's work outside the home practically impossible even when other

* Extracts from *Sotsialnaya zashchita*, No. 2, 1990.

15

conditions are conducive to it. Perhaps that is what strengthens the tenacity of feudal-bey customs in regard to women.

Unemployment is leading to politicisation of women. I myself was witness to the spring pre-election hustings in Moscow which were well attended by women. I particularly remember a banner several women were carrying: 'Give us work, housing, food and justice!'

What measures are being planned to take the social tension out of the women's issue?

It is interesting to see the reaction of Moscow City Council to the strike threat from nursery workers. The Council Chairperson Gavril Popov proposed allocating 500 roubles each to families using nursery services, i.e. the sum which the state allocates for the annual upkeep of each child in a day nursery. Popov's measure would enable some mothers to stay home to look after their children. With nurseries made self-financing, the state would no longer subsidise them, and their upkeep would be the responsibility of parents. Consequently, only that part of the community with large incomes could afford to use the nurseries. That would undermine one of socialism's great gains, making such institutions accessible to all.

How our current politicians pale into insignificance beside Lenin. Public canteens, creches and nurseries are, he said, 'those simple, everyday, relatively inexpensive facilities that could actually liberate women, actually reduce and even eliminate their inequality with men in terms of their role in social production and everyday life.' He called for model practical work in this area 'without grandiloquence, without fuss, without endless chatter about system plans'. Yet now our politicians are advocating a retreat to the traditional division of labour by sex whereby society belongs to men, and women's lives are restricted to the narrow confines of the home and family.

Amongst the welter of disinformation about women and the family, you will find the idea that women work exclusively for the sake of money. Once society can raise itself to a higher economic level and enable women not to work, women will gratefully grab the opportunity and flock to the ranks of housewives. That will be a sign of a civilised society in the eyes of some scholars and politicians.

In actual fact such views do not reflect the genuine interests of women and the family. A study of women's opinions has shown that a career in addition to the family has a high place in their hierarchy of values. Of course, material stimulus for work is of considerable significance. The results of a survey made by the Academy of Social Sciences in 1988 reveals that only one per cent of women said they were indifferent to the amount of remuneration they received. Millions of women are today the sole breadwinner in the family; these are mainly single mothers. Worried letters are being written to newspapers and magazines. The following is typical: 'I know exactly what trying to exist on a twenty-rouble grant for myself and my child means. I've done all I can, earned some extra cash from dress-making, and my parents have helped out. Now it's all behind me. Yet politicians are trying to tell us we should bring up children by ourselves, without relying on aid. Well, you know what they say: life for drowning persons is in their own hands.'

* * *

Women are well educated. As many as 61 per cent of the country's specialists with higher or specialised secondary education are women. They make up 60 per cent of engineers, 70 per cent of agronomists, livestock specialists and veterinary surgeons, and virtually 100 per cent of librarians and bibliographers.

Women are active in science: they comprise 40 per cent of scientific workers, 13 per cent of doctors of sciences and 28 per cent of candidates of sciences.

Only half a million women have nonetheless made it to management level. A million women have reached the next rung down, being in charge of workshops, departments and farm sectors. Exactly what percentage of women has made it to the top in management is not shown in the statistics. But it must be shamefully low.

* * *

Just as bad is the position of women whose husbands are alcoholics or drug addicts. Even in a fully normal family the pay of one person is insufficient to keep the whole family. We cannot ignore the high level of divorces (every second or third family on average ends in divorce), with the woman commonly taking responsibility for material provision for the family.

When we talk of material stimulus for working women, we should also bear in mind the enormous importance of moral stimulus. In our survey we asked 'Would you continue working if you won enough money to keep you for the rest of your life?' Only 6 per cent of the women replied that they would give up working, including 5.6 per cent who had children. To the same question 7 per cent of men replied in the affirmative.

The interviewing I have carried out at various factories confirms women's motivation for work. The most typical responses have been: 'No, I would not quit my job. I feel myself somebody in my job. At home my work's taken for granted'; 'I have an interesting job'; 'I'm attached to the group I work with'; 'You can't live just on the interests of your husband and kids'; 'At home you've got to do everything and the family takes you for granted as their servant'; 'I wouldn't leave my job. Why should my husband live a full life, while I'm tied to the pots and pans?' As many as 75 per cent of those interviewed were against traditional views of women in the family and men in society. This is a world-wide trend. Despite the affirmation of some economists that in a civilised society women don't work, the whole world is witness to a growth in female employment; this is happening particularly in economically advanced capitalist countries where the scientific and technological revolution has reached such a high level.

The work skills of women are growing more slowly than those of men. For example, only a third of women doctors have a seniority rating and only a quarter have improved their qualifications.

Women's average work rating in all industries is lower than that of men. In particular, a third of women have the lowest (first or second) rating in the building industry, about 42 per cent in the paper-making industry, 37 per cent in light industry and 33 per cent in the food industry; men, on the other hand, make up between 10 and 16 per cent at the lowest rating levels in those industries.

Vocational training does little to help women. In 1988, women made up 30 per cent of those on training schemes, and 37 per cent of those who had improved their skills.

*   *   *

It is noteworthy that what private factory owners in the West are achieving today was already being carried out by Soviet state policy in the 1920s for levelling out the social status of men and women. Since then we have drawn further and further away from that objective.

Women's social protection and the country's economic development require from politicians conditions in which women would be competitive in the labour market. The present policy aimed at increasing women's time off for caring for young children is actually bound to bring about a situation where women will be cast to the sidelines of economic and political life.

Reference to the experience of a number of countries in Eastern Europe may explain merely insufficient study of the consequences to which similar reforms have led. In Hungary where in 1967 women were given a paid work-free leave of three years to look after a young child, a whole series of serious problems arose. Many women, not wishing to lose their skills, wanted to return to work, but couldn't because of the lack of nursery places. The lengthy break from work had an adverse effect on the quality and competitiveness of the female labour force. Legislation did not resolve the birth rate or divorce problems, and Hungary today has one of the lowest birth rates in the world. The socio-economic status of women has actually diminished, as the country's leaders have officially admitted.

Eva Gunnarson, a Swedish sociologist, told me in an interview last March that: 'After women have stayed at home with a child for eighteen months they often cannot resume their old job. Men don't always put it into so many words, but they take it for granted that a woman who has stopped work for such a long time has completely lost her skills for the job.'

Attempts under perestroika to find a way out of the economic, social and demographic crisis at women's expense can only create the semblance of problem-solving. Such a policy has no future.

In our desperate times, when we are shifting to radically new production relations, we must retain the notion of recognising motherhood as women's social function and hence it is the state's and entire society's responsibility to establish conditions that will enable women to combine vocational and public activity with motherhood and family obligations.

* * *

The lower the skills the smaller the wage packet. On 1 January 1988 some 16 per cent of men and over 43 per cent of women took home average monthly earnings of 150 roubles; the respective percentages were 35 and 14.5 for between 200 and 300 roubles, and 11 and 2 for over 300 roubles.

Even the starting conditions differ. Some 40 per cent of men and 72 per cent of women received up to 150 roubles a month as young specialists.

Where on earth can women earn a decent salary? It is possible to add on between 20 and 80 roubles a month through all manner of increments: higher work rating levels, responsibility allowances, extra payment for heavy and unhealthy jobs. But only 36 per cent of those receiving such extra payments are women.

* * *

The first Soviet labour code in 1918 banned the use of women's labour for heavy and unhealthy jobs. We later found that we had to classify such jobs, so a list was drawn up in 1932. During World War II women replaced men in all areas of the economy, but it was only in 1957 that women were released from underground work in the coal and extractive industries.

In 1978 the government and trade unions passed a resolution, No. 320, which confirmed the existing list of jobs in heavy and unhealthy conditions it which female labour cannot be employed. According to government regulations all women had to be released from such work by 1 January 1981.

'You can make a report'
T. Gnidenko

Or so said Dr A. Kozlov on behalf of construction union leaders in response to the work of scholars at the Research Institute of Labour Safety and Industrial Disease attached to the USSR Academy of Medical Sciences, when they reported on the working conditions of women house-decorators.

I have been following the fortunes of this study for three years. There were good reasons for it being made. In 1985 the Research Laboratory of Public Safety, which had been studying infant mortality in Moscow, drew the attention of the authorities to the fact that women employed as house-decorators were more likely than others to give birth to children with inborn defects. The USSR Health Ministry financed further study.

But then a new economic mechanism began to operate and the scientists had to master self-financing and cost-accounting. They naturally felt that the Construction Ministry would be interested in the health of its female workers and would be happy to cooperate in their work. They were in for a shock. The person responsible for the uniform technical policy in construction soon disabused the doctors, telling them it was the Health Ministry that was primarily concerned with medical issues, so let it provide the funds.

It seemed that the trade union of construction workers and those employed in industrial construction materials would offer a helping hand, especially as its leaders were endeavouring to show that they were restructuring themselves to protect their members in deed not just in word. And an answer did come from the trade union leadership a year ago. The letter, signed by the union secretary V. Bogdanov, asked about the interim results of the investigation. I asked Dr L. Serebryany, one of the researchers what had subsequently transpired. He told me the union had done nothing at all. Evidently, it was too concerned with arranging its agenda for the forthcoming meeting of the union's presidium.

All the same, the group of 28 scientists, including doctors and candidates of medical, biological and physics/mathematics sciences and engineers completed their work. It makes uncomfortable reading. In conformity with the 'Work Safety Classification', the working conditions of women house-decorators belong to the harmful and dangerous categories (3rd class, 1st degree). This is confirmed by the presence in the working zone air of harmful substances in the 2nd and 3rd dangerous categories – benzol, toluene and xylene – in concentrations that considerably exceed the permissible. The level of dust is twenty times above the norm, the work is extremely heavy, and the static and dynamic pressure on the motor apparatus is high . . .

It is this that leads to many family tragedies. It is now known that women house-decorators frequently suffer early or late miscarriages, still births and primary infertility, and pregnancies are complicated by toxicosis, iron-deficiency anaemia, vegetative joint dystonia, etc.

The children of women house-decorators more frequently than others have to be hospitalised through diseases of the respiratory system, the skin and the cardio-vascular system. The women themselves are among the most widespread sufferers of the same diseases. So we have yet more confirmation of child pathology according to the 'organ to organ' principle.

Today the report by scientists of the Research Institute of Labour Safety and Industrial Disease is with the State Building Industry. It will be used for claiming additional allowances for house-decorators. All the same, such an approach to the medical conclusions does not in any way solve the problems of health; on the contrary, it only makes them worse. It fetters women by financial chains to their harmful and dangerous workplaces. We have more than enough examples of that.

According to statistics of the USSR State Statistics Board, as many as 5,746,581 people, including 952,315 women, received allowances and compensation in the building trade in 1985 for work in harmful conditions. Payment for enhanced rating levels went to 1,146,791 people, of whom women made up 203,667. A total of 1,692,936 people are entitled to additional time off, of whom women make up 219,641. Free special food rations go to 72,696 people, of whom 10,433 are women. Free milk is handed out to 9,953,387 people, of whom 194,325 are women who usually take it home for their families.

Economic stimulus not only makes it difficult for women to leave heavy and harmful jobs, it practically forces them to remain until they become invalids. According to the same statistical sources, women are employed in the very jobs that have long been banned to them: electric welders, pipe layers, drillers, woodcutters, loaders, road workers and so on. However odd it may seem, women are fighting to return to their familiar hell. In March 1987 the USSR State Committee on Labour acceded to the numerous demands of women and permitted them once again to take the wheel of buses and lorries.

All the same, I think that many women would not ruin themselves on a building site if they could help it. One might cite the many surveys, including those made by the construction union, that show the unsupervised use of building materials, including varnish and paint, and the lack of a proper work regime in harmful and heavy working conditions. Last year my colleague from Krivoi Rog, T. Milenina, carried out a mini-survey in the local construction site trust. It turned out that the construction laboratory of the trust makes no chemical analysis of its paints, even though it receives them without any testing certificate. So there is no check on the degree of harmfulness of the materials, and consequently no way of deciding the work regime payment or responsibility for it.

Such a situation exists almost everywhere in our country, even though the construction union possesses detailed information about it.

*   *   *

The State is formally responsible for women's work safety. Article 68 of the Fundamentals of Union and Republican Legislation on Labour directly states that women are forbidden to do harmful and heavy work. In fact, according to the most recent statistics, 8,000 women are employed in banned trades. You'll find them at the coal face and as bulldozer drivers.

Up till now many women work not only at heavy and harmful jobs, but in particularly difficult and dangerous working conditions. In industry, women make up 44 per cent of all workers employed in such conditions.

*   *   *

N. Izmerov, Head of the Research Institute of Labour Safety and Industrial Disease, has told me that scientists are simply fed up demonstrating the harm done by house decorating to a woman's organism. The scientific work being undertaken at the Institute is by no means the only research on the subject. The sources quoted in the report mention 74 other studies on the subject. They include work by dedicated doctors who have spent many years studying problems in the construction industry. For example, there is Professor V. Retnev of the Leningrad Institute of Higher Medical Training. Studies have been made in many different areas of the country: the Soviet Far East, the Ukraine, Lithuania, Novosibirsk, Georgia, etc. All without exception have come to the same conclusion. Yet practically the entire burden of house decorating continues to be borne by women.

Professor Retnev feels that we need no further proof. It is time to put an end to such studies. It is time to review the list of industries and jobs with heavy and harmful working conditions at which women's work is banned. We must stop women working at house decorating.

And after all that . . . 'You can make a report, comrades!' Do trade unionists, so-called protectors of the working class, really see in the conclusions of scientists merely lecture material? We would like to know the opinion of leaders quoted by the delegate Dr Kozlov. After all, Alexander Yakovlev, Chairman of the Trade Union of Workers in Construction and Industrial Building Materials, is a people's deputy and votes in the Supreme Soviet for a humane, socially-oriented perestroika policy . . .

*   *   *

It is reckoned that women suffer problems at work because of family circumstances caused by child-bearing.

How do things stand in giving priority to childbirth? Of the total number of employed women in 1987, 2.8 million were released for looking after children up to one year of age, and 1.7 million were at home caring for children between one and one and a half years. Naturally, all of them have had experience of maternity homes and in most cases were dissatisfied with the experience. According to our survey, almost half the women remarked on the unhygienic state of general facilities, and a quarter of the women reported on the insanitary state of the wards. In 1988, as many as 7,000 women had sepsis diagnosed in the post-natal period.

We Feminists
Natalia Ivanova

'As far as I remember I have always felt my lack of full social value. As a child there was the double standard of morality for girls and boys. At work, to get a managerial post a woman has to be several "goals" in front in terms of knowledge and work qualities than a male competitor. In the family you are in a servant status. Even in love you have to wait for a man to notice you. The position of women in our society has long seemed to me to be degraded . . . '

My guest, Valentina Konstaninova of the Academy of Social Sciences, breaks off to greet visitors entering her office, then answers the telephone.

She is quick, precise, assured. She doesn't at all resemble the put-upon little woman you might imagine from what she was saying. Just the opposite. Perhaps that's how it has to be in our society: for any chance to break through you have to have enormous passion for it.

'Then I began to write up my doctoral dissertation on the women's movement abroad and fairly swiftly realised that I had long shared their feminist views. Of course I had not realised that that was what they were called. What is a feminist? Many things to many people. Feminists are fighting not merely for women's rights, but for a two-sided emancipation of society. After all, the position of men is also abnormal in society. Here we have to study Western experience of the women's movement very carefully.'

'Tell me, you talk a great deal about the very rich experience of the women's movement in our own past. But many of its achievements were later dismantled during the war and never restored. Yet surely we have a few achievements for which the West is still campaigning. Is the West interested in this experience? And why don't you refer to it?'

'It's true, Russia did have rich experience of the feminist movement. But not what you imply in your question. In the early part of the century the feminist movement was eroded by the labour movement and submerged within the confines of the class approach to resolving social problems. After the 1917 Revolution everything was concentrated on women's participation in social production. Meanwhile, our lives remained in a patriarchal state.

'I don't know, it may be that our grandmothers did feel happy sitting on a tractor, but I doubt it. After all, that was only part of emancipation. Apart from the quality of work, women are no less eager to fulfil themselves in other spheres – in their personal lives, in public affairs, having some sort of hobby. Otherwise they become robots. That's the sense in which I say we lag behind the West.

'First, our women are removed from politics. Compare us with Norway: eight of their Cabinet ministers are women (including the Prime Minister) out of a total of 18. Sweden has 8 out of 21. Of the 14 senators in West Berlin eight are women. What do we have? Poor old Biryukova. That's the sum total of our representation. And it's the same at every level of power. Furthermore, public awareness turns out to be even more reactionary under perestroika: the number of women deputies has actually fallen, so that today they make up only 15.7 per cent of all people's deputies.

'If a woman does engage in some form of public work it is at the lowest level, and usually the most formal, boring work where it is impossible to fulfil oneself. That's the second point.

'Finally, even in production where one would think women's gains are most marked, the situation is far from rosy. For example, only 14 per cent of industrial managers are women; most managers are men. Moreover, when you look closer you realise that the equal pay principle is also an illusion, yet another myth. Surveys show the real differential in average earnings is 3 : 2 in men's favour; and in some industries women receive only a third of men's pay.

'That is why the feminist movement regards its main task as the campaign against the sort of stereotyped thinking that bedevils our society.'

* * * [bɪ'devl] мерзать, мучить

Our mortality rate for women in childbirth is between two and four times higher than in most (one-time) socialist countries, and between four and seven times higher than in Germany, the USA and Finland.

The infant mortality rate is also high as a consequence of poor health care for women and children: in 1988 the figure was 24.7 per 1,000 births, which makes the USSR 1.6 to five times worse than advanced capitalist countries.

'Before we talk of the tasks ahead, I'd like to be clear what the Soviet feminist movement is.'

'It started up a couple of years ago, when I met a few like-thinkers at an international conference in Tbilisi. We realised that we shared the same views and made up a sizeable research team: philosopher Olga Voronina, historian Natasha Zakharova, demographic economist Asya Posadskaya, and myself, historian and sociologist. Each of us had our own experience and our own ready material.

'As a result of our cooperation we decided to set up LOTOS – the League for Liberation from Social Stereotypes (*Liga osvobozhdeniya ot sotsialnykh stereotipov*). The League retains its initial nucleus, but many others now take part in our work. We have made contact with women's movements in Great Britain, France, West Germany, the USA and the Scandinavian countries.

'Finally we are in the process of creating a Gender Studies Centre. The term "gender" is known only to a few people in our country, since nothing of that nature had ever existed, even though such centres are well established from advanced European states to the least developed African countries. There are many women's and men's centres abroad. We decided to combine them and conduct studies on both sexes.

'Gender studies are concerned with physiology or biology, they consti-

tute a whole nexus of problems associated with the status of each of the
sexes: at work, in politics, in the armed forces . . . Many surprises lay in
wait. Specialists the world over consider that the most pressing issues are
today associated with the gender approach to status.'

'What success have you had? Do you think there are real changes in
society under the League's influence? Or are transformations coming without feminist ideas?'

'A great deal has been accomplished in the two years LOTOS has been
in existence. Our discussion itself is a sign of the times. We have broken the
monopoly of the Soviet Women's Committee to speak on behalf of Soviet
women – and that's a breakthrough. People are beginning to talk about us
around the world. Even at home a large number of people evidently share
our views.'

'Can you tell me what those views are?'

'The main thing is to give women back a sense of their personal worth,
so that they are no longer second-class citizens, but have equal opportunities with men in all aspects. As they are by nature. Inasmuch as men have
"conceded" to women the unnatural right to lay asphalt on roads and
sleepers on railways and women have coped with such work, women can
certainly manage everything else. We are for making women subjects,
rather than objects, of policy, enabling them to take full part in its formula-
tion. We are for equal participation of women in public life at all hierarchical levels of leadership. We are for equality of women at work, in culture
and ethics. No less important is it for men to return to the family. Children
very much need the salutary influence of a father and husband.'

'Nonetheless, the opposite is surely the popular demand today: returning
women to the home and children, returning traditional values to our society
and on that basis to reanimate public morality. Despite all my respect for
equality principles, it would seem our morality began to disintegrate when
women forgot their natural role in life. How do feminists relate to that?'

'So you think that since a woman has biological characteristics, she has
to give birth, she has to have a family, and all's well with the world? But not
everyone is the same. Perhaps a woman wants to engage in politics or
public work. We have to understand her, accept her right to do so (just as we
do for men) and secure conditions in which she can implement her choice.

'In the Soviet Union we are all used to thinking that a woman's natural
state is to have children and bring them up. That is precisely what gender is
all about – the social gender imposed by society. But let's take men. After
all, no one says that their natural state is that of a sire bull. Some are more
emotional and gentle and perhaps would prefer to be more concerned with
the upbringing of children. And why not? The trouble is that it isn't done.
Men have to be breadwinners, defenders of the fatherland, they must be

aggressive and thrusting. They are innovators, stimulators of progress. This is an artificial division of the sexes. All people are different and everyone has their own vocation.

'What if we do return women to the home and get men to earn more so as to keep the family? What then? Women would become economically dependent on men, which would end in their psychological dependence. What sort of person would we be producing? History provides the answer: a slave. We've already been through all that; it's time we realised that a return to the past is reaction. How can we build a new humane society with reactionary ideas in our heads?'

'What is the relationship between feminism and perestroika?'

'I can't give you a simple answer. On the one hand, we now have the right freely to express our views, and that is a great blessing. On the other, however, perestroika of the economy hurts women more than men. When redundancies are being made they are the first to be fired and last to be hired, especially young women. The social sphere suffers: it's more profitable for a manager to pay for a pregnant woman to take time off than to maintain a creche and nursery in the plant.

'But the main gain is that we are becoming a society of equal opportunities, a society without a rigid reinforcement of social roles. Feminism, therefore, will acquire an increasingly loud voice; that is inevitable. And in the immediate future we shall establish a women's party. It is time for our women to stand up for their political rights – that is the most urgent task. Maybe that, too, will be a product of perestroika.'

* * *   [inevitable] неизбёжный неминуемый

The USSR can boast the greatest number (2,700,000) of marriages every year out of all socialist and advanced capitalist countries (apart from the USA). But it also has more divorces (950,000).

Development of pre-school institutions is one way the state can help working women. Statistics show that 17.4 million Soviet children – or 58 per cent of eligible children – attend creches or nurseries. The application list is much greater; some 1.9 million children are on the waiting list. As many as 1.1 million children go to nurseries where the number of children is greater than the legal limit. As a result, nursery children are frequently sick. Loss of working time through the need to care for such sick children amounted to over 230 million person-days in 1988 – i.e. 800,000 persons did not work on each separate day.

In 1987 the length of paid leave to care for a sick child was increased to 14 days. But the state provides fully paid leave for seven calendar days and only half pay for the rest.

Part Two
Young People

misgive - внушать недоверие, опасени
дурные предчувствия

отноц

enabled
давать возможн
paltry - жалкий

3 Trends in the Development of Soviet Youth

Igor Ilynsky

INTRODUCTION

For a long time, the myth persisted that Soviet young people were 'the happiest', 'the healthiest', 'the best educated', simply 'the best' in the world. The USSR did not suffer from the problems that plagued other societies: drug addiction, alcoholism, prostitution, suicide. Soviet youth were somehow outside the historical process. It is a paradoxical fact that the UNESCO Data Bank still contains no information on the 66 million Soviet young people.

The past 75 years saw the formation of paternalistic attitudes that were indispensable to the totalitarian regime. Such attitudes imply that the ideologically blinded older generation gives its 'paternal' attention and love to young people only in such an amount and in such a form that it deems necessary, and young people have to respond by giving the Party and the state humble thanks for their good grace and patience, demanding nothing more. This attitude to young people prevails even now. *преобладает*

It was young people who acted as the shock force of collectivisation of agriculture and of industrialisation; they were the cheap, reliable and dynamic labour force in developing Siberia, the Soviet Far East and Far North, and in the building of new towns, power stations, railways and vast plants. This 'cheap' workforce enabled billions of roubles to be invested in production, and paltry kopecks to be spent on youth's social needs.

Young people were praised to the skies for their labour enthusiasm, yet feared for their political activity. Outside politics, paternalism implanted cautious, wary, mistrustful relations, full of misgivings and apprehensions. As a result, young people found themselves in the background of political power. The number of young people in political administration steadily diminished, which resulted in decrepitude in the rulers and helplessness in the ruled.

The spiritual basis of paternalism was dogmatism and authoritarianism. The acme of good manners was 'communist consciousness' – the ability of the disciple to memorise and rehearse after the teacher without deviating from society's ideological and political standards.

31

In the sphere of culture, paternalism meant intolerance and repression. Young people's cultural creativity was suppressed at birth. Any aspect of youth culture in ideas, science, literature, music, dance, fashion or general demeanour was not tolerated. Society was ever wondering how best to combat those 'evil people' who refuse to accept from the older generation the ideals, values and goals which the 'fathers' impose upon the 'sons'. Yet young people naturally want to introduce new ideas and values, expressing their own goals and attitudes, needs and personalities to fit the new times. Even now the concept of 'youth culture' or 'subculture' or 'alternative culture' is unacceptable, even absurd, to the great bulk of the older generation; the words 'unofficial' and 'informal association' are perceived only in a negative light.

All this led and continues to lead to frustration, pessimism, bitterness and alienation from society, the state, from the adult world, from the older generation and their ideals. Young people have made a significant contribution to perestroika: they were the first to demand a ban on Marxist-Leninist courses in colleges and universities; they staged numerous demonstrations and strikes all over the country. It was the mass hunger strike of Ukrainian students that brought down the government of the Ukraine. The majority of young people, however, are apathetic, numbed, hypnotised. The market will certainly bring them to their senses: they will be the first victims of a market economy. It is possible that young people will rise in revolt and spark off actions by the still numerous reactionary forces. It could be that young people will unintentionally become the gravediggers of perestroika. It takes little time for reaction to set in, and it can last for decades. One should remember that the French Revolution turned to violence in two years and a military dictatorship in seven.

YOUNG PEOPLE IN THE EARLY 1990s

Soviet youth is made up of nearly 66 million people between the ages of 14 and 30 among over a hundred nationalities, inhabiting a territory that covers a sixth of the world's land surface. The differences in social and economic development between regions in the USSR are so great that the younger generation may well be born and grow up in completely different historical epochs. Differences range from almost complete illiteracy among some young people in remote areas of the Far North and Soviet Central Asia to fully educated (10–11 years) in Central Russia, the three Baltic republics, and over most of the Ukraine and Belorussia. In one and the same republic, they range from primitive farm workers to outstanding scientists discovering new technologies at industrial plants. Their social range requires early (15–16 years of age) marriage for most girls, large families (ten or more children) and feudal family customs in such Central Asian republics as Tadzhikistan, Turkmenia, Uzbekistan and Kazakhstan or relatively late marriages and predominantly one-child families in the Baltic republics of Estonia, Latvia and Lithuania. Their thoughts range from elementary problems of survival (what to eat? where to live? how to buy clothes and shoes?) that beset millions of young people, particularly schoolchildren and students, to complex problems of self-realisation: what is life for? how can we be useful to society and humankind?

So 'Soviet youth' is a fairly abstract notion. Any discussion of Soviet youth 'in general' and 'as a whole' risks skating over essential differences, leads to gross errors and crude conclusions. All the same, some generalisations are necessary in order to work out a general policy, to determine priorities. Let us attempt to give a brief outline of the youth situation in Soviet society today.

Young people make up 43 per cent of the 158 million able-bodied people employed in the Soviet economy; 80 per cent of young people work in material production. Over 50 per cent of those employed in advanced technologies (electronics, radio-technology, computers) are young people. With their natural aspiration for new forms of life and work, new techniques and technologies, young people are the most important resource for our chaotic fledgling market economy. We cannot create a market without youth participation. We cannot base our economy and labour on ideological slogans, moral exhortation and political power as we used to do. On the other hand, we cannot establish a new and effective economy without altering attitudes to work.

Economic reform is taking place against the background of young people's alienation from labour – as it has taken shape over the last three score years and ten. Soviet production had been so organised that it discouraged innovation, enterprise and high quality. Productive and creative work has lost its value in the eyes of young people. Today the most prestigious trade is that of salesperson. Young people are eager to go not where commodities are made, but where they are distributed. Many youngsters want not to earn money, but to receive it – and to receive a lot of it in any (even illegal) way. Only a third of young people believe it possible to attain material well-being by honest endeavour.

Many young people do not avail themselves of the opportunity to work: some half a million youngsters prefer not to work. Over the last five years there has been a sharp increase in the number of young people not working.

It is generally recognised today that the intellectual potential of society suffered enormous losses. This is due not only to our lagging behind in the social and natural sciences, but also to our backwardness in economics and technological sciences, in the low level of training of engineering and management personnel. Young people are alienated from education; the values of work skills and knowledge have been lost. Wages and material well-being are unconnected with education. A professor now earns less than a bus driver. The number of secondary-school leavers who wish to continue their education is diminishing. Surveys show that only a third of the students at technical colleges consider it important to acquire good vocational training. Many just 'kill time' at college as well as at work.

Even the existing intellectual potential is badly used. For various reasons 60 per cent of university and college graduates do not work according to their qualifications; in many cases it is materially more worthwhile to be a manual worker than an engineer.

On the whole, young people welcome a radical reform of the economy, even though they appreciate they will be one of the major victims of market relations. The Komsomol (Young Communist League) has itself helped to set up over a thousand cost-accounting youth trusts; and some 10 per cent of young people are engaged in cooperative and other profit-making firms. Nonetheless, the crippled economic psychology, allied to legal and political instability, are scaring away young people from new forms of economic affairs. In 1989, only 1.3 per cent of the 2.2 million school leavers went to work in cooperatives. In the countryside, there are only a few individuals who dare to rent land or set up private farms; only 30.5 per cent of the able-bodied rural population are young people.

In so far as they are alienated from the old economy, young people do not believe yet in establishing a new one. When asked, however, 'if they had an opportunity to work abroad, what would they do?' only 16.4 per cent out of 1,600 young people answered that they would want to take a permanent job; 65.8 per cent would take a temporary job. Of the total, 82 per cent said they would take the first opportunity to go West in order to find their own way.

That is the ideological verdict of the younger generation on the social system they live in. Psychologically, it represents a new explosion of negative emotions, for it is clear that the West could accept only a small part of these 50 million people. Economically, it means that our society faces a 'brain drain', the loss of the best qualified workers and the most enterprising people.

Profitability has already removed young people's right to work. Surveys show that over 20 per cent of young people are likely to be made redundant in the near future. Already we have over six million people unemployed, mostly in Central Asia. The market will simply aggravate the situation. Some experts forecast an unemployment figure of 15, 20 or even 25 million

The painful economic and political processes are developing against a background of a deterioration in young people's material and social situation, and they are aggravating them. What can a young person think of the country's economy if the money he or she earns is some 130 roubles a month? What can a student think of socialism if the monthly grant is a mere 40–45 roubles? What can most young married couples talk about in the kitchen if their monthly income averages 111 roubles per family member, or is only 75 roubles a month for three dependents? How can young people think about 'renovating' socialism if only one in ten young workers lives in a separate apartment in the sixth year of perestroika, and if seven out of ten live in a hostel or have to rent a room? Of 4,000 young people surveyed in 1989, 42 per cent said they were disappointed with perestroika; only 22.3 per cent expected their lives to improve in the near future.

Society's inability to provide economically for young people and to implement social programmes, especially to render assistance to young families, has led to serious demographic problems: a fall in the birth rate, and an increase in divorces, one-parent families and the infant death rate.

For many years the Soviet state neglected the health of young people (medical service per capita expenditure is 22 times less in the USSR than in the USA). Over 40 per cent of Soviet people, mainly the young, are limited in their work ability owing to ill health; some 10 per cent of young people suffer from nervous disorders.

The dramatic picture of young people's economic and social situation is aggravated by poor legal protection. Traditionally, laws concerning young people were incorporated into general legislation, and most are long outdated.

SOCIAL TRENDS IN THE EARLY 1990s

Where is Soviet youth going? The main direction appears to be towards a pluralism in outlook. The number of supporters of dialectical and historical materialism has considerably fallen in society generally and among young people in particular. It is becoming increasingly evident that Marxism-Leninism and its main principle, dialectical materialism, apply largely to the nineteenth century. Neither Marx nor Engels, nor Lenin, could suspect the discoveries made after their deaths in both physics and psychology. At the time that they were elaborating their theories, they were unaware of the later philosophical interpretations of value, freedom and necessity in ethics. So much in science and philosophy is understood quite differently today than it was in the time of the founders of 'scientific communism' that today's young people, even if they do not understand philosophical subtleties, are well aware that Marxism-Leninism has no right to claim to be 'the only genuine scientific and true world outlook'.

Only 29 per cent of young people surveyed in 1989 (out of 8,000) believed that Marxism-Leninism determines social development. As a result of student pressure, all Soviet educational establishments have had to abandon courses in dialectical and historical materialism, the political economy of socialism, and scientific communism. Now Marxism-Leninism is only studied in the context of philosophy alongside pragmatism, phenomenology, existentialism, neotomism, Christian evolutionism and structural functionalism. Many young people are taking considerable interest in ancient Indian philosophy. But the most popular philosophies today are religious; Christianity and Islam, along with other beliefs, are today experiencing a true renaissance.

While Marxism-Leninism regarded itself as both a class ideology and a world outlook, working as a 'guide to action' and a means of political struggle, so the tendency to increasing ideological and political pluralism is a natural result of an increase in the pluralism of world outlook. Today, when the demagogical function of Marxism-Leninism is blatantly apparent, most young people treat the teaching and the ideal it is based on with derision. Only 8.4 per cent of the 8,000 young people surveyed believed that the future belonged to communism; and most of those were schoolchildren, unskilled workers and others with low education.

At the same time, there are some young people who not only ardently believe in communism, but also defend Stalinism. To the question 'Do you think Stalin was guilty of murdering millions of people, and are people right to condemn him?' 35.8 per cent said 'yes, absolutely right', 40.6 per cent replied 'partially right' and 4.6 per cent said it was wrong to condemn Stalin.

Young people include advocates of anarchism (about 1 per cent) and of capitalism (some 13 per cent); some favour the restoration of the monarchy in Russia. Fascism also has its followers. About half the respondents rejected both capitalism and 'existing' socialism; they seem to favour a 'third way'.

In general, youth consciousness and life are strongly politicised. Young people are critical of everything that went before, yet are also critical of the present. In this sense one may say that today's younger generation is the most political in our entire post-1917 history.

But what kind of politics is it, that is the question. In today's politics there is nothing resembling the submissive 'political activity' that was for years implanted in young people and that manifested itself when, 'by Party will', 'by command of the current leader', young people went where they were sent, did what they were told. Youth politics today are anything but conventional. This unconventionality consists in young people acting on the principles of self-awareness, self-determination – i.e. they act independently. Such people are difficult if not impossible to manipulate. Even the Komsomol, which used to act according to the notorious formula 'If the Party ordered, the Komsomol obeyed', has now declared equal partnership relations with the Communist Party and often differs from Party decisions and assessments.

The forms of political activity are quite unconventional, including strikes, hunger-strikes, protest letters to the press, proposals of alternative ideas and projects, and severe criticism of the Komsomol and Party. Even traditional forms of activity (demonstrations, conferences, rallies) are now as different as chalk from cheese from what they were in the past.

It would, however, be an illusion to think that all young people – or even a majority – are engaged in political activity. Not more than 15 per cent of young people are acting for perestroika or trying to make practical changes. Soviet youth is divided into two large groups. One demonstrates quite a high level of intellect, aspiring to democratic freedoms within the framework of cooperation with progressives among the older generation. The second, much the more numerous, belongs to the 'silent majority' that, at best, reads newspapers, listens to the radio, watches TV and observes the political 'games': some with distrust, some with dislike, some with utter indifference. In the popular culture variant, millions of 'infantile' young people resort to violence to the tunes of Western or home-bred rock groups, develop a cult of crude physical force, gang up and are ready to follow any demagogue who appeals to their primitive image of honour and justice. This 'silent majority' is the object of special interest for the various political groupings and parties, including the newly-formed youth organisations.

Well over 60,000 youth groups have sprung up all over the country. This shows that a youth movement is developing which is replacing the former monopoly youth organisation – the multi-million Young Communist League. It was not so long ago that the Komsomol alone had the right to represent, express and safeguard youth interests in society and government. Yet the Komsomol failed to perform its function, which is why the various youth groups have appeared.

The slow tempo of perestroika has stimulated radical moods in society, especially among young people, who are radical by nature. The wave of radicalism has given birth to political extremism. Our 1989 youth survey showed that 10 per cent of young people considered the use of force necessary to achieve democracy! This is understandable in that the cult of violence (for so many years people were forced towards happiness along a road of blood) has formed a special type of repressive consciousness in millions of people. So people think in violent terms when society is unable to resolve its social, economic and political problems. Both on the 'left' and on the 'right' there are partisans of extreme measures, coercive methods. This results in two opposing notions: 'dictatorship' and 'democracy', fusing into such paradoxical word combinations as 'the dictatorship of democracy' and 'democratic coercion'.

Extremists actively make use of young people who, in many cases, become the principal actors in violent dramas. All the mass ethnic revolts since 1986 (Yakutsk, Alma Ata, Sumgait) leading up to the bloody events in Georgia, the Fergana Valley, Nizhny Ulun and Moldova were actually 'youth acts' since up to 90 per cent of their participants were young people. Students hunger-strikes are also coming into fashion.

Crime is constantly growing among young people. During 1989 alone juvenile delinquency rose by 20 per cent; organised crime has risen sharply. As many as 1,200 organised youth gangs operate in the Soviet Union today. Hundreds of teenage hooligan groups are active in the big cities. According to the Ministry for Internal Affairs, Moscow has 160 such groups while the Tatar capital of Kazan has 63 groups involving some 1,700 members. The press talks of the infamous *Lubery* from the Moscow suburb of Lubertsy and 'Kazan gang warfare'; youth gang warfare involves so many young people in some cities that it is beyond police control.

Drop-outs, drug addicts, prostitutes and alcoholics are widespread among young people. Since 1985 drug and toxic addiction has trebled among teenagers. Recent years have seen the appearance of new marginal groups – migrants and refugees who live in poor conditions and reinforce the criminal elements.

In other words, criminal life has become a permanent feature of significant numbers of young people. Perhaps this is the most damning evidence of the moral and spiritual crisis of youth; it is a terrible national calamity, a tragedy for the country whose future depends on youth.

The psychological atmosphere of the youth environment is best described in terms of 'apathy', 'pessimism', 'nihilism', 'torpitude' and 'indifference'.

Leningrad sociologists surveyed 1,100 'drop-outs' between January and August 1990 in the cities of Moscow, Leningrad, Sochi, Kustanai, Tiumen, Rostov and Nizhny Tagil. Their findings showed that 70 per cent experienced a sense of loneliness. More than 50 per cent had contemplated suicide; some 33 per cent said that more than once they had been in a situation where they thought 'it was better to die than to live'. The country currently has an annual suicide attempt rate of 800,000: as many as 72 per cent of those committing suicide are under 29 years of age, and 63 per cent of those attempting suicide.

SOME CONCLUSIONS

All the above-mentioned trends are taking place against a background of a generation conflict. According to surveys undertaken in late 1989, only 20 per cent of young people share the ideological and political views of their parents. Since then the situation has deteriorated. The parents have no spiritual, moral or cultural values to pass on to their children. All they have is guilt for past mistakes and crimes; their legacy is an extremely impoverished, hungry and disillusioned nation with a huge budget deficit and rapidly mounting foreign debts.

The older generation has no ideals or aims that could attract or inspire young people. Most young people see nothing positive even in perestroika in that they see it as an attempt to 'renovate socialism'; perestroika was conceived ultimately in defiance rather than as a development of socialist history, as a negation not as a continuation of the past.

All the same, there is a large number of parents who 'will not forego their principles' (as the notorious Nina Andreyeva letter defending Stalinism put it) and who repeatedly talk of certain 'socialist values'. There is the 'Marxist Platform' within the Communist Party. Even President Gorbachov often speaks of the 'people's socialists choice' even though the people have no idea when they actually made that choice.

Left to the mercy of fate, the most intelligent and active part of youth is searching for new values, new constructive ideological goals. We are witnesses to the birth of a new outlook that is being built on the foundations of common human values rather than on class values. Young people who subscribe to that philosophy want to live in a society of harmony, peace, concord and humanism, in social conditions conducive to their development and the most complete flowering of their abilities.

But there is another part of youth which, while protesting against existing order, often chooses as its ideologists certain rock idols with their macho, distorted values. It is such idols rather than teachers or constructive youth leaders, who often set the tone for the thinking and behaviour of millions of teenagers. Distancing themselves from adults, such young people gang together with their peers and idols and thereby reinforce their own sense of loneliness and isolation from the adult world.

In an analogy with Greek mythology, one might say that previous generations acted like Chronos, father of the young gods: being afraid of his

children's independence he devoured them. Today, Soviet young people are
in the position of one of Chronos's children – the young god Zeus – who
refused to accept his fate, rose up against his father and killed him.

Everyone now wonders what is going to happen. For the situation is
rapidly getting out of control, and the future is unpredictable. Both the
extreme left and the extreme right realise that the country stands on the
brink of civil war. The sources of such a war are seen in the insubordination
of some republics, the arrogance of certain new political parties, the populism
of individual politicians, and the intrigues of the military and the KGB. Yet
the main danger might well come from an unexpected source: from young
people. It is unexpected because neither the public nor the politicians realise
how explosive the youth situation is; everyone is preoccupied with global
problems, and the youth problem seems too remote.

In the meantime, the potential for dissatisfaction, fear, hatred, anger and
aggression has reached its limit within the youth milieu. The scale and
acuteness of youth, especially student, revolt have grown considerably of
late. In our view, the possibility of a youth rebellion or even a youth
revolution is extremely high. To avert this, there must be an immediate
change in the attitude of society and the state of young people. The change
must come today, not tomorrow; and young people must feel it markedly.
They must see that in their talks on a radically new youth policy, the state,
the trade unions, the political parties and youth organisations are in earnest;
they are intent on creating new conditions and motivations for young people
to realise themselves and develop a sense of their own worth and dignity.

4 Urban Youth: A Sociological View

Ludmilla Koklyagina

The development of contemporary civilisation based largely on industrialisation has engendered a rapid growth in towns and cardinal changes in
residential structure. Urbanisation as a logical consequence of industralisation
has occurred at different rates and in diverse forms in various parts of the
world; but the growth in number of towns and cities has been a universal
indicator of the process. The classical American and British literature of the
turn of the century, no less vividly than the work of Frederick Engels, has
given us a picture of the growth of giant cities and especially of the fate of
the little person lost in this world. Today, over a hundred years after
urbanisation began in Europe and the United States, those patterns and
examples are being felt in exceedingly diverse ways. Here are a few lines
from one letter among many received from our respondents during a 1989–
90 postal survey.

'I'm a failure,' writes a 22-year old man who had come to Leningrad
from a small town in the Kurgan Region of the Urals. 'I no longer wish to
go on living. I suffer days and nights of despair, much more than before. But
it's not just that which is driving me to suicide.' He goes on to describe the
situation in Leningrad so sociologically that the letter could easily have
been signed by over a third of young people living in hostels for ages,
without the slightest hope of escaping. Thus, '. . . the residential permit has
forced me to choose work I don't like and which isn't what I'm qualified
for, utter loneliness, chronic lack of money, uncomfortable living quarters
(even though the hostel's in the city centre) . . . To all the rest I could add
that my head often buzzes with the notion that I'll never marry. Probably
from my inferiority complex. Here I am in the centre of Leningrad, yet I feel
as if I'm in some flyblown village as I walk the winter streets often after
midnight. It's a paradox yet, however odd it sounds, when I'm somewhere
in the suburbs I always seem to see people on the streets even at ten o'clock
at night – it's like an emptying of the soul.'

Nostalgia for life in a small, 'pure' town where he lived until leaving
school ends with the young man trying to find any way out of his dilemma
– John Braine's path to 'room at the top' takes the form in Soviet conditions
as follows: 'I love hoarding things. I'd go through hell to track down goods

in short supply or latest fashions . . . I'm simply desperate. Though I've only been in Leningrad a short while I've already managed to make various contacts (I buy imported instant coffee, condensed milk, Indian tea, all sorts of sweet boxes, various tinned meat, vanilla and so on). You think I'm boasting. By no means! I'm just describing my consumer status and giving you examples of my enterprise.' The letter finishes: 'One thing's clear: I want to live better, I need to marry a Leningrad girl to get my residential permit quickly so as I can do the work I like . . .'

The American tragedy of the late nineteenth century has not yet come to Leningrad. A 22-year old describes how he has to find 'room at the top', but you have a feeling similar to what remains from a Dreiser novel after reading these letters.

One could refer to them merely as a special Soviet phenomenon; after all, history never repeats itself. All the same, the life of young people in Soviet cities in the late 1980s and early 1990s is uncommonly close to that illuminated in classical literature.

Inspired by Stalinist industrialisation, the process of Soviet urbanisation has deep roots in the analysis of sources of industrialisation, despite affirmations to the contrary; it relied on the baneful destruction and impoverishment of Russia's traditional settlement structure, especially its villages. Yet its highest growth rates occurred in the postwar 1950s. The increase in average annual growth in urban population was due to the growth in industrial production and the mounting rural migration to the towns. Even in these years we could discern trends with which the West did not have to deal – increasing differentiation between types of urban settlement and between territorial communities within regions owing to urbanisation. The highest rates of urbanisation were in the traditionally industrial areas of the country, while the least urbanised areas during the highest urbanisation rates actually 'lost people' through an outflow of the young.

Such a detailed analysis of urbanisation in different areas of the USSR is important because this was a time when the generation of parents of today's youth started their work activity. These facts provide a more structured picture of the types of parent families of young townspeople – whether they comprise native town-dwellers or migrants – which found its reflection in differential conditions of education and training for life.

By the mid-1960s, relying on state statistics, we can clearly see the manifestation of two predominant types of area in terms of settlement structure: a self-reproducing settlement structure within a region, and regions 'giving up' their population, largely young people, with a rapidly changing settlement structure.

These processes set the social characteristics of townspeople – the parents of the present younger generation. Bearing in mind that by contrast with the urbanisation process in European states, the assertive tempos of the five-year plans were apparent for three or four years in the same assertive rates of urbanisation in the USSR. The major proportion of urban population came from those leaving the countryside which made up more than half the Soviet population right up to the 1950s.

Former villagers who had migrated to the city continued to preserve their links with the countryside. This was evident in certain manifestations of a typically rural way of life – desire to have their own home, to have an allotment to grow extra food for their family and for sale (not for recreational purposes), and to retain contacts with relatives who constituted the main community contacts along with neighbours. While in the major cities of the European part of the country and the capitals of the Baltic, Belorussian and Ukrainian republics urbanisation encouraged migrants to grow accustomed to a typically urban way of life, in the old Russian towns, largely medium and small in size, it 'hampered' the development of an urban lifestyle and led to an even greater differentiation than in the big cities because of the high rate of rural–urban migration. It is therefore not surprising to find in sociological and demographic work certain conclusions on differences between towns that possess the same size of population and between different areas of the country; these differences are found to be much greater than corresponding differences between town and country in certain regions. The fate of small towns and rural settlements deserted by young people – and therefore immediately 'aged' several times over, thus losing the potential for development – is tragic.

A considerable number of studies by well-known Soviet economists and sociologists, like T.I. Zaslavskaya and R. Ryvkina, have already been directly concerned with rural settlements. However, until recently only a few researchers had touched upon the fate of small towns that had suffered and, in certain regions, shared the fate of rural settlements. The departure of young people for the big cities not only complicated their socio-economic development, but primarily interfered with the development of those towns as a connecting link between the village and the large city; this had considerable impact on the social development of villages.

The origins of today's town-dwellers are important in analysing the status of various groups of urban youth. We may single out the following:

(a) The above-mentioned industrial development of a country in need of a constant flow of labour power was one reason why the parents of today's urban youth came to the city, thereby supplementing the army of industrial workers.

(b) The educational situation means that a large part of secondary, junior technical and higher educational institutions are located in the cities. Since the younger generation spends a substantial period of its life in education this enhances the role played by education in the destiny of migrant-parents and, furthermore, successive waves of migration relating to the educational path of the younger generation itself.

(c) Naturally, we must not forget romantic factors among reasons for migration – i.e. a desire to discover the world, a passion for new discoveries and adventures.

Since the 1970 census the proportion of young people between 16 and 29 among the urban population has changed in an undulating fashion, reflecting demographic processes (i.e. the diminishing share of young people in the Soviet population as a consequence of World War II, the fall in the birth rate during the 1970s, etc.). In 1970 almost one in every four town-dweller was young (between 16 and 29). By 1979 this figure had increased to 27.6 per cent, but had fallen back to 22.2 per cent by 1989. We must also mention the obvious aging of the urban population today – the presence of at least four generations which have become urbanites at different times and for different reasons.

Young people constitute a large part of the urban population in what was until recently typically agrarian areas whose urbanisation period was mainly in the 1950s and 1960s – the republics of Central Asia, the Transcaucasus and Moldavia.

The urbanisation process has brought changes to the proportions of urban and rural populations and left its imprint on the structure of young people. More than 37 per cent of young people from 16 to 29 live in towns of the largest republic, the Russian Federation, which accounts for half of urban youth. Over 14 per cent of the above-mentioned youth group (or 21.2 per cent of all urban youth) live in Ukrainian and Belorussian towns, 9 per cent (or 14 per cent of urban youth) live in Central Asian republics, 4 per cent (or 5 per cent of urban youth) live in Transcaucasia, some 2 per cent (or 3 per cent of urban youth) live in the Baltic republics, and 0.8 per cent (or 1 per cent of urban youth) live in Moldavia. The proportion of young people in the youth group is 68 per cent, which somewhat exceeds the share of the urban population in the total Soviet population, 66 per cent.[1]

Even with an unquestionably wider information base for analysing the objective situation, and with new statistical handbooks from the State Statistics Committee, we cannot make a more profound analysis of the situation because of the averaging out of the statistics. If we take statistics on young people living in different sized towns, large, medium and small capitals, million-plus cities, we will see at once how difficult it is to draw general conclusions. So only sample surveys can form an important part of this analysis.

A few words are in order on the *Paths of Generation* research or, rather, about that part directly concerned with urban youth analysis. In studying the lives of the younger generation, we take indicators of migration of various youth groups from one type of settlement to another and the reasons for that migration; and we take a whole series of indicators describing the youth environment at the moment it acquires secondary education and later.

The problem of identifying young people from their environment, their residential milieu and the social consequences of urbanisation is an important aspect of the analysis, which unfortunately is absent from the earlier work of Soviet sociologists.

We cannot explain the statistically high level of migration from one town to another and from one area to another as shown in state statistics merely by the high rate of industrial development and the ploughing up of new land. The educational factor was a major accelerator of youth migration in the late 1970s, when more than two-thirds of the Soviet younger generation had to leave home to acquire the compulsory general secondary education (up to 17) mainly in the towns. An even more important migration factor that for some time did not show through was the mounting differentiation in living standards in various types of settlements and areas. Our comparison of figures by longitudinal research and of those gleaned from earlier material, including an analysis of youth plans, enabled us to single out one very interesting trend reflecting this process. On the scale of life choices, the importance of such values as a trade or profession and social position gradually began to edge out the place of residence, which had taken either first place or shared first place with choice of job and social status. The letter from our respondent cited at the beginning of the chapter just goes to show that as a result the place of residence could not for many youngsters replace a favourite job and accustomed milieu. But the abstract desire to live in a big city is causing serious human tragedies for the majority.

The most serious questions remain housing, income and the close nature of young people with their unresolved problems.

Although it would be wrong to claim that the great bulk of young people wish to live in the cities – and, furthermore, in big cities – our research material enables us to see that potential migration (or intention to change place of residence) is much lower than real migration in several areas. The big city normally attracts the youth of industrial regions – such as the Urals, the Ukraine and the central part of Russia. At the same time, the industrial-agrarian areas provide another model of migration orientation, where the main factor is the small town and even a rural-type settlement. Is this a desire by young people to live in less hectic conditions, with lower pretensions and less uncertainty about their own powers, or is it simply a fear of the big city with all its problems? We have no simple answer; in each case we have to look at the entire set of factors, including the social background of the young people, the type of secondary education they have acquired and where they have studied.

Unfortunately, the objective situation – to gain an education and trade, and to work in one's trade or profession – means living far from the parental home in two out of three cases.

Research into the living conditions of those completing their education in the different types of secondary schools and colleges mentioned above confirms the hypothesis that differences in housing are closely connected with the type of secondary school or college which young people attend. Pupils at secondary schools normally continue to live with their parents while they are studying, and their proportion among students at technical and trade colleges, where they comprise some 60 per cent, is fairly high. Of these students less than a third live in hostels during their studies. On the other hand, acquiring an education and a farming skill as well as study in non-production colleges means changing one's place of residence and taking a place in a hostel at the age of 15 or 16 for 40 per cent of all such students. A few years later, by the time they leave school or college, the youngsters living in hostels will be very different from their erstwhile schoolmates.

From time to time newspapers, radio and television make critical remarks about a particular trade school or college where the authorities seem to have lost control of the students. They debate the excesses of smoking and drinking, and early sexual relations among the young people. More than any other educational institution, the one that gets most criticism is the so-called trade school (PTU – professionalno-tekhnicheskoye uchilishche). These establishments have earned themselves an unenviable reputation. The curious fact is that in trying to raise the reputation of such colleges in the eyes of the public, the people in charge laud the excellent facilities and variety of trades offered, and they play down the weaknesses, such as the low level of training of students coming from incomplete secondary schools (where students have a much lower success rate than other school pupils) and the poor discipline record.

The real picture of negative habits spreading among students therefore covers up an already complex set of stereotypes – namely that the secondary schools are for good students – although a certain deviance has developed there too – while technical college students are virtually 'programmed' for negative behaviour.

The desire for imitation and a heightened sense of hankering after everything new and unusual, as well as a desire to appear more adult, in certain circumstances will encourage the all-round development of a young person's personality; in some, however, it leads to a deformed view of everything around and an inclination towards negative forms of conduct. In the latter this occurs normally in the absence or weakening of natural social control from adults.

At the level of everyday consciousness, for some reason there has developed the idea that today's youth listens to no one and rejects everything and all authority, especially that of their parents. At the same time, the findings from our research in virtually all areas show that parents are the most important authority figures for graduates of secondary schools and colleges; this particularly applies to the mothers, whose opinions are listened to by between a quarter and two-thirds of all students. It applies less to fathers. On the whole, however, parental authority remains higher in contrast to that of young people's peers, teachers or lecturers. Parental advice is less often rejected by graduates when taking important decisions.

The research showed that 15–16 was the major age 'peak' in taking up smoking and drinking, while a sex life begins at 14–16. From the viewpoint of age psychology, it is precisely this age that bears the 'difficult' tag, in that the physiological maturation of teenagers is much faster than their social development.

It is this age period that coincides with study in the senior classes of secondary schools and trade colleges, and as a result of the problem over the location of educational institutions (since they are mainly in big cities or towns) two-thirds of teenagers are taken away from their natural social milieu into hostels and apartments. Thus, in the Tula Region one in ten technical college students and one in five students at trade school live in hostels. If we include those who live outside the parents' family, we have 7 per cent of school leavers, virtually a third of trade school graduates and a quarter of technical college graduates; in Estonia the corresponding figures are 5 per cent, 59 per cent and 44 per cent; in Tadzhikistan 3 per cent, 33 per cent and 26 per cent; in the Sverdlovsk Region 1 per cent, 78 per cent and 37 per cent.

We have deliberately ignored here the average indicators of housing conditions of graduates of secondary educational institutions, since those customary 'averages' can only distort our impression of the real situation. However, the figures we cite do show the general trend. Almost a third of students at trade school and technical college during the 'difficult age' are deprived of natural social control because of the lack of a suitable network of secondary educational institutions which corresponds with the settlement pattern of the regions. In other words, young people, especially those from the countryside, have to leave their parents' home to gain a secondary education and a trade.

One objection to this approach to the problem is the idea that life away from parents teaches young people independence and helps them to mature socially. Proponents of such a view remind us of positive examples from the past, citing young 14–15 year olds who have left the parental home to go to work and have become completely independent people, growing up swiftly. There are two objections to such a view. First, to leave the parental home to gain secondary schooling does not alter the major form of youth activity since young people continue to have to study, and second, independence assumes material autonomy, i.e. the ability to satisfy their own needs for clothes, housing, food and other factors – in other words, self-reliance. But this does not happen, as our research shows.

The new environment of trade and technical college students in hostel conditions substantially differs from what the home provided. We would single out two of its key characteristics. First, today the sex and age composition of groups of school and college students shows a concentration of girls in schools and boys in technical colleges. As regards the various vocational schools, the composition depends on their profile: in some, young women, in others young men dominate. So, there is no normal environment in which girls and boys can study together, enabling them in a certain measure to smooth over the various negative behaviour patterns from young men (for example, that of bad language). Second, technical college students tend to come from a fairly poor background; their parents tend to have low education and often material levels. Primitive stereotypes of behaviour and orientation on physical force are usually the characteristics of such an environment. In particular, from a quarter to a third of technical school leavers, according to various regions, state that their parents often punished them; this is a much higher figure than for schoolchildren. Naturally, it is difficult to imagine in such circumstances that negative habits acquired at home will easily be overcome. Further, they are likely to spread much more quickly when one is surrounded by people from a similar background.

Thus, those who do not smoke at all among school leavers consist of between three-quarters and four-fifths depending on the region. There were fewest smokers among school leavers in Belorussia and the Kurgan Region; among trade school students the proportion of those who did not smoke at all ranged from 40 per cent in Estonia to 76 per cent in Belorussia. Technical college students occupy an intermediary position: the share of non-smokers ranges from 48 per cent in Estonia to 74 per cent in the Kurgan

Region. The biggest smokers to be found among all students (smoking up to half a packet of 20 a day) are those at technical college; their proportion is virtually the same in all regions, comprising about 30 per cent.

The problem of the campaign against drink and smoking cannot be fully resolved without fresh generations of young people reproducing the 'army of drunks and smokers'. Many research projects are studying this problem today; it has interested us here purely within the context of the general characteristics that concern the lives of the younger generation. There are fewer non-drinkers than non-smokers among graduates of secondary schools and colleges. And schoolchildren are once more in the lead: more than 60 per cent of them in Belorussia, and the Tula and Kurgan Regions, 57 per cent in the Kharkov Region, 47 per cent in Estonia and 42 per cent in Sverdlovsk Region said that they hardly ever touched spirits. At the same time, non-drinkers among technical college students comprise: 38 per cent in the Kharkov Region, 36 per cent in the Sverdlovsk Region, some 30 per cent in the Tula and Kurgan Regions and Belorussia, and 23 per cent in Estonia. Further, those who 'partake fairly often' came to 7 per cent of school leavers in Estonia, 20 per cent of technical colleges and trade schools, 15 per cent of vocational colleges, while in the Tula Region the figures were 3 per cent of schoolchildren, yet one in ten graduates of technical colleges and trade schools.

The great bulk of graduates of secondary schools and colleges regard themselves as infrequent drinkers (at parties only), and make up a half of all respondents.

We may draw preliminary conclusions on whether the existence of bad habits among school and college students is by chance or has some under-lying cause. It is certainly not coincidental. The reasons are to be found not only in the failings of educational work within the colleges and schools – and in the hostels to which we could devote a special study – but also in the imbalance between educational developments and the existing residential pattern, i.e. the principles on which schools and colleges are located and staffed. This is not so much an educational as a social problem, inasmuch as it lays the foundation for a person's path in life. Perhaps it was still possible yesterday to accept that cadres had to be trained faster and at any price, but now we are posing quite a different question.

An inalienable facet of this problem is that of the future potential of our society, particularly the future health of our young people, since their overall state of health and capacity for work stem from their living condi-tions. The present research did not aim at a detailed analysis of such problems. Almost nine-tenths of the young people in our survey noted that they are in good health, and are not prevented from taking part in work and play along with their peers; at the same time, one in ten cannot take a full part because of health reasons.

Virtually all students had suffered infectious and common cold diseases (least of all among Tadzhikistan students), but we are left with serious cause for thought about the fact that from a tenth to a quarter of those surveyed say they suffer from chronic illnesses. Let us remind ourselves that the average age of young people in the survey was 17–18. Clearly, the problem of shaping a self-maintaining awareness which, at a higher level, is part of the struggle for human survival, should be seen as more than averting the threat of world nuclear war. Bad habits do not appear out of thin air. We have to do all·we can to seek their causes in the circumstances in which young people live today.

NOTES

1.   *Molodyozh SSSR. Statistichesky sbornik* (Moscow: Molodaya Gvardia, 1990), pp. 4–35. All other references and data are taken from the unpublished study *Paths of a Generation* under the supervision of M. H. Titma.

Part Three
Privilege and the Market

5 The End of Privilege?
Mervyn Matthews

Virtually everyone who has an interest in Russia would now readily concede that Soviet society possesses an easily recognisable elite. This fact was
not always widely appreciated. The existence of elitism in a rigorously
'socialist' society was for decades carefully concealed in official pro-
nouncement. And so loud was the blare of Marxist-Leninist propaganda, so
inaccessible was Soviet society to objective study, that many people in the
West were inclined to accept, in large measure, Soviet protestations of
egalitarianism. Indeed, such was the lack of awareness of the phenomenon
that Milovan Djilas's interesting, though unoriginal, book on the so-called
'new class', created something of a sensation when it appeared in 1957.

Of course, eminent western scholars (like M. Fainsod, W.W. Kulski and
others) did much to dispel egalitarian illusions, at least with regard to the
Soviet political elite. But they were often regarded as overly critical and
'cold warish'. And a few Western observers (particularly sociologists of a
Marxist cast of mind) were only too ready to ignore Soviet elitism, or
downplay its significance. Fortunately, from the 1970s onwards, the Soviet
elite was increasingly explored by outsiders, and the truth about it became
more readily available. Even so, elitism in the USSR should never have
enjoyed the sort of concealment it did, nor benefited from so much scholarly indifference in the West.[1]

It has, need we say, a long history. It was born in the turbulent days after
the Revolution, and became, even before Lenin died, a central element in
the Soviet edifice. Despite stringent censorship, there were soon fair indications of its existence, had one sought them – in the system of state honorifics,
wage differentials, housing laws, social security provisions, etc. Much
valuable testimony was provided by journalists and émigrés.

Perestroika and glasnost brought exceptional opportunities for analysis
and discussion inside the Soviet Union itself.* Native observers were
allowed, and indeed only too ready, to make incisive comment. As a

---

* The unexpected developments of August 1991 have made several paragraphs of this paper
particularly inapposite. Like many observers of the Soviet scene the writer anticipated a
decline in the status of the CPSU, rather than its sudden dissolution as a bureaucratic entity.
However, we imagine that the perspective as of early 1991 is still of interest; much of our
comment remains valid; and the reader may be intrigued by our references to the possibility of
abrupt change.

consequence, the press became awash with facts and criticism, together with (rather feeble) defence from beleaguered groups. It appears that (unlike Western Marxist-Leninists) Soviet citizens have always been keenly aware of elitism in their society. Many of them also seem to be highly resentful of it, either because they find it ideologically unacceptable, or simply because most of the privilege is perceived to be ill deserved. Officials who basked in it throughout their careers are now held responsible for the economic disaster which has struck the land. Elitism, in its traditional Soviet form, is under attack. We are now, in a sense, witnessing another extreme reaction: for elitism can surely be a healthy phenomenon in certain well-recognised circumstances, and may even be deserving of some protection.

There are, it would seem, four principal reasons for the new criticism, all intimately connected and easily perceived. The first is political freedom, which raises the real possibility of a changed social order; the second is a certain commercial freedom, which will evidently undermine old administrative practices; the third is critical (and destructive) utterance in the media; and the fourth is nationalism, which sharply diminishes the power of the centre.

Gorbachov obviously did not anticipate the thrust of these forces when he started out: and he may well have done a U-turn or two, had it been possible. We believe that he intended to change the old order, renewing and revitalising it, while retaining a framework of Party supremacy. He wanted a small opposition for purposes of competition and useful criticism, not the total collapse of the old centralist order. Obviously, if there is collapse, the old forms of privilege have to go with it. Yet for all his shortcomings, Mikhail Sergeevich must be credited with having effected a political miracle, in this respect as in several others.

The object of this paper must, in the circumstances, be limited. We shall endeavour to review the current pressures on old-style privilege in the USSR, and consider how they are being countered by existing elite groups. The task is not an easy one. Profound changes are still afoot: the picture is confused; and although the information at our disposal is many times more voluminous than it was, it is unorganised and scattered. We cannot be sure that important facts have not been overlooked, and ask the reader's indulgence if they have. We would hope, however, to assess the situation generally, on the basis of recent developments. At the same time the possibility of more unexpected developments, even cataclysmic change, must be kept in mind. The whole Soviet system has suffered many shocks since Gorbachov came to power.

In terms of elite groups, we shall focus only on two: the Party elite, and the country's top economic managers. They are important components of the elite as a whole, and since they have been most in the limelight, are easier to write about. The Party elite is anyway closely allied to what might be termed the state/administrative elite, the bureaucrats who head state organisations. The managers may be *the* new class of the future. We shall have brief comment on the KGB and military. A discussion of all elite groups, including the intelligentsia, creative artists, diplomatic personnel, etc., is scarcely practical and would require a more lengthy analysis than we can undertake here.

THE POLITICAL ELITE

One should probably begin by affirming that the mass membership of the CPSU was never, in any true sense, an elite, being too numerous (19.5 million in October 1988) and too lacking in influence.[2] In the past people entered the Party mainly to improve their career prospects at the workplace. However, the CPSU has always been characterised by a strongly hierarchical structure, and for purposes of analysis here it is convenient to think in terms of three types of more elitist membership.

The more active rank and file members could find themselves elected to some 400,000 positions in a hierarchy of territorial committees, ranging from the local *gorkom* (town committee) to the Central Committee of the CPSU itself.

Positions were held from two to five years, but there has usually been a large proportion of re-elections, giving longer tenure. Membership of these committees has traditionally yielded not only political influence at the said level, but also personal contacts which could be useful over long periods. The second kind of special membership involved a full-time career in the Party apparatus, which exercised political power on centralist lines in all localities. Its size and exact configuration have long been shrouded in secrecy, but it was generally thought it number over 100,000.

The third type of membership comprised what might be thought of as the Party elite proper, and core of elitism in the USSR: it included all Party 'bosses', from the first secretaries of large towns, districts and regions up to the Politburo in Moscow. As we well know, there has always been a considerable overlap between the three categories; elections were largely bogus; central control was effected through the nomenclature system; and the Party in turn intermeshed with state and 'social' organisations. In terms of life-style the whole bureaucratic elite enjoyed superior access to goods and services through administrative rather than commercial channels, and a highly protected standard of living. In a sense Party elitism reached its peak with the promulgation of the 1977 Constitution, Clause Six of which termed the CPSU 'the leading and directing force in Soviet society, the nucleus of its political system and of all state and social organisations'. Until Mikhail Sergeevich came to power most observers considered this structure to be virtually immovable.

The changes actually taking place may be summarised as follows. First, we have the much-commented fact that the Party elite is losing its monopolistic control of the state machinery. This is an intricate topic, and the situation is still, at the time of writing, highly unstable. Certain tendencies are nevertheless clear. Gorbachov assumed new powers as President, not as head (or General Secretary) of the CPSU. The old All-Union Politburo was side-stepped first by the Presidential Council, and then (after November 1990) by Gorbachov's Federation and Security Councils. In the Russian Federation, a decree of the Supreme Soviet forbade the simultaneous holding of authoritative state powers and any other responsible position in a state, political or social organisation.[3] The state legislature (one must now talk of legislatures), though heavily weighted with CPSU members and overshadowed by the new nominated organs, acquired a new public image and some influence on government.

The replacement of the old, powerful USSR Council of Ministers by a new Cabinet of Ministers, also outside the Party structure, and the possible weakening of the centralist producer ministries as the economy lost its command structure, all betoken a weakening of the old Party apparatus. The alignment of forces in the localities is not clear (even within Russia) but must eventually reflect the changed relationships in the centre. The mass Party members, formerly meek and united supporters of the elite, are overtly split, as witnessed by the appearance of the oppositionist Democratic Platform. By late 1990 Gorbachov appeared to be strengthening his own powers without direct reliance on the old Party levers.

Secondly, the new configuration of politics was leading, in the late 1980, to a cutback in the size of the full-time Party apparatus, at least from the republican levels down, and a loss, or potential loss of power by the territorial committees. This was not the first time that the apparatus has been reduced, but this particular reduction seems to have been the most specific for many years.[4] Under the terms of a decree of the Central Committee passed on 10 September 1988 a new simplified structure was proposed for republican and lower territorial offices, involving an overall closure of 1,064 departments, or 44 per cent of the 2,418 in existence. The data as published were deliberately incomplete: they did not cover the highest, All-Union organs, nor reveal the number of transfers. But the republican and territorial staff cuts varied from 30 per cent to 10 per cent, and evidently totalled a little under 12,000. In social terms, career prospects plunged for many.[5]

Thirdly, the Party elite has lost its veil of secrecy. The current revelations may be regarded as having started in 1986 with the uncovering of corruption and bribery among Brezhnev's family and close associates. Personal criticism of the late leader culminated in the accusation in April 1988 that he had awarded himself unmerited medals, and by the removal of his name from public places. Indeed a drive was then started to re-establish pre-revolutionary place names, removing those of famed communist leaders.[6]

With the advent of glasnost criticism of the Party elite quickly became a recognised genre in the press, with two specific focuses: the failure of this elite to manage the country properly, and its undeserved privileges. The outspoken weekly *Argumenty i fakty*, for example, actually seemed to specialise in it (which is why we have used it for many of our references here). Boris Yeltsin, President of the Russian Federation, joined in with a book of his own. The new periodicals (appearing with or without authorisation) have also devoted considerable amounts of space to it, sometimes with articles of a sensational character.[7]

Let us take, as an example of serious, negative treatment, the results of a survey of 2,500 respondents, organised by the All-Union Centre for the Study of Public Opinion, and published in *Moskovskie novosti* on 15 April 1990. Over 60 per cent of the sample thought that the CPSU had pursued wrong policies, and nearly 90 per cent that it had restricted national growth. Over two-thirds blamed the Party leadership, including 37 per cent past, and 29 per cent present leaderships. On the other hand, only 17.4 per cent thought the Party as a whole was to blame. No less significant was assessment of the role and authority of the Party in 'making the country great'. Sixty-two per cent thought the USSR would not have been a great nation without it: but positive assessments fell from 39 per cent for the period of the Revolution and Civil War to 2–3 per cent for NEP, the Khrushchov years, the Brezhnev years . . . and perestroika.

Only 5.8 per cent thought that local Party organs reflected the will and opinions of the mass membership, and 12.3 per cent believed public confidence in the Party could be re-established. Obviously, the Party, and the Party elite in particular, must suffer a loss in prestige as a result of such revelations, for public dislike, formerly unmapped, is now openly, and most disadvantageously, expressed.

High salaries are always an especially sensitive matter, and those of Party officials (absolutely secret after the 1920s) are now published. They can only serve as an extra focus of envy, given the published national average of 220 roubles a month, and a minimum 'full' pension of 70. Gorbachov's own salary passed into the public domain in November 1990 and was given as 2,400 roubles a month, or 1,400 roubles after tax. According to figures published in February 1990 the salaries of the Party apparatus in the Ukraine (and presumably in other republics, as they had been fixed by the Central Committee in Moscow) ranged from 870 roubles a month for secretaries of the Central Committee down to a minimum of 280 roubles for a modest instructor (i.e. junior officer) at the town and district level. By way of justification, some average salaries in the production sector in Kiev and local regions were given. They varied from 1,125 roubles for managers of large enterprises to 240 roubles for milkmaids. However, other Party benefits (as everybody knew) would also have to be taken into account: we shall consider these separately below.[8]

Next, there is the spectre of the new, oppositionist, elite. A political opposition is already very much in evidence, not only in Moscow and the republican capitals, but also in local government (at least in Russia). Noncommunist deputies aspire to play an active role; the local administrations, despised under Stalin and neglected under Khrushchov and Brezhnev, are assuming a new importance; and there has been talk of allowing them to levy their own taxes. The role of the local Party office is in question.

As yet opposition politicians publicly embrace non-elitist ideals, attitudes and life-styles. They also have many of the characteristics of the political elites we know in the West; a populist stance, an insecurity of political tenure, pluralistic concepts of political life and economic function, vulnerability to criticism, etc. Conversely, the oppositionist elite lacks the characteristics of its Soviet predecessors – secretiveness, final control of political machinery, the support of the KGB and military, access to restricted supplies and services. It maintains that under a democratic order a new national leadership would have to forego the practices of the old one.

Beyond that, the republican Party elites must inevitably suffer from any break-up of the union. Of course there have always been nationalists in the non-Russian organs of the CPSU. But the insistent centralism of the system meant that all roads led to Moscow, and the centre could always offer help. The nomenclature system ensured All-Union cohesion and stable ordering. The presence of non-Slavs like a Pelshe, Rashidov or Kunaev in the Politburo, with local nationals in higher Party bodies, gave a kind of assurance. The rise of irredentist nationalism outside the CPSU has meant that the local elites have become more vunerable on this count. Not only may they be blamed for economic failure, as at a national level, they tend to trail an association with hated Russian domination.

THE ENTERPRISE MANAGERS

The managers of economic enterprises are the second major group on whose fate we wish to comment. They are, in many ways, less homogeneous than Party and state officials, and only a limited number of all managers could, by virtue of their income, responsibilities and nomenclature status, be considered to fall truly within the elite. In November 1988 there were said to be 475,000 managers of 'independent enterprises'. When we examined the managerial *elite* as of the early 1970s we hypothesised a total of some 17,000. Having in mind the growth of the economy, we would now propose a figure somewhat bigger. But the problem need not detain us, as we are concerned with new trends and pressures, rather than social delineation. Suffice it to say that enterprise managers form a much smaller elite group than Party and state officials.[9]

There is, we must remember, a profound difference between their prospects. Whereas Party officialdom faces a popular threat of suppression, or virtual exclusion from power, good production managers will always be needed. The problem lies in switching their activities from an administrative to a commercial base, with possibly more meritocratic forms of advancement.

Though much involved in the perestroika processes, enterprise managers have so far escaped the intense criticism which has been the lot of Party/ state administrators. This may be because managers are commonly thought to be less responsible for past failure, and more deserving of support. A man who runs a macaroni factory may be involved in administration but he is obviously doing something worthwhile, even if his output plans are unfulfilled. The usefulness of an official sitting in the local *obkom* (regional Party committee) is less evident. At the same time, we would argue that the position of most managers, especially the managerial elite, is becoming significantly less secure than it was.

The first reason for this lies in the policy of turning the traditional, centrally administered enterprise into a more independent unit which produces and actually sells desirable goods in market conditions. The new enterprise law of July 1987 was a major step in this direction. It involved changing wage and bonus systems to encourage contractual, rather than 'command' relationships (both inside and between enterprises), more efficiency, independence, and higher earnings.[10] This must lead to more differentiation. Managers of units which could face the new pressures and perform better stood to benefit: but unviable enterprises and sections now faced the danger of closure. In fact, the official figures for 1988 showed that between 3 per cent and 21 per cent of enterprises in all production and service branches of the economy were loss-making.

Inside the enterprise, the manager may now find that he is vulnerable from below. He may be blamed not merely for unfulfilled plans and forfeiture of bonus, but for staff reductions, and even closure. He may face the novel prospect of unemployment himself. The strike committee has made its appearance, an event unthinkable but a few years ago. Any connections he may have with Party committees have become less useful. New rules stipulate that he has to stand for regular re-selection by his employees. It is difficult to judge how realistic this process is, and we have so far seen no comprehensive data on exclusions. According to the national statistical handbook, however, by 15 November 1988 27 per cent of the managers of individual industrial enterprises had been elected by their workforces.[11] Changes in economic management have so far been limited in scope, mainly on account of their social cost, impracticability, or opposition from vested interests, especially the planners and ministries. The proposed growth of the private sector is another cloud on the managerial horizon, though one not as yet to be greatly feared, as the new private sector is small and problem-ridden.[12]

Another concern for the higher-paid members of the elite, both in administrative and production hierarchies, is the new system of income tax. One long-standing feature of Soviet reality was a tax system, introduced in 1943 and hardly modified later, with a maximum rate, for state workers and employees, of up to 13 per cent. It was therefore low and non-redistributive. True, rising nominal wages intended to increase the proportion of salary deducted from all earners, but by 1988 the full deduction would have been only about 22 roubles from the average wage of just under 220.

From September 1990 tax rates in the upper brackets were raised significantly. The payment on 220 roubles would still have been about 24 roubles, but that on, say, 1,200 roubles (which we may take as a 'threshold' elite salary) would have risen from about 151 roubles to 247 roubles. Someone earning 3,001 roubles, however, would be paying 1,046 instead of 385 roubles. Though these rates are modest by Western standards, it must be borne in mind that the Soviet elite is much poorer. Also unsettling is the fact that half a century of tax quiescence is now at an end.[13]

PRESSURES ON ELITE BENEFITS

A major advantage of belonging to an elite, especially in conditions of widespread shortage, is the enjoyment of a relatively high standard of living. The long-established system of distributing goods and services through administrative channels has been considered unjust enough to warrant on-going consideration at the highest levels. In 1989 the Supreme Soviet of the USSR set up a Deputies' Commission on Benefits and Privileges, while the Presidium of the Supreme Soviet of the Russian Federation established its own Commission for Ordering (*po uporyadocheniyu*) Benefits and Privileges. Their work seems to centre on restricted access to consumer goods and services, special medical care, personal transport, and personal pensions. The USSR Commission was said to be concerned not with procuratorial 'investigation' of these matters, but with elucidating their causes and proposing change.[14]

Privileged food supplies have become a matter of growing contention as the shops have emptied and rationing spread. The main, and most resented, form was the closed distributor, or *raspredelitel*. Two other less exclusive but useful channels were workplace buffets (with take-home sales) and weekly orders, also delivered at the workplace. These systems offered three benefits in one: the provision of foodstuffs unobtainable in the shops, acquisition without queueing, and in some cases, extremely low prices. We must also not forget that higher salaries gave largely the same families the possibility of buying fresh produce in the collective farm markets, where (according to official figures) prices were two and a half times higher than in state shops.[15] The few well-placed citizens who could get foreign currency or vouchers were also able to use the foreign-currency and Beriozka shops offering a selection of virtually unobtainable (to Soviet citizens) goods to foreign tourists, foreign residents and diplomats.

A crack-down in this sphere apparently started in January 1988, when under the terms of a decree of the USSR Council of Ministers, the foreign-currency shops were forbidden to serve Soviet citizens. On September of the same year the most notorious government *raspredelitel*, situated on Granovski Street in central Moscow and trading under the comforting name of 'Curative Dining Hall', was closed. Its five thousand chosen customers were obliged to look for other sources of nourishment.[16]

On 1 February 1990 the USSR government introduced a decree which envisaged the abolition of all special food supply systems for Party, state, economic and social organisations. According to the text of the article in *Pravda*:

The so-called base no. 208 [in the capital] which had supplied high quality groceries to about 400 organisations, from the USSR Council of Ministers to Mosfilm and [elitist] fishing and hunting societies, has been reorganised. Henceforth it will serve 26 orphanages, 12 children's homes, the Botkin Hospital (in its entirety, not only the 'privileged' block), the Sklifosovski sanitorium, and children's hospitals . . . The dining rooms and buffets of ministries, administrations, All-Union and republican organisations are being detached from 'special supplies'. A trickle of produce will be directed for state receptions and presentation purposes, but in a significantly reduced quantity. The governments of the union republics have been entrusted with taking like decisions. This was done in the Russian Federation a few days ago.[17]

Transport is a sensitive subject in so far as public services are inferior, while private cars are extremely expensive and difficult to get. The total of passenger cars for 1988 may be estimated at only fifteen million. Furthermore, many of the vehicles in private ownership, given the shortage of spare parts, high prices and harsh climate, must have been in a poor state, so the figure may not reflect usability.[18]

The high quota of cars available to bureaucrats has been raised a number of times in published interviews. Vehicles supplied to the Central Committee were among the matters the Democratic Platform had hoped to discuss at the 28th Party Congress in July 1990. V. Ginsburg, a member of the USSR Supreme Soviet Commission on Privileges, claimed that in 1989 there were about a million official cars in the USSR, each of which cost, with garaging, repairs and chauffering, between 8–10,000 roubles a year. No doubt as a consequence of public criticism the USSR Council of Ministers had (he said) passed a decree cutting the number of official vehicles by 40 per cent. However, Ginsburg expressed doubt as to whether the decree could, or would, be implemented.[19]

The health-care facilities available to the general public, although basically free, have always been mediocre or poor. For the man in the street better service could be obtained only at fee-paying clinics or from private practitioners. People in senior posts, by contrast, had access to relatively good, but restricted, medical services – polyclinics, hospital wards, sanatoria and rest-homes. Most of these were run by the Fourth Directorate of the USSR Ministry of Health. At the same time powerful organisations like the CPSU, the USSR Council of Ministers and the Komsomol were at liberty to establish their own, and did so, particularly for recuperative and holiday use. After a barrage of criticism, the USSR Council of Ministers, by a decree of 12 October 1989, abolished the Fourth Directorate, and transferred its institutions elsewhere (a matter to which we shall return below).[20]

Personal pensions, originally established by Lenin for individuals who gave exemplary service to the socialist state, have become another source of contention. In 1988 they were still enjoyed at the All-Union, republican and local levels by 338,219 persons, out of a total contingent of 58.6 million pensioners.[21] The maximum personal pensions varied between 140 and 250 roubles a month, while the national average for normal pensions was 80 roubles in the state sector, and 55 roubles among peasants. The Russian Supreme Soviet abolished not only all personal pensions throughout the republic as from 1 October 1990, but also additional privileges (presumably the rent reductions, favoured travel and holiday arrangements, etc.) which such pensioners employed. The practice of awarding personal pensions for work in social organisations and membership of the CPSU was actually declared illegal. 'It is a secret for no one,' wrote V. Romanenko in *Argumenty i Fakty*, 'that at times the question of personal pensions is decided by a narrow circle of persons, without the opinion of fellow workers or any account of the recipient's work. Apart from that, they are sometimes awarded to persons who have abused their official position.'[22]

Elite housing is another major problem. The practice here has been for privileged citizens to get space well above locally-approved norms, in blocks of flats which are well situated and either built by the organisation for which they work, or ceded by the local authority. In addition, it is easier for persons of influence and high income to buy accommodation in the private sector, as prices are high and mortgage repayments, even at low rates of interest, beyond average means.

The most striking revelation recently to come to our attention concerned two separate blocks of flats in the desirable Oktyabr district of Moscow, one built by the CPSU Central Committee and the other by the USSR Council of Ministers (*Sovmin*). The district housing officer, A. Zhokin, gave a very frank interview about abuses involved. The district housing commission had found, in the autumn of 1990, that although the actual ownership of the blocks was not in question, blatant irregularities had occurred in the allocation of all flats in the CPSU house, and nearly all in the *Sovmin* house. The Russian regulations stipulating a maximum of twelve square metres per dweller, together with the statutory six-month limitation on leaving new space unoccupied, had been ignored. Apart from this there were apparently breaches of the militia restrictions on residence in Moscow. On the other hand, 40 per cent of the permanent inhabitants of the district were still living in communal (i.e. shared) flats, and there were 22,000 people on the local waiting list.[23]

All the privileged tenants had received, or were due to receive, far more space than they were entitled to: many had moved under false pretences (because their previous norms did not warrant rehousing); and many of the flats had been left empty for long periods. Much of the accommodation was destined for immediate occupation by officials called in from other parts of the country, which (given the local waiting lists) was considered to be obviously unfair. The surplus space in the CPSU block alone equalled 130 flats, that in the *Sovmin* block (which had been frozen by the local Soviet) amounted to 180.

To put the matter in even better perspective, in 1989 the district had received, for all the people on its housing lists, only 189 flats, and in 1990 only 101. Thus, the living space illegally allocated in the two blocks exceeded the annual allotment for the whole district. Also, it was of vastly superior quality, the average construction cost being 446 roubles a square metre, against 271 roubles for council housing in Moscow, and 233 in Moscow Region.

An associated problem is that of the state dachas (country homes), which, given the problems of holidaying, are a valuable benefit. E.M. Primakov, head of the USSR Commission for Privileges (and also a Candidate Member of the Politburo) mentioned the matter no less than three times in a published interview. He gave a defensive assurance that all such dachas had been taken from their former occupants, though he then contradicted himself by saying that only 'the first two members' of the Politburo still had them, while some of the older officials deserved special treatment. He claimed, incidentally, that he himself had received only eight days' holiday for the whole of 1989. He had been criticised for using an official plane when he left Moscow, despite the fact that this accorded with the rules then in force.[24]

WHITHER PRIVILEGE?

The pressure on Soviet elite groups and their life-styles are many, but it would be wrong, in our opinion, to assume that such pressure will be overwhelming. The forces which support elitism are numerous, and it is to these that we now turn.

One should, perhaps, begin with some sound generalisations. Laws of social development are curious things, and often turn out to be untrue: but the existence of elites of one kind or another in all modern societies nevertheless seems to have a certain firm inevitability. In any case, it is difficult to think of a society, socialist or capitalist, from which they are absent. Vilfredo Pareto's theory of elites evidently contained truths as well as absurdities. There is little indication that the Soviet populace as a whole still adheres to rigidly egalitarian ideals: it may believe, as do some people in the West, that elitism can be positive if it is accessible to the deserving, open to public scrutiny, and serves to stimulate social progress. In theoretical terms the ultimate disappearance of all elites from Soviet (or Russian) society thus seems highly unlikely. One would expect elitism only to acquire other forms.

Secondly, even if the existing Soviet elite is dissolved, the likelihood is that it will be replaced, as we have indicated, by new groupings. The latter, indeed, are already striving to consolidate, and form political counter-elites. New trade union movements will generate their own national leadership. A new media elite is certainly being born. The church is re-emerging as a powerful social force, and although one sees few changes in its phalanx of leaders, they are becoming more prominent.

The private sector is producing its first 'businessmen', though that process is only in its earliest stages, and the term may be scarcely appropriate. Conditions are highly restrictive, and likely to encourage, at least in the short term, what Max Weber called 'booty' capitalism – unhealthy variety, subject to state intervention, and lacking guarantees for long-term development. Soviet capitalists, in any case, might be very heterogeneous, with poor and rich among them. Nevertheless the seed has been sown. As for the world of criminality, there is every indication that a powerful new-style mafia is in the making, and this, too, will have its place in the picture.

If the Soviet Union does disintegrate, each republic must, according to this argument, generate its own elites. There has been much talk about a military coup; if this disaster should occur, then the country might well acquire a ruling military elite characteristic of Central or South America. All of these scenarios should at least provide ample research opportunities for the next generation of scholars. Increasing contacts with the West may render new Soviet elites more like their Western counterparts in life-styles and attitudes.

So much for new growth. At the same time it is obvious that the existing elite, though under sore pressure, is by no means finished. In fact, it is currently putting up a strong rearguard action. Although CPSU membership is beginning to fall, it still far exceeds any other organised political grouping. Over the first six months of 1990 some 350,000 people left the Party, but 54,800 joined. In terms of Party history this outflow is highly unusual, and may of course turn into a flood. It is a cause for concern, but given the size of the membership, hardly alarm. A lot of people follow Gorbachov in thinking that the Party can be revitalised, despite the predominance of die-hards at the top of its hierarchy.[25]

In the republics the CPSU has shown an ability to retain popularity by intensifying its nationalistic colouring. In the recent elections in Georgia, for example, the local Communist Party lost power, but remained the largest single party in the republic.[26] It would seem likely that CPSU members, at least in the lower age-groups or less senior posts, have useful political experience which they can offer to the public, plus a strong incentive to change their spots.

The Party apparatus still has possession of most, if not all, Party buildings, offices and printing facilities, usually located on prime sites. In September 1990 it was revealed that the Internal Affairs Ministry deployed 1,900 militiamen to guard state offices, and some 10,000 to guard 'Party organs, the entrances to houses of members of the Central Committee[s] and obkom secretaries'.[27] The central apparatus in Moscow still occupies the same highly prestigious premises. The question of removing Party offices from hundreds of sites here and elsewhere is fraught with problems. A recent letter in *Argumenty i fakty* revealed that even the withdrawal of a Party committee from its premises at a coal mine in the provinces prompted the local *raikom* (district committee) secretary to brand the move as a 'dangerous precedent'.[28]

An attempt to raise the question of Party property by the Democratic Platform at the 28th Congress was easily defeated. The Platform's declaration also revealed that the Party had a reserve financial fund of 4.9 million roubles, with annual incomes of 1,612,860,000 and 1,587,600,000 roubles from members' contributions and publishing respectively. In 1990 the cost of maintaining this apparatus was still running at 51 million roubles. However, criticism of costs did not prevent officials getting a pay rise in 1989.[29]

In 1990 the Moscow Oktyabr district Soviet achieved some fame as the first to offer, in its premises on the Shablovka, an office to a Party other than the CPSU, namely, the Democratic Party of Russia. We found, on visiting it in June of that year, two rooms and a telephone. This may be regarded as a startling departure from past Soviet practice, or an extremely modest advance for a city of nearly nine million inhabitants.

Party control of the media remains absolutely overwhelming. True, the figures for the opposition press might at first sight seem impressive. By September 1990 the State Committee for the Press had received 622 applications for the registration of new periodicals (not all political), of which 188 had been authorised. A less reliable source declared, in October of the same year, that there were 400 'socio-political' journals in existence, most of which were democratic in political orientation. According to the 1985 statistical handbook, however, there were no fewer than 1,524 'official' journals and 8,427 newspapers, all (at that time) under Party control and state censorship. We have no information on the print-runs and periodicity of the new titles, but there is little doubt that (given paper shortages, problems of finance and distribution) the volume of print was, relative to the Party-controlled press, tiny. At the centre the opposition has yet to get anything approaching a fair share of radio and TV time.[30]

The future of the economic managerial elite, or perhaps one should say, *an* economic elite, seems to be relatively assured: in the present economic circumstances there is little more to be said on this score. Change there must be: but managers are in a sense a meritorious elite, and we would suggest that the main changes here will be in turnover and type. Perhaps leading positions in the group will pass into the hands of engineers who have been able to get extra training or experience abroad. Perhaps the top Soviet managers will (of all groups) most resemble their counterparts in the West, narrowing the wide gaps in outlook and experience which at present divide them.

Though our discussion has centered on the Party and managerial elites, it behoves us to touch on the KGB, as representing possibly the best case of elitist self-defence. In conditions of glasnost, the organisation's dreadful history, and continuing surveillance activities, soon became a focus of criticism. But Gorbachov himself seemed to be treating it with caution and respect: and, in fact, very little of substance has been revealed about it.

It has run its own artificial glasnost campaign, designed more to improve its image than provide information on its activities. Such a policy is deserving of study for which we have no space here. The main developments may, however, be listed as follows: continued secrecy about numbers and function; emphasis on an apparent concern with legality, and the fact that the organisation has rid itself of guilty Stalinists; emphasis on the continuing need to counter a foreign enemy; and the provision of scraps of information about spy-catching and daily hard work. It has started to put out its own thick journal.[31] Its regular columns in newspapers, TV programmes and published interviews are invariably flattering, and there is even a tendency to dwell on its humanistic leanings. We are told there has been a profound reorientation of its work from politics (or 'ideology' as it is euphemistically called) to the struggle with the new mafia.[32]

An officer who broke the code of silence and divulged real or unflattering information has been dealt with harshly, and may be under threat of criminal prosecution.[33] Some anonymous letters have been published saying that public defamation of the KGB is ill-deserved. The organisation has always prided itself on top-quality recruitment – an interview in the provincial press recently revealed that only one candidate in five or six was taken.[34] A role in fighting crime would also seem to be important and long-term.

Consequently, even on this sort of basis, the elite status of the KGB remains, in our view, secure. We have seen no authoritative information on its running costs or premises. Most people seem to be convinced that the surveillance apparatus has remained untouched, and is ready for use in future, if need be. In some respects the Soviet military enjoys the same advantages since Russia will always need a considerable defence force. At the same time the regular officer corps faces heavy cuts, and may lose the certainty of universal two-year conscription. Most modern elites would presumably have to include leaders of the security sectors.

As for privileged life-styles, they will not be easily suppressed, especially in conditions of acute shortages of consumer goods and services: transmogrification will prove easier than abolition. The application of market forces would result in a restriction of benefits to relatively few recipients, again the most wealthy.

There is a strong possibility that blessings enjoyed by the Party apparatus (specifically the Central Committee) may pass in a slightly different form to members of the new supreme state bodies. As for income (or legally declared income), figures recently published show that differentiation has in fact become greater under Gorbachov, as old wage ceilings have been removed, and state minima virtually abandoned.[35] The income tax reform, though striking, was not sufficient to discourage high earners.

Many elite benefits already administratively distributed and long enjoyed cannot be taken back. True, food supplies, transport and health arrangements can be altered fairly easily. But the collective farm markets will presumably retain their commercial prices and elite character; private cars will be available, in the first instance, to people who can afford to buy them. Personal possessions, if acquired within the law, cannot normally be sequestrated: unless a cataclysm occurs we can expect no massive redistribution of wealth holdings in the short term.

Housing is not easily transferred either. Under Soviet housing law, which is unlikely to be changed in this respect, no family can normally be moved without the provision of satisfactory alternative accommodation. Even elite families illegally settled cannot be put out on the street; and if threatened, many, no doubt, could invite relatives to move in with them, thus lowering their space norms. We have not, for reasons of space, considered the inequalities of Soviet education, but there is little doubt that the access to superior facilities, and the job-getting connections enjoyed by the children of the elite, will be largely retained.

Developments in the health service may provide an indication of what is to come. Under the terms of a decree passed in June 1988, certain self-financing arrangements and further privatisation are being encouraged. On the other hand, the disbandment of the Fourth Directorate did not have the looked-for effect, and as Yuri Tsavko, a member of the USSR Commission for Privileges, angrily revealed, its facilities were simply being made available to other select administrations.[36]

When the Bolsheviks came to power, many members of the bourgeoisie continued to benefit by offering their professional services to new masters.

The existing Stalinist-engendered elite will presumably do the same, though possibly in easier circumstances. We have written elsewhere that Gorbachov's social policies, at least in the late 1900s, were not so much egalitarian as moderately differentiative, designed to encourage honest effort and positive outcome. Gorbachov's fate presently hangs in the balance, as do many of the social policies he promoted. The anti-elitist forces which have been unleashed are powerful indeed. But one result of the present turmoil will in all probability be a reform of Soviet elitism, and not its suppression.

NOTES

1. See M. Fainsod, *How Russia is Ruled* (Harvard, 1963), later to be rewritten and 're-orientated' by Professor J. Hough; W. W. Kulski's *The Soviet Regime* (Syracuse, 1954) was excellent but never really achieved the prominence it deserved. A text which represents the other category would arguably be David Lane's earlier *Politics and Society in the USSR* (New York University Press, 1972). Despite its title it virtually ignored elites, the oppressive functions of the KGB, and the censorship.

   The popular success of bland, uncritical writing by various hands is striking, perhaps a reflection of some Western readers' desire to believe that Soviet-type socialism (in some ways) really worked. It is sad that the failings of such analysis should only now be vividly demonstrated inside the USSR, after so many years of social injustice. The relaxed atmosphere of Western campuses (or comfort of Intourist hotels) are evidently not conducive to indepth analysis of Soviet reality.

   In the West the long silences were broken by M. Voslensky's *Nomenklatura* (OPI Ltd, London, 1984) which dealt with the theme in a competent if journalistic fashion. Hendrick Smith's *The Russians* (Penguin, 1976) had an interesting chapter on elite life-styles. Mention should be made of my own work, *Privilege in the Soviet Union* (Allen & Unwin, 1978), though it has long been out of print. Other titles, but of a more literary character, could be listed.

2. *Spravochnik partiinovo rabotnika* (henceforth *SPR*), *vypusk* 29, 1989 (Moscow, 1989) p. 589; also *SPR*, *vypusk* 24, 1984 (Moscow, 1984).

3. *Argumenty i fakty* (henceforth *AiF*), No. 25, 1990.

4. Khrushchov attempted reductions of 25–30 per cent by his decree of 24 March 1956 (*SPR*, Moscow, 1957, p. 406).

5. *SPR*, *vypusk* 29, 1989, pp. 307–12. We are not aware of any official data on the present size of the Party apparatus. One would imagine that 12,000 was some 10 per cent of the whole.

6. For criticism of Brezhnev see *Pravda*, 3 April 1988, commented upon in *The Independent*, 4 April 1988. Detailed references to bribery and corruption around Brezhnev and in Central Asia, may be found in *Keesing's Contemporary Archives*, Volume XXXII, p. 34,752; Posev, Nos 1 and 3, 1987; *Radio*

Liberty Research Bulletin, 30 January 1987, No. 49/87 and 23 February 1987, No. 79/87.

7. See the popular sheets '*Tainy kremlyovskovo dvora, Gazeta moskovskovo otdeleniya informatsionnovo agentstva Belsamizdat*), Nos 1, 2, 1990 (extracts from Boris Yeltsin's book *Confessions on a Given Theme*); '*Antisovetskaya pravda*', June, November, 1990: *Svetskie vedomosti, Spetsvypusk* No. 1, 1990 (Minsk).

8. *Pravda Ukrainy* 14 February 1990; for figures in Belorussia, see *AiF*, No. 37, 1988; *Sotsialnoe razvitie SSSR, statisticheski sbornik* (Moscow, 1990), p. 92.

9. *Narodnoye khozyaistvo SSSR* (henceforth *Nar. khoz.*), 1988, p. 327; *Privilege in the Soviet Union* (London, 1979).

10. *Nar. khoz.*, 1988, p. 621. For some discussion of the social impact of this measure (as viewed in 1988) see our *Patterns of Deprivation in the Soviet Union under Brezhnev and Gorbachov* (Hoover Institution Press, 1989), p. 20.

11. *Nar. khoz.*, 1988, p. 327.

12. By April 1989, according to official data, the private sector employed only 1,951,000 persons in cooperatives, while 734,000 were registered for 'individual labour activity' out of a total labour force of 129,900,000 (*Nar. khoz.*, 1988, pp. 34, 321, 329).

13. See *AiF*, No. 33, 1990; S. N. Dyrdov and E. A. Avdoshina, *Spravochnik po nalogam s naseleniya* (Moscow, 1984), pp. 24, 32, 41. The new rates in the upper brackets of the state-employed were close to the old high rates for private enterprise. The figures given here are generally accurate, but the reader should bear in mind that tax regulations are complex.

14. *AiF*, No. 48, 1989; No. 49, 1989; No. 39, 1990. The USSR Commission is sometimes referred to simply as the 'Commission on Privileges'.

15. Our own (frequent) purchases at the Rizhski Market in Moscow in June 1990 would suggest that the differential was much greater. See also *Privilege*, p. 38.

16. *Independent*, 29 January 1988; *Pravda*, 13 February 1990.

17. *Pravda*, 13 February 1990.

18. *Sotsialnoe razvitie, statisticheski sbornik* (Moscow, 1990), p. 142; *AiF*, No. 49, 1989.

19. *AiF*, No. 31, 1990. The Democratic Platform complained that in 1990 alone the Party apparatus was supposed to receive 1,300 cars, whose free market value would be four to five times greater than the official price paid to them. See also *AiF*, No. 49, 1989; No. 36, 1990. G. Bochkov, an economist in distant Krasnodar, stated (without quoting a source) that *nomenklatura* officials alone had the services of two million chauffeurs.

20. *AiF*, No. 48, 1989; No. 11, 1990.

21. *Nar. khoz.*, 1988, p. 86.

22. *AiF*, No. 39, 1990.

23. *AiF*, No. 37, 1990.

24. *AiF*, No. 10, 1990.

25. *SPR*, 1989, p. 589; *AiF*, No. 40, 1990. The standard study of these movements is to be found in T. H. Rigby, *Communist Party Membership in the USSR, 1917–1967* (Princeton, 1968); see in particular pp. 51–4. Most significant falls in membership were due to purging.

26. *Independent*, 2 November 1990.

27. *Sovetskaya militsia*, No. 9, 1990, p. 28: *AiF*, No. 43, 1990 gave a figure of 980 'Party and economic buildings – the premises of CPSU district, town and regional committees, ministries and administrations'.

28. *AiF*, No. 35, 1990; For further examples see *Demotcraticheskaya Rossiya*, No. 2 August 1990, N. Travkin's exposition.

29. *AiF*, No. 31, 1990; *Ogonyo*, No. 10, 1990, Early in 1990, KGB officers were also said to have had a rise (*AiF*, No. 22, 1990).

30. *AiF*, No. 38, 1990; No. 43, 1990. *Pechat SSSR v 1985 godu, statisticheski sbornik* (Moscow, 1986), p. 9.

31. *Sbornik KGB SSSR (Yezhemesyachnik)*, with the subtitle 'Sovershenno sekretno', no date. We have seen only a twenty-four page special issue to celebrate the 45th Anniversary of Soviet victory in the 'Great Patriotic War'. It was on sale for the (then) hefty sum of two roubles, and for some reason printed in the *Stavropol Pravda* press. The text is historical with spy adventures from true life.

32. *AiF*, for example, has frequently offered them space – see Nos. 10, 22, 24, 25, 1990; see also *Vechernii Frunze*, 16 December 1989; *Sokolniki*, April 1990.

33. O.D. Kalugin, a former officer, aroused considerable public attention by television appearances and a press article in which he hinted at the size of the KGB apparatus and its harmful functions. He was stripped of his state awards by a decree of the Presidium of the Supreme Soviet of the USSR of 29 June 1990, but proceeded to fight back in the courts. *AiF*, No. 39, 1990; No. 43, 1990.

34. *Vecherny Frunze*, 16 December 1989.

35. This fact may be elucidated from the table in *Sotsialnoe razvitie SSSR, statisticheski sbornik* (Moscow, 1990), p. 110. The income curve has flattened and moved to the right.

36. *SPR, vypusk* 29, 1989, p. 435; *AiF*, No. 11, 1990.

6 The Black Marketeers under Perestroika

Ian Bremmer and Raymond Taras

The existence of a black market in the Soviet Union – known also as the underground or parallel economy – has been the subject of considerable interest on the part of Western specialists on the USSR. Research has proven to be largely speculative, however, given the elusiveness of empirical data bearing upon the scale and operations of this economy. What little we have learned about the subject has been provided by a small number of scholars such as Gregory Grossman, Aron Katsenelinboigen, Herbert S. Levine and Dennis O'Hearn.[1]

The significance of the black market in the Soviet Union would seem to merit further study. This is perhaps most readily apparent from an economic perspective, specifically in the black market's relief of monetary overhang. Simply put, monetary overhang occurs when an abundance of money chases a scarcity of consumer goods, and it has characterised the government-subsidised consumer-agricultural sector for decades. If the *cost* of goods has been accessible to most Soviet citizens, then as a consequence the *goods* themselves have not. Underlying shortages of many goods, therefore, are often caused by excess demand rather than a breakdown of production. The widespread nature and highly inflated prices of the Soviet black market may be explained by its function to 'relieve' this imbalance between an abundant money supply and a scarcity of desired goods. With private initiative supplying sought-after merchandise at market-determined prices, inroads are made into monetary overhang without the politically risky adoption of policies which increase state-fixed prices.

Thus, while Soviet per capita income may be considered significantly but not drastically lower than that of Western states (2,000 roubles annually, or about $3,400 at the pre-October 1989 official exchange rate), the Soviet people have had few options regarding the expenditure of money that they have accumulated.[2] Soviet medical care and education are free, housing is extremely inexpensive, and consumer goods are either virtually unavailable or of inferior quality, leaving little legal outlet for Soviet income. The well-supplied black market acts as a necessary escape valve for excess roubles.

The black market is also noteworthy as a social phenomenon, involving large numbers of disaffected individuals engaging in what Timothy Colton

72

calls 'exciting behaviour': 'In the Soviet Union in recent decades, the most egregious displays of exciting behaviour have been the spiral of the "second economy" and of official corruption (which feeds the second economy)'.[3] Soviet citizens escape from a stressful social and political situation not through migration, passive acquiescence or political action but through depriving the system of their talents.

Thirdly, the black market is important as a psychological phenomenon. With the (up until recently) relative impermeability of Soviet national borders, the black market has represented one manner in which its citizens may realise how well their standard of living compares to that of the world around them. While foreign broadcasts of glorious living conditions in the West could perhaps be dismissed by Soviet people as mere propaganda, the knowledge that it takes two weeks of labour to purchase one pair of Western jeans is far tougher to dismiss.

The far-reaching importance of the black market has not been lost upon the Soviet government. Indeed, in recent years, the Soviet leadership has acknowledged the existence, and even vitality, of the black market. In one of the first high-level official statements on the subject, then First Deputy Prime Minister Geidar Aliev noted at the 27th Party Congress in February 1986: 'There is a black market where goods that are in short supply are often sold.' He went further to identify the existence of profiteering and bribery 'even among, unfortunately, Communists and the leadership'.[4] While Aliev's candour did not save him from political disgrace shortly after the Congress, Gorbachov's administration has, in a variety of policy decisions since then, addressed the issue of a dynamic, if legally suspect, second economy in an otherwise moribund state-managed economy.

The first of these decisions was Gorbachov's continuation of Andropov's 'Operation Trawl', which sought to punish Soviet citizens who were found, without reason, away from their workplace during working hours. Black marketeers, as well as absentee workers, were targeted in KGB street round-ups. In December 1985, a law against social parasitism and speculation introduced the death penalty for certain kinds of economic crimes. Included among them was trade involving large amounts of hard currency.

The most important of the new policies was a law passed by the Soviet Parliament in November 1986 which attempted to regulate and profit from the second economy rather than to combat it. In this way Gorbachov strove to make resort to 'illegal paths less necessary by giving rein to local initiative.[5] The law legalised 29 types of private enterprise ranging from the manufacture of furniture, clothing and sports equipment to the repair of cars and domestic appliances. The provision of private services, such as transporting goods, painting apartments and tutoring students, was also legalised. The intent of the law was to harness the momentum of economic entrepreneurship, found hitherto in the alternative sector, to the state sector.[6] Although the price structure reflecting such private initiative would be considerably higher than that which traditionally prevailed in the public sector, it would generally be comparable to that in existence on the black market.[7]

Gorbachov decided in October 1989 to devalue the rouble to 10 per cent of its previous tourist exchange rate. The existence of black market exchange rates, which as long ago as 1970 offered Western visitors ten times as many roubles for their foreign currency as the Soviet state bank, presented Gorbachov's rational restructuring drive with a severe challenge. Finally in 1989 he confronted the dilemma with the agonising recognition of the rouble's low value. Devaluation was, in a sense, an 'achievement' of the thriving black market which, since its implementation, has led to the market's partial erosion.

That the Soviet black market has been thriving is largely due to the existence of an irrational price structure. A direct attack upon that structure may not be feasible. Abel Aganbegyan, chairman of a special economic commission that has reported directly to Gorbachov, has recognised that price reform is a two-edged sword. Aganbegyan, who has publicly opposed the system of massive state subsidies which allows staple goods (milk and bread) to be sold to consumers below the costs of production, nonetheless has only proposed the implementation of gradual price increases to be spread over many years. He has added that: 'In the nearest future, one mustn't expect any deep or radical reform of retail prices'.[8] The dangers of an inflationary spiral or, even worse, stagflation, are real: while Finance Minister Boris Gostev estimated in late 1988 that inflation was running as high as 1.5 per cent annually, other Soviet economists privately revealed that the real rate might be closer to 7 per cent.[9] The removal of state subsidies and price controls would accelerate price increases and might result in 'Hungarian-type inflation' (10–20 per cent annually), or even 'Polish-type inflation' (over 50 per cent).[10] IMF-type austerity measures imposed in the USSR would have unprecedented political implications.

The introduction of 'rational' market-responsive pricing mechanisms would, therefore, in some ways mirror the operational principles of the black market and, consequently, could engender the same kind of social injustices. Prices would be determined by both the scarcity of goods and consumer demand as on the black market, and would thus reflect their real market value. A contradiction could easily develop between, on the one hand, the suppliers and purchasers involved in the free-market sector, and on the other, those citizens left out of it. This, in turn, could increase the relevance of class-based antagonisms.

For these reasons, it seems important to examine in greater detail the dynamics of the black market. What are the driving forces behind black market trade and how does the black market operate? Who are the principal participants in the black market and what is its structure? What have been the effects of Gorbachov's perestroika on the black market? Are these effects consistent with the economic reforms that Gorbachov plans to implement? Finally, what is the combined impact of perestroika and the black market upon Soviet society? It is to these questions that we now turn.

BLACK MARKET DEMAND: WESTERN GOODS AND HARD CURRENCY

While a black market exists for scarce Soviet state-manufactured goods and administered services and, we may note further, for black market produced goods and provided services, the scope and magnitude of these sectors is impossible to verify owing to their nature as businesses run entirely among Soviets. Without Western participation in the process there is no opportune niche for observation. It is the market for Western-imported goods, where personal scrutiny is possible, which therefore comprises the grounds of this study.

Western goods and hard currency have considerable value for Soviet citizens. With the exception of high-ranking officials and some members of the intelligentsia who enjoy the privilege of shopping at special stores where a full selection of high-quality goods is stocked, these items are generally unavailable in the Soviet Union. The vast majority of Soviet people may only make such purchases on the black market.

Once on the black market, most Western goods are sold directly to consumers. Black market professionals' profit margins in these transactions have tended to be quite high, with the resale value of most goods being double that of their cost.[11] The difficulty in obtaining the goods, finding a buyer, and transporting the goods all help explain this mark-up in, until recently, a non-profit oriented economy.

In turn, small and relatively inexpensive Western goods are often used as a substitute currency. Cigarettes, chewing gum and ballpoint pens, for example, are greatly valued by Soviet citizens and often serve as gifts for the procurement of favours. From getting reservations at a crowded restaurant to finding the best seats at the Kirov ballet, these goods are almost universally acceptable in the Soviet Union and appreciated far more than a few roubles. More expensive goods, such as a bottle of French cognac or a fine pen and pencil set, can serve as *prinosheniye* (literally 'bringing to'), an acceptable and, indeed, often expected way for Soviet people to obtain favours from individuals in authority. Soviet black market 'professionals', who have easy access to these types of goods, are frequently engaged in *prinoshenie*, and even treat gifts of Marlboros or Wrigleys as their 'calling cards'.[12]

Utility for hard currency in the Soviet Union, on the other hand, is somewhat less self-evident. In most Soviet cities there exist 'hard currency' shops, or Beriozkas, which cater to the shopping needs of foreign tourists. High-quality Soviet goods are available there, as well as Western goods such as cigarettes, alcohol and chocolate, but payment is accepted exclusively in hard currency. As until very recently it had been illegal for Soviet people to possess hard currency (with the exception of those who travelled abroad), there had also been a formal ban on Soviet citizens entering Beriozkas. Nonetheless, many people obtaining hard currency on the black market made a practice of frequenting them or, more often, convincing Westerners to visit and purchase goods for them. Of course, with the lifting of restrictions concerning both the possession and expenditure of hard currency, this has become a more attractive outlet.

The majority of Soviet demand for hard currency, however, comes from those citizens seeking to travel abroad. Would-be travellers have always faced difficulties in obtaining enough hard currency to live and make purchases in Western nations because they have only been allowed to exchange their roubles for an extremely small amount of hard currency at the official rate. In 1989, this amounted to little over $300 or £200 a month for the average citizen.[13] For these people, black market hard currency 'supplements' are the rule rather than the exception.

Once in the hands of black market professionals, hard currency is either distributed directly to the consumer or used by the marketeers to bribe officials and purchase Beriozka items which are, in turn, sold to consumers. Additionally, the usual channels of distributing goods to outlying Russian areas and the non-Russian republics are not as important for the hard currency market. Many Soviet people who travel abroad live in the major Soviet cities (Moscow, Leningrad and Kiev); demand for hard currency is thus conveniently highest where it is in greatest supply.

Profits on hard currency tend to be lower for Soviet professionals than for trade in goods. Black marketeers buying dollars for approximately 7–8 roubles in early 1989 could reasonably expect to receive 12 in return.[14] This 150 per cent return was still smaller than the 200 per cent average return on Western goods. In 1990 reports from both Soviet sources and Western travellers point to a maximum black market purchase rate of 255 roubles to the dollar and a sell rate of around 30. The profit margin in this case is still considerable.[15] Whether before or after devaluation, therefore, Gorbachov's slogan of 'raising the authority of the rouble' would appear to be largely rhetoric.[16]

THE SOCIOLOGY OF THE BLACK MARKET: PARTICIPANTS AND STRUCTURE

The profit margins in black market trade, as well as the types of goods sought from the Western traveller, vary greatly depending upon the Soviet trader. Due in greatest part to the relatively unknown character of the Soviet black market, Western scholars have exhibited a tendency to oversimplify, or ignore altogether, the subtle distinctions among different sectors of black market trade. This has led to the conceptual consolidation of black marketeers into a quasi-monolithic bloc: Belikova and Shokhin, for example, distinguish only between *vezuny* (those bringing in goods), and *nesuny* (those marketing them).[17] In reality, black market professionals fall into three different categories, each of which has a unique way of going about their business.

The first type of black marketeers are the entrenched professionals, who distinguish themselves by conducting their business in major Intourist hotels. They, along with the artistic intelligentsia who receive royalties in hard currency, constitute the bulk of the few rouble millionaires in the Soviet Union. They may be found in greatest numbers in Moscow and Leningrad, but also operate in other large Soviet cities. Buying large amounts of goods and currency from the Western tourists staying at these hotels, entrenched professionals facilitate their trade by stocking Soviet goods such as fur hats, Soviet army clothing, caviar and lacquer boxes on the premises. In addition to the Soviet goods and prerequisite roubles, entrenched professionals occasionally have drugs available for black market dealing. Those not carrying drugs usually have connections within the hotel for such trade.[18]

In the black market system, retrenched professionals act as the hubs of distribution. Dealing in large quantities of goods, they do not have the time to trade with Soviet consumers directly. Instead, they trade with black marketeers operating outside the hotel. Often, entrenched professionals working in Moscow and Leningrad come from non-Russian republics, siphoning goods back to their homeland. It is not uncommon for the largest Russian Intourist hotels to have black market 'representatives' from several different republics (most commonly Armenia, Georgia and the Ukraine).

As would be expected, entrenched professionals are full-time black marketeers. While they officially hold legitimate jobs, in reality they either bribe their managers into 'forgetting' to report their absence or pay someone else to work in their place. They *never* work alone, most often having one partner (and sharing a hotel room) but occasionally working in groups of three or four. They tend to be older than other professionals, usually having started their 'career' in the black market by trading on the streets.[19] Two additional factors which distinguish entrenched professionals are their profound lack of politicisation and the considerable involvement of women in their ranks. While an entrenched professional may make political statements in order to improve relations with a potential customer, his overall set of political attitudes tends towards indifference. Also women, rarely active in other sectors of the black market, are often found amongst the ranks of entrenched professionals, sometimes even organising the group themselves.

An entrenched professional has two main advantages over other types of black marketeers. Of primary benefit is the high level of security gained from operating within the confines of the hotel. Sheltered from the open trading of the street, entrenched professionals do not have to worry about arrest by the militia or blackmail from the civilian 'raiders' (discussed below). Almost as important, they also have a steady inflow of Westerners immediately accessible for trading. In the relaxed hotel environment, meetings are quickly set and deals are easily concluded. Additionally, most of the Westerners comprising the hotel's captive market are tourists who do not actively search out black market trade and are consequently unaware of the market value of their goods and currency.

These advantages, of course, do not come without their price. The operations of entrenched professionals are well known and tolerated by the hotel's administration, but they demand a share of the professionals' takings in return. As might be expected, there are a great many people who must be paid off. The doormen, the receptionists, the cleaning women and the hotel management all receive their cut, and while the lower levels of administration tend to accept their payment in roubles (of negligible cost to the entrenched professional), the hotel management expects quality Western goods and hard currency. Additionally, just like Westerners staying in the hotel, entrenched professionals must pay for their room in hard currency. This expense typically amounts to over seventy dollars per day and well over one hundred in the most modern hotels (where, in turn, the most money can be made).[20] For these reasons, prices offered by these professionals to tourists for Western goods and currency are extremely low.

Relatively little of the total volume of black market trading in the Soviet Union takes place in the Intourist hotels, however. The bulk of the traders are 'wandering professionals', who operate in high density tourist areas such as main shopping districts, national museums, outside Beriozkas or outside Intourist hotels. They are a more heterogeneous group than their

entrenched counterparts and vary in degrees of sophistication.[21] For example, some wandering professionals linger about the city streets looking for
Westerners, while others, armed with copies of the touring schedules of
Western groups staying at certain hotels, wait outside during the times they
have planned to arrive and depart.

Wandering professionals typically carry a small amount of tradable goods
with them – a lacquer box or two and a fur hat is the usual complement –
but have large amounts of Soviet currency.[22] Indeed, it would be rare to find
a wandering professional carrying less than one thousand roubles on his
person. Their business is conducted in any location which is close to the
initial meeting area but not frequented by pedestrians, such as the stairwells
of apartment buildings, back alleys or city parks. If they meet Westerners
with large quantities of goods to trade they generally attempt to schedule
later appointments to meet in a 'safer place' – typically their apartment.

Wandering professionals, like entrenched professionals, tend to be full-
time black marketeers and never work alone. While usually approaching
Westerners individually, once trading commences the pro's 'partners' will
turn up. The number of wandering professionals working together can be
considerable, with groups of four or five being common and some number-
ing even seven or eight having been reported.

Without having to pay off a hierarchy of hotel workers or pay for a hotel
room, wandering professionals have few overhead expenses. Even with
their offering of consistently higher prices than entrenched professionals on
both currency exchange and Western goods (see Table 6.1), wandering pros
can still command an extremely high profit margin.

Hand in hand with this high profit margin, however, is the serious risk of
being caught. The most immediate threat to the wandering professional is
the Soviet militia. If a Soviet trader is apprehended, the first and second
arrest bring stiff fines. While the exact nature of these fines are neither
published nor disclosed by black marketeers, they are sufficiently steep to
make wandering professionals extremely concerned about facing arrest.
The baseball adage, 'three strikes you're out', is the literal punishment
facing a Soviet black marketeer who is unlucky enough to be arrested thrice
for illegal trading. In this case, the trader's city registration papers are taken
away and he is exiled from the city. The option of bribing an official to
avoid arrest exists, of course, but also carries its dangers, as many authorities who are faced with a choice between accepting a bribe or arresting the
trader and taking his money anyway invariably opt for the latter.

A recent phenomenon that has also posed a threat to the well-being of
wandering professionals are the Soviet civilian 'raiders'. These are street
vigilantes who attempt to blackmail black marketeers by threatening to turn

Table 6.1 Entrenched vs. wandering professionals: Moscow and Leningrad
1989 (roubles)

| Commodity | Moscow | | Leningrad | |
	EP	WP	EP	WP
US Dollar	5	7	5	8.5
T-shirt	15	20	10	15
Used jeans	50	70	50	70
Chewing gum (10 pack)	10	10	10	12
US cigarettes (1 pack)	5	8	5	5
Sunglasses	5	8	No offer	10
Cassette tape (Rock)	5	8	5	10

EP – Entrenched professional
WP – Wandering professional

NB: The results in this table are based upon offers to Western professionals.

them in to the authorities. When raiders come across a black market deal in
progress, they approach the traders and demand money. If the request is not
granted, the raiders will summon the militia and identify the professionals
involved. Some particularly sophisticated raiders stake out a high-tourist
area for several days to learn of all the black market activity taking place
before making themselves known. Refusing to pay the raiders may be costly
for black marketeers, for even if they manage to avoid arrest, they have to
change location – a costly and time-consuming process at best.[23]

In addition to the two groups of professionals, there exists a third partici-
pant type: personal traders. Personal traders hold regular jobs and deal on
the black market only to acquire Western goods for themselves, close
friends or family. While black market professionals may be thought of
generally as 'middlemen', most Soviet citizens can be considered 'personal
traders' in that they are only willing to 'trade' with a Westerner who has an
item which they desire for personal consumption. The tradeable goods they
offer in return are their own belongings, such as rabbit fur hats or old army
uniforms. Accordingly, personal traders rarely consider currency exchange
and, while they offer higher prices on any given commodity than a professional, they will hardly ever purchase a commodity in quantity.

Because of their non-professional nature, personal traders fill the niche of
custom-order black market trading. If a Westerner is searching for a particular commodity not carried by a professional, his best hopes of buying it are
with personal traders, who will take the time and effort to find it so that they

may in turn obtain something they desire from the Westerner. Professionals, on the other hand, will not spend time tailoring a personal order when they could be more profitably trading with other customers.

Just as there exist different types of Soviet black marketeers, there are significant distinctions among Western traders. The overriding cleavages separating them are their extent of black market knowledge and level of black market activity.

The vast majority of Westerners who trade on the black market are tourist traders or 'dudes'. They have little, if any, knowledge of the black market and only trade if the opportunity presents itself. Entrenched professionals make their main business trading with dudes who are unaware of the black market value of hard currency and Western goods. As we see below, tourist traders have been the only source of rouble stabilisation in the Soviet black market; that is, they have operated close to the artificially inflated official exchange rate for currency.

Semi-informed traders, or 'pseuds', have accumulated some information about the value of their goods and currency, either from having visited the USSR before or from knowledgeable friends. They typically bargain with traders and occasionally come to the USSR prepared with tradeable items. They are also particularly willing to exchange hard currency, which they generally consider the easiest way to make a clear profit.

There also exists a small group of Western professionals, or 'shrewds', who travel to the Soviet Union primarily for the purpose of black market trade. While amongst these professionals are citizens of many Western nations, their numbers are by far the greatest among the neighboring Finns and nearby Swedes who travel to Leningrad or Tallinn for a day or weekend trip. These professionals know where the heaviest black market activity takes place and usually have several personal contacts in their destination city. By purchasing sought-after tradeable goods before they travel and making several initial meetings at different places to price the market, shrewds maximise their profits, thus exhibiting what Colton might have called 'entering behaviour'. Western professionals always deal in quantity and sell their goods to wandering professionals to command top prices.[24]

Participation on the demand side is virtually ubiquitous, with all but the outmost extremes of society engaging in some form of black market activity. The impoverished (pensioners, collective farm workers) barely have enough money to survive even given the irrational Soviet price structure. At the other extreme, the very privileged can travel abroad themselves with sufficient legally obtained hard currency for personal expenses and, in the Soviet Union, have access to special stores stocking Western goods. For both of these groups, monetary overhang does not apply. Aside from the extremes, however, black market trade occurs almost without exception throughout Soviet society.

Given the participants on both the supply and demand side of the black market, the question of structure becomes relevant. Typically, illegal market structures are depicted similar to that of the Western drug market, where there exists a vertical hierarchy and distribution is controlled at every point from supply to demand by an imposed organisation from above. The emphasis placed by the Western media upon problems of organised crime in the Soviet Union would seem to lend credence to the validity of this analogy yet, upon closer scrutiny, the black market structure appears to be somewhat anomalous.

With the sole exception of the entrenched professionals, who normally distribute their goods to wandering professionals as opposed to the Soviet consumer, there is no evidence for hierarchical lines of authority in the black market. The central distinction among black marketeers appears to be that of market niche and not market function. All professionals participate directly in the supply end of the market; most follow the goods all the way through to demand. Without compartmentalising function, each marketeer becomes something of an individual proprietor. The findings therefore point away from the possibility of there existing 'kingpins' who control large-scale black market activity. Indeed, apart from the small groups formed to guard against capture, facilitate trade and ease boredom, black market professionals simply do not seem to have organised into larger groups. This would seem to be the primary reason why the *reket* and militia pose a threat to them. The proper analogy to draw would thus seem to be that of the private shopkeeper trying to stay in business while avoiding (or paying off) the mafia. The only major difference would appear to be that the service provided by the black marketeers is, *de facto* if not always *de jure*, illegal.

PROFIT-TAKING ON THE SOVIET BLACK MARKET

Until recently, in both the cases of Western and Soviet black market professionals, the highest profit margins involve the trading of Western goods. However, the margin of difference between currency and goods trade, considerable in the mid-1980s, has decreased drastically. Indeed, it now seems that, with few exceptions, currency trade has become more profitable. Before we discuss the implications of this shift, we should first look more closely at its properties.

Let us introduce an index to measure the market-determined value of goods – the Black Market Multiplier (BMM). It represents the number of times over the official exchange rate prevailing for the dollar that a commodity would bring when sold on the black market. In other words, if a $1 pack of cigarettes brought 5 roubles in 1986, that would represent an effective exchange of 5 roubles for $1, or $0.20 for a rouble. With the official exchange rate at $1.4567 for a rouble, the BMM would equal approximately 7.3.

We may now cross-price various commonly demanded Western goods on the Soviet black market. From Table 6.2 it is apparent that returns on these goods in 1986 varied greatly.[25] From a pair of used jeans bringing a BMM of 7.3, to a pair of sunglasses bringing 17.0, profit margins have fluctuated wildly depending upon the commodity in question. There was little change in the profitability of these goods in 1989. Some merchandise – most notably blue jeans – increased in value, while others decreased, but on the whole the profitability of common Western goods remained stable.

Profit margins on exchange of hard currency, however, were quite another story. In 1986, one dollar was worth, on average, three roubles on the black market, as opposed to an official exchange rate of 0.6865 roubles (see

Table 6.2   Prices in Moscow and Leningrad: consumer goods, 1986 and 1989 (roubles)

| Item | Moscow | | Leningrad | |
	BMP 1986	BMM	BMP 1989	BMM
Pk cigarettes ($1)	10	14.6	8	13.2
10 pk gum ($1.39)	15	15.7	12	14.2
Sunglasses ($3)	35	17.0	10	5.5
Cap ($3)	15	7.3	15	8.2
T-shirt ($4)	25	9.1	20	8.2
Used jeans ($10)	50	7.3	70	11.5
Sweatshirt ($15)	100	9.7	75	8.2

BMP – Black market price
BMM – Black market multiplier

Table 6.3). This amounted to a BMM of 4.4, quite insubstantial in comparison with profit margins on goods trade. By early 1989, however, a dollar commanded from five to eight roubles and by mid-1989 at least ten roubles (sometimes even fifteen). The BMM for hard currency in 1989 had thus more than doubled from approximately 7 to 15.[26]

Comparing indices for currency exchange (CEI) and consumer goods

Table 6.3   Rouble/dollar trade: 1986 and 1989

City	BME 1986	BMM	BME 1989	BMM
Moscow	2/1 – 3/1	2.9 – 4.4	5/1 – 7/1	8.2 – 11.5
Leningrad	2/1 – 2.5/1	2.9 – 3.6	5/1 – 8.5/1	8.2 – 114.0
Pyatigorsk	2/1 – 2.5/1	2.9 – 3.6	—	—
Tbilisi	2/1 – 3/1	2.9 – 4.4	—	—
Yerevan	2/1 – 2.5/1	2.9 – 3.6	—	—
Bukhara	—	—	6/1 – 8/1	9.9 – 13.2
Samarkand	—	—	3/1 – 6/1	4.9 – 9.9
Tallinn	—	—	5/1 – 6/1	8.2 – 9.9
Tashkent	—	—	5/1 – 8/1	8.2 – 13.2
Yalta	—	—	7/1 – 8/1	11.5 – 13.2

BME – Black market exchange
BMM – Black market multiplier (BMM = BME/Official Rate of Exchange, Rbl :
    US$)
Summer 1986, official exchange: $1.4567 : 1 Rbl / 0.6865 Rbl : $1
Winter 1989, official exchange: $1.6480 : 1 Rbl / 0.6068 Rbl : $1

(CGI) allows this change in relation to be expressed graphically (see Figure 6.1). Looking at the CGI, the gentle downward slope is apparent. This represents slight diminishing profitability. The CEI, on the other hand, slopes upward sharply, starting from a relatively low BMM but then over-taking the CGI. Essentially, this means that over the course of two and a half years, the rouble, in its relation to hard currency, was devalued by roughly 30 per cent in relation to its previous black market value.

This unofficial devaluation of the rouble was essentially caused by two main factors, both of which were the products of Gorbachov's reforms. First is the marked increase in Soviets travelling abroad. What was in the past a privilege granted to very few Soviet people has become increasingly routine, with people generally now needing only an invitation from a Western citizen to obtain the necessary passports. While precise data concerning this growth is unavailable, the American State Department has issued a report stating that in 1987 the number of Soviet people visiting relatives in the United States was 6,000 – four times the average of such visitors from 1980 to 1986.[27] Not surprisingly, demand for hard currency has drastically increased as a result.

Just as glasnost has enabled more Soviet citizens to travel abroad, so too has it brought greater numbers of visitors to the Soviet Union. But, curiously, Westerners have had less impact on rouble equilibrium than East

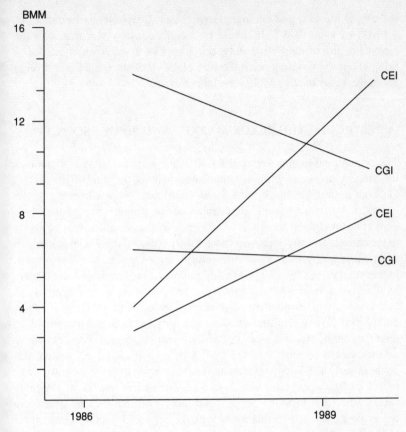

Fig 6.1   *Currency exchange and consumer goods indices Moscow and Leningrad 1986 and 1989*

Europeans, who have given Soviet professionals unwanted competition for hard currency. The chief group driving down the rouble's value has been made up of the Poles and, to a lesser extent, the Romanians. Both, significantly, share the longest contiguous borders with the European portion of the Soviet Union and also rank first and second in population among Eastern European nations.

Perhaps most significant of Gorbachov's efforts to contain the rouble's downward spiral was the devaluation of the rouble for tourists to 10 per cent of its previous rate. The black market was by no means suffocated by the cut, but profit margins were substantially reduced. Although data on recent prevailing rates are less extensive than in 1986 or 1989, it seems clear that the rates in Moscow and Leningrad have risen to 25 roubles to the dollar, for a BMM of about 3–3.5. It should be mentioned, however, that with the recent floating of the Polish zloty, one source of demand which helped to bring about the devaluation in the first place – Polish competition driving down the value of the rouble – no longer exists.

PERESTROIKA, THE BLACK MARKET AND SOVIET SOCIETY

The economic dilemma facing the Gorbachov administration is to counter inflationary pressures while simultaneously halting the slide of the rouble. On both counts the black market has contributed to a worsening of the situation. Yet it now seems inevitable that the primary impact the black market has had upon the Soviet economy – increasing the prices of goods to the consumer – also represents a necessary option if the Soviet leadership is to secure long-term economic reform. Retail price increases would, however, reverse many long-standing policies. For decades Soviet leaders have taken pride in combating inflation; an about-face on this issue would be very hard to manoeuvre. Similarly, it is difficult to foresee Soviet citizens rallying around perestroika, which demands higher productivity, while accepting lower personal disposable income. Soviet workers, whose salaries would be most affected by this policy, would be devastated. Already in early 1989 a Soviet industrial worker on an average monthly wage of 150 roubles could only buy about $20 on the black market, in 1990 this figure was closer to $5! A Soviet pensioner on 60 roubles was effectively receiving $2–3 – a sum that a black marketeer could obtain in one minor transaction. If, as has been estimated, the average Muscovite had to work 56 hours to be able to purchase a pair of Russian jeans, he would have to work nearly 80 hours to buy a pair of used Western jeans (see Table 6.2).[28] The issue of relative deprivation is, therefore, pertinent to this phenomenon.[29]

Rouble devaluation is a step towards higher consumer prices. While devaluation indeed makes Soviet exports cheaper, at the same time the few Western goods now imported for hard currency become increasingly unaffordable. The Soviet trade balance would improve if Soviet goods became more attractive overseas in terms of price *and* quality, but the problem would remain to induce Soviet workers to improve the quality of their output while simultaneously putting Western goods further out of their reach. The danger becomes increasingly apparent that Soviet workers will find it not worthwhile to work for a day's wages. The move to a domestically convertible rouble, similar to Poland's currency policy, means its value may be determined not by rational international forces (e.g. confidence of Western money markets in Soviet reform) but by internal demand for consumer goods.

Demand for hard currency is, in practice, demand for market consumer goods. While it is true that many goods have decreased considerably in price on the black market since 1986, such as T-shirts, chewing gum, cigarettes and sunglasses, these goods are non-durable or low-scale ones (see Table 6.2). The new 'hot goods' on the Soviet market include ski jackets, Walkmans, and electronic keyboards – all personal consumer items that are expensive because of the difficulty of bringing them into the Soviet Union in large quantity. The price of these goods may decrease too if the influx of tourists increases to meet the market demand; however, as we have observed, as the demand for one set of goods decreases, demand for another set appears in its place. In other words, while the commodities may change, the market remains the same. Real problems of domestic consumption, therefore, may not be resolved through rouble devaluation.

In the face of these difficulties, the most rational option of the Soviet authorities would seem to be to stay the course with perestroika in the hopes of riding out the devaluation through the achievement of the long-term goals of economic growth and free trade. In a speech at the 27th Communist Party Congress in 1986, Gorbachov stated, 'By the end of this century, we intend to increase the national income nearly twofold while doubling the production potential and qualitatively transforming it. Labour productivity will go up by 2.3 to 2.5 times.'[30] If perestroika managed to accomplish these goals, then the decline in real wages would necessarily turn itself around. With increased productivity and competitiveness, Soviet terms of trade would improve and, eventually, the Soviet Union could not only enjoy full trading relations with Western nations, but also meet much of the domestic demand for goods. In this scenario, the Soviet rouble could become fully convertible at a reasonable rate of exchange (an aim that Gorbachov has mentioned on numerous occasions), and full selections of Western goods could be available in Soviet stores.

Thus, improved productivity and competitiveness may result when domestic prices reflect scarcity. In this situation, the drive for profits by both deregulated state-owned and private sectors would fuel productivity. As previously mentioned, the result of such a policy might be an inflationary cycle, accompanied by all the strains upon worker morale this implies.

It is possible that productivity and competitiveness could occur while price controls on consumer goods were maintained. In late 1988, leading Soviet economist Nikolai Shmelyov proposed that price decontrol should be postponed for several years while the production of goods is expanding.[31] In this case, real income would be safeguarded while a greater availability of consumer goods would be simultaneously generated through increased productivity. Yet it is difficult to imagine how even the most optimistic increases in productivity planned by Soviet economic forecasters could dent the goods shortages currently experienced on the Soviet market. In short, maintaining price controls ensures a continuation of scarcity of Soviet goods, and scarcity is the motor force of the black market. Our conclusion is, therefore, that apart from the negative psychological and ethical consequences of a vibrant black market, its persistence poses a threat to nothing less than Soviet national security. For the ability this market has already demonstrated to 'strangle the rouble' may have medium- and long-term efforts on overall Soviet strength in dealing with the world around it.

At best, therefore, a policy of doing nothing will be met by a continuation of the present black market patterns; at worst, the rouble could plummet to a point where its potential for recovery would be extremely bleak. The 'strangulation of the rouble', accelerated by an influx of Western tourists and East European 'shrewds', could do much to sabotage the Soviet economy.

NOTES

1.   See the following articles by Gregory Grossman: 'The "second economy" of the USSR', *Problems of Communism* (September–October 1977), pp. 25–40; 'Notes on the illegal private economy and corruption', in US Congress, Joint Economic Committee, *The Soviet Economy in a Time of Change* (Washington: USGPO, 1979), pp. 834–55; 'A tonsorial view of the Soviet second economy', *Berkeley-Duke Occasional Papers on the Second Economy of the USSR* (December 1985); 'Inflational, political, and social implications of the current economic slowdown', in Hans-Hermann Hohmann *et al.* (eds), *Economic and Politics in the USSR: Problems of Interdependence* (Boulder: Westview Press, 1986), pp. 172–197.

      See also: Aron Katsenelinboigen and Herbert S. Levine, 'Market and plan, plan and market: the Soviet case', in Morris Bornstein (ed.), *The Soviet Economy* (Boulder, Colo.: Westview Press, 1981), pp. 61–70; Dennis O'Hearn, 'The consumer second economy: size and effects', *Soviet Studies*, 32 (April 1980), pp 218–34.

2.   'Stepping out', *The Economist*, 14 January 1989, pp. 62–4. Indeed, the devaluation of the rouble has eroded Soviet real wages to a fraction of that figure. Unless otherwise noted, all currency conversions given here are based on the pre-October 1989 exchange rates. For the devaluation, see *New York Times*, 26 October 1989. For other ways of converting roubles into hard currency, see Jeffrey Burt, 'Turning roubles into dollars', *Bloc* (December 1989 – January 1990), pp. 19–20.

3.   Timothy J. Colton, 'Gorbachov and the politics of system renewal', in Seweryn

Bialer and Michael Mandelbaum (eds), *Gorbachov's Russia and American Foreign Policy* (Boulder, Colo.: Westview Press, 1988), p. 154.

4. Mikhail Gorbachov, *Political Report of the CPSU Central Committee to the 27th Party Congress* (Moscow: Novostil, 1986), pp. 24–60.

5. Thane Gustafson and Dawn Mann, 'Gorbachov's next gamble', *Problems of Communism* (July–August 1987), pp. 1–20. This law took effect in May 1988.

6. See Libor Roucek, 'Private enterprise in Soviet political debates', *Soviet Studies*, No. 40 (January 1988), pp. 46–63.

7. Moreover, Soviet studies have found that 83 per cent of the population overpaid for goods and services in one form or another anyway. Galina Belikova and Aleksandr Shokhin, 'The black market: people, things and facts', *Soviet Sociology*, No. 28 (March–April 1989), p. 57.

8. *Wall Street Journal*, 3 March 1986. For Gorbachov's programme objectives, see Mikhail Gorbachov, *Perestroika: New Thinking for Our Country and the World* (New York: Harper & Row 1987).

9. *New York Times*, 3 November 1988.

10. These margins have probably decreased considerably as a result of the October 1989 rouble devaluation.

11. The existence of *prinoshenie* within the official economy is also widespread: Marshall Goldman referred to a Moscow food store manager who amassed a personal fortune of some $1.5 million by providing a variety of 'deficit' consumer goods to only those customers who offered him personal gifts. What was even more consequential politically was the fact that he had secured the protection of officials at the highest level of the Ministry of Light Industry, who had become his quasi-partners. *New York Times*, 3 November 1988.

12. *New York Times*, 22 November 1987.

13. *New York Times*, 21 November 1988.

14. At this rate of twelve roubles to a dollar, a Soviet citizen looking to purchase hard currency from a black marketeer must pay nearly *twenty* times the official rate of 0.6068 Rbl : $1.

15. It is the Westerners, therefore, who have taken the largest cut in profits since the devaluation. Given the recent curtailment of demand from East Europeans (owing to the changes in their economies) and the increasing glut of hard currency on the market (with increasing tourist rates) this should come as no surprise.

16. *Pravda*, 26 June 1987.

17. Belikova and Shokhin, op. cit., p. 52. This is a somewhat less than helpful distinction. On the Soviet black market, both of these functions are most often fulfilled by the same person.

18. Along with the issue of drugs is that of prostitution. While prostitution merits separate treatment, it is clear that some group or racket (*reket* in Russian) profits considerably from it. According to one Soviet source, of an average 15,000 roubles earned by a prostitute per month, about 10,000 is skimmed off the top by the *reket* (Larisa Kislinskaya, 'Crime in the USSR', paper delivered at the annual meeting of the American Association for the Advancement of Slavic Studies, Chicago, 5 November 1989). We have no evidence, however, that the *reket* is necessarily organised by entrenched professionals.

19.   This would seem to be the case because of the large capital requirement for establishment into an entrenched professional slot, discussed further below.
20.   The cheapest hard currency rooms in Leningrad's fashionable Hotel Pribaltiskaya, for example, cost $150 a night.
21.   A graphic alternative terminology to distinguish entrenched from wandering professionals is the parasitic versus predatory underworld. See Gregory Gleason and Peter Lupsha, 'Soviet political corruption in comparative perspective', paper delivered at the annual meeting of the American Association for the Advancement of Slavic Studies, Chicago, 5 November 1989.
22.   If they are stopped for questioning by the militia, the money is far less conspicuous than, for example, a case of caviar.
23.   Premium areas for black market trade have professionals competing for them, who consider the area their 'turf'. Newcomers are, as would be expected, not welcome.
24.   The disappearance by late 1989 of 'high ticket' items (gold, silver, jewelry, precious stones) in Soviet stores gave 'shrewds' less incentive to engage in trade. Indeed, the Western professional may become an endangered species following rouble devaluation.
25.   To gain accurate comparisons here, the same items were used over and over again as 'sample goods' to price the market.
26.   Regional and seasonal variations exist, but are not statistically significant.
27.   *New York Times*, 28 February 1988.
28.   Keith Bush, 'Retail prices in Moscow and four Western cities in October 1986', *Radio Liberty Supplement*, No. 1/87 (21 January 1987), pp. 1–30.
29.   On the issue of deprivation and inequality, see David Lane, *The End of Social Inequality?* (London: Allen & Unwin, 1982). On the question of morality and the black market, see Peter Wiles, 'Political and moral aspects of the two economies', in Hans-Hermann Hohmann *et al. Economics and Politics in the USSR*, pp. 198–213.
30.   *New York Times*, 26 February 1986.
31.   *New York Times*, 3 November 1988.

APPENDIX 6.1

NOTES ON RESEARCH METHODS

The black market in the Soviet Union is a matter of great sensitivity: the fiction both sides must live by is that 'We pretend they [the authorities] don't exist, they pretend we don't exist.' For this reason, any empirical data-gathering of a 'non-existent' subject must necessarily be established upon less rigorous methodological canons than a comparable survey in a liberal-democratic state. In short, we are not dealing with the traditional sources used by Sovietologists.

The bulk of the hard data presented in this paper was gathered through a series of open-ended ten to fifteen minute interviews with more than fifty black marketeers in Moscow, Leningrad, Transaucasia and Central Asia. While the nature of the interviews precluded formal question and answer sessions, common themes – such as the top prices offered for currency and certain goods, competition, methods of distribution, and the risks involved in trading – appeared throughout.

Interviews with Western student groups visiting the Soviet Union offered an alternative perspective of the black market, and substantiated much of the data accumulated from the black marketeers. While this is not to imply that every student contacted had dealt extensively in the Soviet second economy, the overwhelming majority had been approached by black marketeers and a slight majority did engage in black market trading of some sort. In total, three groups (for a total of over 60 students) in 1986 and five groups (over 80 students) in 1989 were interviewed.

A final, invaluable source of information came from a series of intensive interviews with what we would refer to in the West as 'well-informed sources'. These were people peripheral to but knowledgable about the black market. Information obtained from these sources that could not be verified in the field was corroborated by more than one interview subject. Much useful information was left out of the paper for lack of supporting evidence.

Editor's Footnote
This chapter was written before the further drastic devaluation of the rouble in May 1991, which decreased its value five times in relation to Western currencies (e.g. one pound sterling was equal, at the tourist exchange rate, to 50 roubles, instead of the previous 10), and the withdrawal of 50-rouble and 100-rouble notes from circulation. Both measures were calculated to undermine black marketeering. They do not appear to have been successful, for the reasons given in this chapter.

Part Four
Social Care

7 Charity and the Churches
Suzanne Oliver

Before the Revolution of 1917, charitable and philanthropic activity was very much an accepted part of the church's responsibility towards society, which it sought to serve according to Christian principles. Monasteries in particular were not only great centres of pilgrimage and spiritual enlightenment but exercised a valued social ministry in the community. Feodosiy, Father Superior at the Kiev Monastery of the Caves, built a church and a hostel in the grounds of the monastery for the crippled, the blind and the homeless: a tenth of the monastery's income and harvest was set aside to supply their needs. In many cases, monasticism carried with it social obligations to care for the sick and the poor, to show hospitality and to teach.

Parishes also were active in charitable work: in the sixteenth and seventeenth centuries nearly every church maintained a hostel for the needy. The reforms of Peter the Great, however, did not have a favourable effect on the social ministry of the church, and it was only towards the end of the last century that such activity was resumed on a large scale. In 1914 St Petersburg alone boasted 33 parish-based charitable organisations, which between them commanded a budget of over 5 million roubles. The churches also maintained 1,000 'charity beds' in the hospitals, 800 orphanage places and 200 spaces in free accommodation.[1] In the same period, a priest, John of Kronstadt, was well known for his ministry to the poor and the sick.

Individuals from the noble classes, too, considered it their Christian duty to engage in philanthropic activity: in many cases they promoted social welfare programmes and patronised hospitals, some of which bear the name of their benefactors to this day – for example the Kashchenko and the Botkin hospitals in Moscow. An outstanding example of this is the Mary and Martha Society set up at the beginning of the century by Elizaveta Fedorovna, a noblewoman related to the Romanovs. Motivated by a deep religious faith, she devoted herself entirely to charitable causes following the death of her husband. She bought an estate and built there a hospital, a pharmacy, a women's refuge, an orphanage and a soup kitchen – a philanthropic centre which became known as the Mary and Martha cloister. Her hospital gained an excellent reputation and many of the city's top specialists would offer their services free of charge. In 1910, she took holy orders and along with a small band of women devoted herself entirely to the needy. By the time war broke out there were 97 nuns in the cloister. After the 1917 revolution, Elizaveta Fedorovna was arrested and the cloister was abandoned.[2] In accordance with the new positive profile given the church's charitable activity, the Russian Orthodox Church canonised John of Kronstadt on 8 June 1990, while the case for the canonisation of Elizaveta Fedorovna is currently under discussion. The newly elected local Soviet in the Oktyabrsky district, where the Mary and Martha Society was situated, has recently registered a charitable organisation to be run in the grounds of the cloister, under the jurisdiction of priest Boris Kulyakov.

In 1914, the church maintained over one thousand old people's homes and 291 hospitals. In addition there were over a thousand monasteries and convents – centres of social involvement in pre-revolutionary Russia.[3]

THE LEGAL POSITION OF THE CHURCH IN THE USSR

In January 1918, the Bolshevik government issued a Decree on Separation of Church and State and nationalised church property, leading to a cessation of the church's ministry to the needy. The new government wanted to exclude the Russian Orthodox Church from the mainstream of social life, claiming it had been a tool of oppression wielded by the tsarist government and, moreover, had played no positive role in the alleviation of human suffering. In 1929, the Council of People's Commissars and the All-Russia Central Executive Committee promulgated a law on religious associations, which among many other regulations limiting church activity expressly forbade charitable work. Article 17 states:

Religious associations are forbidden (a) to create benefit funds and cooperatives; (b) to provide material support to their members; (c) to organise . . . sanatoria and medical assistance.[4]

This requirement is elucidated further in a book entitled *Religion and the Law* by Genrikh Golst:

All the requirements of this law are subject to strict execution and do not in any degree restrict the rights of believers. In Soviet socialist society all concerns about the provision of citizens' needs, the organisation of leisure time, cultural and educational work among the people is shouldered by the state, the trade unions and other public organisations. Under these circumstances there can be no question of charity of any kind on the part of religious organisations. A decree of the All-Russia Central Executive Committee and the Council of People's Commissars of 8 April 1929,

'On Religious Associations' forbids all charitable activities on the part of the church.[5]

By the outbreak of World War II, the institutions of the church had been virtually destroyed as a result of the Stalinist purges and a strong anti-religious policy. The name of the game could only be survival as far as the church was concerned: only four bishops remained at liberty and all seminaries and monasteries were closed.

THE ROLE OF THE CHURCH IN A SOCIALIST SOCIETY: FLUCTUATING ATTITUDES

Although the activity of the church in all spheres of life in the Soviet society was severely limited by 1939, there were several factors which ensured that church institutions would survive. State attitudes changed with the onset of war and national crisis: the dictates of pragmatism led to Stalin's meeting with the remaining Orthodox hierarchs in 1943, where a concordat between church and state was struck. The church would provide financial and moral support in the war effort; the state, in its turn, would guarantee a limited revival of church institutions. It was discovered that church–state relations could be manipulated to considerable advantage, the church subordinate to, and dependent on the state. The Russian Orthodox Church and other religious bodies were expected to follow the government's foreign policy line postwar: indeed 'peace-making activity' was the only form allowed of what could broadly be termed social involvement. The only possible form of 'charity' – and this is stretching the term somewhat – was to make regular and generous donations to the Soviet Peace Fund and, in more recent years, to the Soviet Cultural Fund. The Peace Fund in particular has been the source of much resentment among Church activists, perceived as little more than another means of taxing church income. Thus we can see how the state was able to play on what are often genuine and legitimate Christian concerns within the broader interpretation of social involvement. Such concerns as the desire for peace and the preservation of cultural monuments have been manipulated to the advantage of the state by providing additional revenue, while the possibility for more direct charitable action has been excluded.

For many years it has been impossible to assess just how much the church has donated to state funds, but with the advent of glasnost some statistics have become available. For example, Bishop Lev of Tashkent and Central Asia, in an interview with *Pravda vostoka*, revealed that out of an annual expenditure of around 500,000 roubles, his diocese gave 141,000 roubles to the Peace Fund and 35,000 to the Cultural Fund in 1988. At 176,000, this constitutes more than 30 per cent of the total expenditure, not to mention the donations the diocese had made to other charitable concerns, although the interview does not make it clear if the total represents only the budget for the charitable donations or the annual budget for the diocese as a whole.[6] An article in *Moscow News* revealed that in 1988 the religious associations of Moscow had donated over 800,000 roubles to the Peace Fund, and 180,000 to the Children's Fund (established in 1987).[7] It is to be hoped that with the gradual improvement of church–state relations more comprehensive statistics will become available.

Ironically, although the churches were debarred until recently from offering aid to their fellow citizens, it was not uncommon for them to send aid to friendly countries abroad. An interview in *Moscow News* with the then president of the All-Union Council of the Evangelical Christians and Baptists, Vasili Logvinenko, revealed that the Baptist churches have been involved in sending aid to Angola, Nicaragua and Ethiopia.[8]

One important factor which has caused a policy change has been the generous provision of aid by the churches, offering relief to the victims of the natural and man-made disasters which have plagued the Soviet Union in recent years. The disaster at the Chernobyl nuclear reactor and the subsequent evacuation of thousands of people created a vast area of need. The early days of glasnost concealed facts about the scale of the disaster which only now are being made known. At the time, Soviet propaganda, using figures such as Metropolitan Filaret of Kiev as its mouthpiece, took the opportunity to condemn the West, accusing it of trying to gain political advantages from someone else's grief. Archbishop Makari of Ivano-Frankovsk attacked the Catholic charity Aid to the Church in Need, which had called on the Soviet government to allow overseas Christian organisations to import aid for the victims without ideological reservations, for supporting the cause of the then outlawed Ukrainian Catholic Church. This illegitimate politicisation of acute human suffering obscured the fact that churches within the Soviet Union had immediately offered financial help and resources. Vazgen I, head of the Armenian Church, informed the then President Gromyko that his church was making a 150,000 rouble donation to the relief fund. Baptists in Kiev also took up collections for the fund and offered accommodation to the evacuees. In 1986, however, the newness of this departure was a source of considerable embarrassment to the state, and Vazgen I felt it necessary to couch his church's offer of help in rather apologetic terms: 'We know that our state has taken all measures to provide flats, foodstuffs and medicines to the evacuated population.'[9] Only in

November 1987 did the state overcome its embarrassment sufficiently to reveal that the churches had donated over three million roubles for the relief of Chernobyl victims.[10]

By December 1988, the time of the Armenian earthquake, it was already becoming more acceptable for the churches to offer aid in a time of crisis. By a strange coincidence, a charitable organisation had been established in Armenia just three months before, following the lead given by the newly established 'Miloserdie' (Charity) movement elsewhere in the USSR, which shall be discussed later. The organisers were thus in a position to coordinate some of the relief effort. Baptist churches in the Russian Federation reported in their information bulletin that 180,000 roubles had been collected over a few days for the Armenian Relief Fund.[11] *Moscow News* revealed that the religious organisations of Moscow had donated a total of 420,000 roubles.[12] Father Mark Smirnov, priest and journalist, said in an interview with the Estonian youth paper that the Russian Orthodox Church had contributed around four million roubles in the first month of the appeal.[13] Concerts were organised across the country by various churches to raise money for the fund as the nation as a whole sought to respond to this new crisis. Undoubtedly the combined effect of the number of national disasters and subsequent revelations about the inability of the state emergency organisations effectively to deal with the scale of the needs were an important factor in changing official attitudes to the acceptability of church involvement in charitable initiatives.

THE REHABILITATION OF THE CONCEPT OF CHARITY IN THE SOVIET PRESS

Over the past few years, one of the major themes in the Soviet press has been the question of the general rehabilitation of moral values in a society which has become cynical and demoralised. The word charity, *miloserdie*, is a word which fell so much into disuse that it was marked as obsolete in Soviet dictionaries: charity, like religion, was considered to be a relic of the past, a mark of condescension to the needy which did nothing to relieve material suffering and injustice. In a state which claimed to provide for the needs of its citizens, any sanctioning of charitable activities would be tantamount to an admission of failure to deliver on its promises. However, glasnost has also revealed to what extent charity is now needed.

A writer who has shown concern in the past for the moral and spiritual state of society, Daniil Granin, published a lengthy article in *Literaturnaya gazeta* in 1987, bringing *miloserdie* out of obscurity and into the forefront

of public debate. He attributes the general decline in moral values in Soviet
society to the psychological and moral effects of the mass repressions of the
1930s, when to display any form of compassion was potentially dangerous:

> Charity has not declined by accident: it was systematically obliterated
> during the time of the dispossession of the kulaks, when people were not
> allowed to help the victims and sentiments like charity were regarded as
> suspect.[14]

Granin goes on to describe the conditions in a Leningrad hospital where
he was receiving treatment: one nurse to 90 people, a lack of auxiliary staff,
run-down, rat-infested buildings and patients forced to lie in corridors
because of lack of space. He tended elderly and dying patients because there
was no one else to answer their need. A subsequent article in the same
newspaper illustrates that Granin's story about the need to bribe medical
staff to get adequate attention was not far-fetched: conditions were so bad
in a Voronezh old people's home that the elderly patients were neglected,
there was only one shower room to two hundred people and the nurses had
to be bribed to perform the most elementary tasks. To make matters worse,
there was obvious mismanagement of funds. A journalist investigating the
home was subsequently intimidated by threats of dismissal from her job.
When the administrator of the home was finally removed from her post, she
was promoted to a more senior position.[15]

In general terms it is now widely acknowledged that there has been
systematic neglect of certain groups in Soviet society – the aged, the
handicapped, the sick and the dying. According to a recent article, again in
Literaturnaya gazeta, the health service is in disarray, inefficient and under-
funded, with no hope of rectifying the situation in the immediate future.[16]
Many of the most basic medicines are in short supply and fewer operations
than needed are performed because of the lack of resources. *Izvestiya*
reported recently that medical workers gathering in Moscow for their annual celebration mounted a protest about the state of the health service,
bearing banners displaying slogans such as 'Soviet medicine is bad for your
health'. A letter written by a Soviet student to *The Times* carried the
disturbing information that there was an acute shortage of disposable syringes and that nurses were often forced to reuse needles on doctor's
orders.[17] Another negative factor is the low rate of pay in the lower ranks of
the medical profession: junior doctors start at 110 roubles a month, and
nurses receive just 80 roubles a month – as a result there is an acute shortage
of medical personnel.[18] 'Social workers' – a new category of workers which

emerged in 1987 to provide some sort of care for the elderly – also receive just 80 roubles a month, a rate of pay hardly likely to attract people to such employment.[19]

It is in the light of this that many responded to Granin's call for charity and supported the establishment of a voluntary charitable organisation. The first, called 'Miloserdie', was established in Leningrad in April 1988: the movement soon spread to over 20 cities, with the establishment of the Soviet Mercy and Health Fund in September of that year and of an All-Union 'Miloserdie' Association in 20 December. These organisations appear to be an agglomeration of various agencies such as the trade unions, the Ministry of Health, the Komsomol, the Soviet Red Cross and other social organisations. While there continued to be an ongoing discussion in the Soviet press on the subject of charity, voices began to be raised in support of church involvement: indeed believers had approached the editorial offices of the paper *Sobesednik*, one of the promoters of the charity venture, offering support in a common cause.[21] Vasili Logvinenko, in the interview mentioned above, had criticised state restrictions on charitable activity, saving:

> Restrictions imposed through laws on charity activities by church organisations prevent normal and natural development. We are helping the needy and sick in other countries, why not help our fellow countrymen? The lifting of restrictions . . . would benefit believers and non-believers alike.[22]

The late Patriarch Pimen, in an interview with *Izvestiya* prior to his meeting with Gorbachov in 1988, also suggested that the church could make a significant contribution to charitable work, explaining that convent nuns could work in hospitals for the gravely ill, or work in homes for invalids and the disabled.[23] The Rector of the Leningrad Theological Academy, Vladimir Sorokin, in an interview with *Meditsinskaya gazeta*,[24] stressed the idea of 'adopting' certain institutions rather than making faceless donations of state funds, while Metropolitan Filaret of Kiev suggested that the church might again be permitted to run its institutions.

In the meantime it is clear that while these discussions were taking place in the press, apparatchiks and ideologists behind the scenes were wrestling with the problem of church involvement in charitable work. Not least among them was Konstantin Kharchev, then Chairman of the Council for Religious Affairs. In a speech to the Higher Party School in May 1988, addressing the whole question of church–state relations and legislation affecting religious organisations, Kharchev's comments regarding charitable activity are a telling illustration of the dilemma in which the state authorities found themselves:

> Let us look at such an aspect of the law on the separation of church and state as the prohibition on charitable activity by the church. In Moscow – and in large towns generally – there is a drastic shortage of junior personnel and of ordinary nursing staff in hospitals. In Moscow alone the shortfall is 20,000. Representatives of the church have applied to the authorities for permission to engage in charitable activities. So what should be the response, yes or no? We can let them empty bedpans, but then again, how will it reflect on the political and moral image of communists if a patient goes to his grave thinking that the Soviet state is incapable of supplying someone to bring him a bedpan? Another reason why we cannot allow the church to engage in charitable activities is that the Catholics will seize upon it: that well-known Mother Teresa has already offered, Protestants, Baptists, Adventists. As for the Orthodox Church, it is in such a cornered position that at present it simply lacks the financial resources for anything like that.[25]

Subsequent developments, however, would indicate that sheer necessity has overridden any ideological scruples: since May 1988 widespread publicity has been given in the press to church involvement in charitable work.

THE NATURE OF CHURCH INVOLVEMENT IN CHARITABLE WORK

It is clear that, in the main, the churches are following the lead given by secular initiatives such as Daniil Granin's 'Miloserdie' Society rather than initiating their own programmes, since they are still hidebound by the 1929 legislation forbidding them to do charitable work and because any offers of help in the past had been met with open hostility. Once believers saw that conditions in society were becoming more favourable they were willing to respond. In addition, the state is now actively encouraging charitable activity: in June 1988 the Ministry of Health issued a statement which said its institutions were free to accept any kind of help offered by believers.[26]

In an interview with *Meditsinskaya gazeta*, Priest Matvei Stadnyuk at the Patriarchal Cathedral revealed that he and other priests from the Cathedral had approached the Moscow health authorities in 1987, asking to be involved in hospital work, with little hope of success at the time. A key influence in changing attitudes, according to Stadnyuk, was the high-profile meeting of Gorbachov and Patriarch Pimen in April 1988, which sent out the unmistakable signal that in some areas at least church and state could share common ground. This, coupled with the pomp and ceremony with which the church was able to celebrate its millennium, gave it the confidence to engage in new initiatives. Parishioners at the Patriarchal Cathedral are now visiting the neurological department at the Basmanov Hospital, with the full approval of the director, Anatoli Solovyov.[27] The popular journal, *Ogonyok*, ran a four-page photo feature on their work with the elderly patients. This work has since expanded, and the parishioners of the Patriarchal Cathedral have been joined by groups of helpers from the St John the Baptist Church in Ivanovo and the Veshnyakovsky Church.

Izvestiya has been carrying regular news items about Orthodox activity for a couple of years, including several articles about Orthodox work in hospitals, old people's homes and invalids' homes. These illustrate that such activity is not limited to Moscow. Believers of Tambov Cathedral have 'taken a lead' in the work in the regional hospital carried out by the regional branch of the All-Union Fund for Mercy and Health,[28] while the Tselinograd commissioner for religious affairs has welcomed the help of believers. Bishop Gavriil of Khabarovsk accompanied the chairman of the local soviet on a visit to a home for invalids and the elderly. According to the chairman, N. Danilyuk, 'the inmates are lonely, they need constant attention and individual care and there are not enough orderlies and nurses. So we welcome the priests' initiative to take charge of the people living in this home.'[29] When a priest in Ufa issued an appeal at his church for helpers at the local hospital, where there is a desperate shortage of medical personnel, both Orthodox and Baptist believers responded.[30] Moscow Radio's world service reported in May 1989 that the Russian Orthodox Church was planning to extend its charitable activities: Archpriest Nikolai Vedernikov said that the church was giving attention to hospitals, old people's homes and mental clinics 'where there is an especially big need for mercy and compassion'.[31] More recently, *Meditsinskaya gazeta*[32] published an interview with Metropolitan Alexis of Leningrad[33] who spoke of plans to open a hospital in a building newly returned to the Orthodox Church. This, however, would not be church-run, but the church would supply some of the equipment and medicines that the Soviet health service is unable to provide, as well as volunteers to work on the wards.

The Baptist church in Moscow was very quick to respond to the new opportunities for social involvement. Barely a week after Gorbachov's meeting with the Orthodox hierarchs, they had organised a programme of visiting at the psycho-geriatric unit at the Kashchenko Hospital. This had small beginnings: at first only 18 women regularly visited the wards, but by May 1989 more than one hundred women were working in four wards.[34] In the main, the women feed and dress the patients, clean the wards, change the bedlinen and talk to the patients – thus providing an invaluable service to the overstretched staff at the hospital. This has been given widespread coverage in the Soviet press. At the end of 1988, Baptist churches reported that for them it had been a year of charity, with churches getting actively involved in hospital visiting across the country. In May 1989 the Baptist publication, *Informatsionny byulleten* (now renamed *Khristianskoye slovo* – 'Christian word') published an article written by the deputy president of the secular charity organisation in Odessa, saying that believers in the town formed a large proportion of the numbers involved and expressing especial thanks for their commitment and support.[35] Leningrad Baptists have recently established a soup kitchen, providing a hot meal for elderly pensioners living below the poverty line.

At the end of 1988, it seemed that while the authorities were willing to allow believers into geriatric and psychiatric wards, where the patients were unlikely ever again to play a part in the mainstream of social life, any involvement with children would be much more suspect. However, during 1989, both Baptist and Orthodox churches have become involved in children's hospitals and children's homes. It is clear that the same degree of neglect and underfunding affects these institutions also, despite the traditionally privileged position of children in Soviet society. Several church figures are members of the Lenin Soviet Children's Fund, established in 1987, including Metropolitan Mefodiy of Voronezh and former Baptist Union President Vasili Logvinenko: since 1987 the churches have been making regular donations to this fund. Much of the churches' individual contributions towards the care of children have been geared towards the provision of funds and equipment. Metropolitan Mefodiy, in an article called 'Charity for children', published in the Orthodox monthly, the *Journal of the Moscow Patriarchate*, told of a new initiative where the Sofrino workshops, which produce church items such as candles, had sponsored a local orphanage and had been buying equipment for it.[36] Similarly, the new Orthodox newspaper, *Moscow Church Herald*, reported that the Danilov Monastery had taken responsibility for Children's Psychiatric Hospital No. 6 and had repaired the furniture, bought a TV and a fridge and toys for the children.[37] Metropolitan Mefodiy received a lot of publicity for donating a house belonging to his diocese to a couple who had adopted six children in the new adoption programme being encouraged by the Soviet government, given the recent severe criticism of state orphanages: indeed Mefodiy himself had criticised orphanages for not preparing children to face the demands and responsibilities of adult life.[38] It is theoretically possible for believers themselves to adopt orphans, although it would be difficult to confirm whether this has in fact happened.

The Moscow Baptist Church has begun a programme of visiting in a boarding school for handicapped children, and churches throughout the country have raised funds for schools or held charity concerts to make donations to the Children's Fund. The Kishinev church bought clothes and crockery for the children's home in the city and did voluntary work improving the grounds and repairing the buildings.[39] *Moscow News* devoted a large amount of space to a story about Adventists in Tula who had helped out in a boarding school, raising funds and doing essential repair work to buildings that were so dilapidated they had been declared a health hazard, making good the deficiencies which the state could not remedy.[40] As well as donating considerable sums of money to the Armenian relief fund, members of the Moscow Baptist Church also visited some of the child victims of the earthquake in February 1989. Doctors commented on the positive effect this visit had had on the children and invited the group to come again.[41] Indeed, the Baptists have reported in their publication that they have actually been approached by health service workers, requesting help in their institutions: following such requests, Baptists inaugurated regular programmes of visiting at the Children's Hospital No. 41 in Moscow and at Children's Home No. 28.[42] Parishioners from the Orthodox Tikhvin Church of the Holy Virgin have been visiting a home for disabled children who have been abandoned by their parents.[43] However, although there is obviously scope for direct personal involvement with the children themselves, it is clear that it is the financial contribution from the churches which is most valued by the state authorities.

One of the more startling developments has been the granting of permission to priests and groups of believers to visit prisons and labour camps. The first of such visits took place in July 1989, when Metropolitan Filaret of Kiev visited the camp at Bucha.[44] Again this activity is an example of the extent to which the state is seeking to enlist the moral and spiritual authority of the church in the rehabilitation of moral values. The rise in the crime rate (in the first six months of 1989 there was a 32 per cent increase on the same period in 1988[45]) has caused considerable anxiety and prolonged debate at sessions of the Congress of People's Deputies: Metropolitan Alexis of Leningrad and Novgorod who, incidentally, was nominated as parliamentary deputy by the Soviet Mercy and Health Fund, stated in December 1989 that the church had a key role to play in the moral re-education of prisoners.[46] In recognition of this, Vadim Bakatin, Minister for Internal Affairs, has given permission for prison visiting. The Baptist churches have also been into camps where traditional methods of political re-education have failed and held meetings which have a strongly evangelistic element. The highly organised Latvian Christian Mission has a comprehensive programme of prison visiting and aims to set up a centre for the rehabilitation of former prisoners, a totally new departure which runs far ahead of any state attempt to reintegrate former offenders into society.

The Latvian Christian Mission is in fact a unique organisation in the USSR.[47] An ecumenical and apparently autonomous organisation, it coordinates many charitable activities within the republic and its representatives have travelled as far as Siberia sharing their experience and expertise. Over 250 women are visiting all the major hospitals in the republic with no restrictions on their activity. In addition, the LCM is negotiating with overseas aid organisations for the supply of medical equipment and medicines and is holding talks with the customs authorities to get customs duty concessions. The organisation also hopes to raise funds for its own 400-bed hospital in Riga. Riga has its share of elderly impoverished citizens and the mission has recently opened a soup kitchen which provides 100 meals a day for those on a pension of under 50 roubles a month. The fact that people from the Mission appear to travel extensively within the Soviet Union indicates that this organisation is perhaps seen by other believers as the model for future Christian charitable concerns. Indeed, now that the initial euphoria about being able to engage in charitable activity has lessened, indications are that there are considerable difficulties to be overcome.

PROBLEMS AND DILEMMAS

The most obvious difficulty the churches face is the continuing legal ban on charitable activity: despite assurances that the 1929 law has been abolished, it is clear that some believers have been reluctant to engage in any activity which remains technically outside the law. In his article reporting on Adventist involvement with a boarding school in Tula, Father Mark Smirnov, himself also a coordinator of Christian charity under the auspices of the Soviet Mercy and Health Fund, had the following to say about the dilemma in which believers find themselves:

> . . . the position of those working for charity is ambiguous: doing good, they risk violating the current legislation pertaining to religious cults . . . This does not match well with the current times: our society is impatiently waiting precisely for such help from believers . . . on the one hand Christians must follow Evangelical ideals and do good. On the other hand, as citizens of their country, they must observe its laws.[48]

For over two years there has been the promise of new legislation affecting religious practice and freedom of conscience in the Soviet Union, but it has been subject to long delay. A draft was recently published in *Izvestiya*[49] which does in fact lift the ban on charitable activity, but is vague about how far the churches can actually go in setting up their own institutions.

In their own analysis of charitable activity, the churches are themselves aware of the difficulties born out of lack of experience in the field which, added to the ambiguities of the legal situation, does not really make for success. The *Journal of the Moscow Patriarchate*, not usually known for openness on church matters, published an article in March 1989 analysing the difficulties which the church now needs to overcome if its work is to be effective. The article sees that the high media profile and expressions of gratitude towards believers cannot be allowed to obscure the realities of the situation:

> Many parishioners who have taken up charitable work on the spur of the moment abandoned it within a month or two. Some of them, especially the young people, proved to be unprepared psychologically for the sufferings of the gravely sick and the dying. The dispersion of believers in the parishes and lack of contact with the local clergy also have a negative effect. The inertia of the stagnation period is still there. The church's estrangement from public life . . . resulted in believers adopting a guarded attitude towards society.[50]

Because of the lack of experience and the lack of adequate pastoral support for those engaged in such activity, the article acknowledges there is a high drop-out rate. To remedy this there needs to be more support and encouragement at a parish level, with the provision of literature and pastoral expertise. These problems, essentially linked not just to charity but to the re-establishment of normal parish life in the Soviet Union, will take some time to resolve.

The journal *Ogonyok* attacked this subject from a slightly different angle. In its coverage of the work of believers at the Botkin Hospital, the journalists did a survey of the Orthodox parishes in Moscow which revealed that few priests were willing to display any new initiative: 'Everywhere they were waiting for some kind of directive.'[51] A telephone conversation with Archpriest Vladimir Sorokin revealed that only four people had persevered with hospital visiting after about four hundred initial expressions of support. Although this article was written in 1988 it illustrates the kind of psychological barriers the churches have to overcome.

Another difficulty is the lack of resources. Although the Russian Orthodox Church has been receiving more revenue since the millennium in 1988 because of an increase in the number of baptisms and church weddings, its resources are stretched to the limit because of new demands to undertake restoration work in recently returned churches. The challenge to the church in the era of glasnost is not only greater social involvement but the need also to establish and expand its institutions on a firmer foundation than was previously possible. Archibishop Kirill of Smolensk has pointed to the need for small beginnings in the sphere of social involvement in order to gain the expertise necessary for larger projects.[52] A constant dilemma for any church – but especially the church in the Soviet Union – is how it can adequately cater to the needs of its flock and at the same time fulfil its mission to society, a dilemma intensified by the current situation.

Interestingly, voices are now being raised in the press which are critical of the way in which the state has used the willingness of believers to engage in charitable work. In an article which appeared in *Literaturnaya gazeta* in January of 1990, Edda Zabavskikh wrote a searing criticism of the various secular charitable initiatives.[53] She holds up Christian charity as an example to be emulated, in contrast to the initiatives of various social organisations and cooperatives which are only engaging in this work because of its publicity value. The church is obviously being used by a state which has failed to deliver on its promise to care for the needs of its citizens. She cites an instance when a doctor being interviewed on television commented on the recent return of a church near his hospital, making it clear that the newly established parish would provide a welcome source of labour power in the hospital wards. Zabavskikh also implies that the funds donated by believers do not always reach the people for whom they are intended. Instead, the churches should be able to set up their own charitable concerns independent of the state. Early on in the charity movement, there were intimations of difficulty in such state-sponsored organisations as the Mercy and Health Fund – the danger being that with such large-scale organisations bureaucracy and inefficiency would hamper their effectiveness. People's Deputy Ilya Zaslavsky, himself active in the charity movement, said during a visit to Keston College that these large-scale charitable organisations attempted to have a monopoly over all charitable initiatives, instead of being organised on the basis of voluntary affiliation supported by such church representatives as Father Mark Smirnov and Baptist charity coordinator Mikhail Zhidkov. Administrative costs also run high, thus creaming off a proportion of funds which could be used more effectively. A recent article in the émigré newspaper, *Russkaya mysl*, by the Orthodox layman Vladimir Zelinsky, makes some disturbing allegations about the siphoning off by local authorities of the relief supplies sent from abroad to alleviate the suffering caused by the Armenian earthquake.[54]

Another article, this time in the *Moscow Church Herald*, said that believers were being exploited by hospital staff, citing an example in Moscow Hospital No. 70 where all the most difficult tasks are given to believers and the medical staff themselves shirk their responsibilities.[55] Any real contact with the patients is met with obstruction and hostility from the staff. The writer maintains that believers are also assigned to those patients the medical staff have 'written off'.

The real solution to these difficulties would be to allow the church to run its own institutions, as Archbishop Kirill stated in a New Year interview with *Literaturnaya gazeta*.[56] Whether this will become a reality remains to be seen.

There are, however, far wider issues to be considered. Clearly the churches and other voluntary organisations should not be expected to shoulder the whole burden of community care in a society where each day brings new revelations about the extent of the need. In the Russian Federation alone, 17,000 disabled people are waiting for accommodation and 100,000 need a health visitor to tend to their needs at home; the situation has actually worsened in recent years.[57] State institutions house 1,100,000 children, many of them abandoned because of some physical or mental disability.[58] Some 43 million people, many of them elderly, live below the poverty line.[59] What is also certain is that economic reform will bring with it considerable hardship with rising inflation and unemployment increasingly likely as President Gorbachov introduces a market economy. The state recognises and is using the moral support the church can offer in a time of national difficulty, but this should not become a substitute for social justice and effective government policies. A recent interview with Russian Social Security Minister, V.A. Kaznachev, has revealed the difficulty his ministry faces, openly admitting that much of the care needed by the elderly and infirm is in fact being provided by voluntary organisations when it should be the responsibility of the state. Kaznachev also hints at the potentially chaotic nature of such voluntary organisations, further endorsing Edda Zabavskikh's critical comments.[60] For her, this constitutes a powerful argument for allowing the churches to run their own institutions. However, the church – or the Russian Orthodox Church at least – is expected to be a prop for government policy, not an autonomous body in society; yet if one takes the numerous articles regarding the rehabilitation of moral values to their logical conclusion, then the church should be free to criticise state social policy if it sees fit. Indeed social and philanthropic issues are likely to become politicised in any society. In Britain, government criticism of the Church of England's *Faith in the City* report is a telling illustration of the problematic nature of this form of social involvement; in the Soviet Union, the wider issues of church–state relations are unlikely ever to be entirely problem-free.

In many societies the church is expected to provide support in the traditionally 'difficult' areas of need. Every society finds it necessary to question the extent of individual and collective responsibility for community care, which in turn implies a deeper understanding of the underlying relationship between the individual and society. No society finds it easy to establish the right principles and achieve a proper balance in this area. What is certain is that in an imperfect world human need and suffering are a continuing reality – the test is how the interplay of forces within society, both charitable and state enterprises, can best serve the interests of the needy. In the Soviet Union, it remains to be seen how far such a balance can be achieved: in the meantime, the churches are providing a much needed boost to the nation's failing health services.

NOTES

1. Statistics taken from an article on charity in *Nedelya*, 18 December 1989.
2. Elizaveta Fedorovna's story was told in an article by priest Alexander Shargunov, in *Literaturnaya gazeta*, 4 October 1989. In it he held her up as an example of Christian charity worthy of emulation.
3. Statistics taken from Trevor Beeson, *Discretion and Valour* (London: Routledge & Kegan Paul, 1982) (revised edition), p. 53.
4. N. Orleansky, *Zakon o religiyoznikh obedineniyakh RSFSR* (Moscow, 1930).
5. Genrikh Golst, *Religiya i zakon*, (Moscow: Yuridicheskaya literatura, 1975).
6. *Pravda Vostoka*, 25 March 1989.
7. *Moscow News*, 9 July 1989.
8. *Moscow News*, 3 April 1989.
9. *Keston News Service* (KNS) 252, 12 June 1986.
10. *Nauka i religiya*, 11/87, interview with K. M. Kharchev, former Chairman of the Council for Religious Affairs.
11. *Informatsionny byulleten*, No. 1, March 1989.
12. *Moscow News*, 9 July 1989.
13. *Molodyozh Estonii*, 28 February 1989.
14. *Literaturnaya gazeta*, 18 March 1987.
15. *Literaturnaya gazeta*, 14 June 1989.
16. *Literaturnaya gazeta*, 8 November 1989.
17. *Times*, 17 October 1989.
18. *Literaturnaya gazeta*, 8 November 1989.
19. 'The Aged in the USSR', William Moskoff, Radio Liberty Report on the USSR, 15 September 1989.
20. *Literaturnaya gazeta*, 14 June 1989.
21. Reported in Oxana Antic, 'Discussions in the Soviet press on allowing the Church to engage in charitable work', Radio Liberty, Munich, 27 April 1988.

22. *Moscow News*, 3 April 1988.
23. Oxana Antic, op. cit.
24. *Meditsinskaya gazeta*, 30 March 1988.
25. *Russkaya mysl*, 20 May 1988.
26. *Ogonyok*, No. 38, September 1988.
27. *Meditsinskaya gazeta*, 17 June 1988.
28. *Izvestiya*, 17 March 1989.
29. *Izvestiya*, 3 May 1989.
30. *Izvestiya*, 29 March 1989.
31. *Summary of World Broadcasts*, BBC Caversham, 3 May 1989.
32. *Meditsinskaya gazeta*, 28 January 1990.
33. Now Patriarch Alexi II, enthroned on 10 June 1990.
34. *Informatsionny byulleten*, No. 3, May 1989.
35. Ibid.
36. *Journal of the Moscow Patriarchate*, November 1988.
37. *Moscow Church Herald*, No. 2, May 1989.
38. *Trud*, 3 January 1990.
39. *KNS* 321, 16 March 1989.
40. *Moscow News*, 8 January 1989.
41. *Informatsionny byulleten*, No. 1, March 1989.
42. *Informatsionny byulleten*, No. 3 May 1989.
43. *Moscow Church Herald*, No. 3, May 1989.
44. *KNS* 338, 16 November 1989.
45. 'Much Ado About Crime', D. J. Peterson, Radio Liberty, Report on the USSR, 15 September 1989.
46. *Leningradskaya pravda*, 7 December 1989.
47. *KNS* 344, 22 February 1990.
48. *Moscow News*, 8 January 1989.
49. *Izvestiya*, 5 June 1990, reported in *KNS* 352, 14 June 1990.
50. *Journal of the Moscow Patriarchate*, 3/89 (English), 6/89 (Russian).
51. *Ogonyok*, op. cit.
52. *Journal of the Moscow Patriarchate*, 8/89.
53. *Literaturnaya gazeta*, 10 January 1990.
54. *Russkaya mysl*, 27 April 1990.
55. *Moscow Church Herald*, No. 10, August 1989.
56. *Literaturnaya gazeta*, 3 January 1990.
57. *Sovetskaya Rossiya*, 18 January 1990.
58. *Sovetskaya Rossiya*, 16 December 1989.
59. 'The Aged in the USSR', Radio Liberty, 15 September 1989.
60. *Pravda*, 21 May 1990.

8 Ecological Disaster Zones

Environmental Concerns and the Soviet Union
Olga Bridges

Environmental pollution is now considered as a major and worldwide problem which recognises no national frontiers. Its causes are many, but primary factors have been the overriding priority for economic growth, the implicit faith in nature as an entirely renewable resource and the lack of public and therefore political interest in environmental quality.

During the last ten years there has been growing public pressure on Western governments to give more emphasis to the quality of food, water and air. In the past decade the EC has issued a number of important environmental directives, particularly on the chemical and microbiological quality of water for both drinking and recreational purposes. These have highlighted, for example, the need to control nitrate and pesticides in drinking water and to minimise sewage contamination of bathing beaches.

With the recent changes in information freedom and the increasing openness of public debate in Eastern Europe it is now possible to obtain a reasonable picture of environmental quality in those countries. This article is concerned particularly with problems of water supply and water quality in the Soviet Union.

It is generally acknowledged that in the 1960s people in the USSR did not know what 'ecology' meant. In contrast, in 1989 a survey of the popular magazine *Ogonyok* showed that 80 per cent of the Soviet people were very concerned about environmental problems and their impact on human health.[1] This public concern was reflected in a decree of the Soviet Parliament in 1989 which defined the measures to be taken in order to help protect the environment.

Even excluding the other republics of the Soviet Union, Russia occupies just over 10 per cent of the world's land mass. It is also very richly endowed with fresh water; much of it is found in Siberia. Lake Baikal alone accounts for about 20 per cent of the world's total fresh water supply. Other lakes and rivers in Siberia account for a further 20 per cent of the world's fresh water.

There are estimated to be some three million rivers in the Soviet Union, but 84 per cent of these are in the north and east in the basins of the Arctic and Pacific Oceans where the population is relatively sparse. In contrast the great centres of population are in the south and west, but only 7.5 per cent of the rivers flow through this region into the Baltic, Black and Caspian seas. As a consequence, despite the overall plentiful supply of fresh water, there is no water reserve capacity in the south-west of the country; indeed at present there is deficit in the balance between water needs and water availability in this region.

This is a classic example of a gross mismatch of resource and population distribution: six times more people live in the south and west of the Soviet Union, but there is one third of the water availability of the north and east. This distribution problem is reflected on a much smaller scale in many countries around the world, including the United Kingdom (the cleanest rivers are in Scotland well away from the major towns).

This imbalance between the location of fresh water and the distribution of the population is the first of four major factors which have led to the deterioration of water quality in the heavily populated areas of the Soviet Union.

The second factor which has caused water pollution has been the concentration of heavy industry in areas where water is plentiful for processing and cooling purposes and unwanted residues are easily disposed of with no prior treatment and hence at minimum cost.

The third factor that has contributed to the problems of water pollution has been the strong pressure for increasing agricultural yield. The need to produce a range of crops even in the most environmentally unsuitable regions of the country accounts for the fact that two-thirds of all water in the Soviet Union is used for agriculture.

Sixteen out of the last 30 years have witnessed serious droughts. Even with normal rainfall it has been found necessary to irrigate some thirty million hectares of the country by canals and waterways. During this process typically between 20 and 30 per cent of the water is lost through evaporation or during filtration (see Table 8.1). Irrigation also creates problems by disturbing natural water sources and frequently produces soil erosion. It may also cause a significant increase in the salt content of the soil.

The fourth factor is particularly important: neither industry nor farms have up till now paid for the water they use. Because water is free, its quality is not valued and efficient use has therefore a very low priority. It is a sad reflection on human nature that when a resource is free to everybody, often nobody feels responsible for looking after it. Another consequence is

Table 8.1 Percentage water loss through irrigation, 1987–88

Republic	1987	1988
Georgia	34.2	32.4
Azerbaidzhan	28.3	28.4
Russian Federation	23.9	23.0
Kazakhstan	20.3	19.2
Ukraine	17.4	19.7

Source: Sbornik statisticheskikh materialov 1989 (Moscow, Finansy i statistika, 1990).

that no capital is realised from the resource and thus little investment is made in it.

So far I have identified four of the major factors responsible for water pollution in the Soviet Union. There are in addition often local factors. Pollution inevitably has multiple causes rather than a single cause.

I would like now to address some of the particular problems which are currently besetting the Soviet Union's water supply. These can be categorised broadly under three separate headings, although often they are inter-related:

(a) contamination of the sea and large-scale environmental damage;
(b) pollution of major fresh water sources;
(c) contamination of drinking water (both microbiological and chemical).

Much publicity has been given in the Soviet press to the tragedies of the Aral Sea, Lake Baikal and the River Volga. Thirty million people of Soviet Central Asia are estimated to be affected by the death of the Aral Sea which was brought about by the zeal of government officials in their desire to irrigate bigger territories for agricultural purposes. Some measure of the scale of this problem is indicated by Table 8.2.

The cost of remedying the Aral Sea disaster is estimated to be 37 billion roubles, five times more than has been spent on clearing up after Chernobyl! Not only have there been very major effects on people's livelihood and on the environment in general but there have been claims of serious effects on human health. Hepatitis is found with increased frequency in babies and adults of the area as well as TB and brucellosis. The salt content of breast milk of the women living in the area is three times higher than the average.

Large-scale disasters attract attention, sympathy and even financial as-

Table 8.2 Changes in the Aral Sea, 1961–1987

	1961	1987
Surface area	66,000 sq. km	36,500 sq. km
Maximum depth	53 m	40 m
Salinity	10–11%	~30%
Wildlife species	178	38
Annual fish catch	25,000 tonnes	0

Sources: A. Sitnichenko, 'Spasat, shtoby spastis', *Sobesednik*, No. 18, May 1990, p. 3; S. Fioletov, 'Proshchanie s Aralom', *Poisk*, No. 11, March 1990, pp. 3–4; M. Shakhanov, 'Gorkaya sol Arala', *Sovetskie profsoyuzy*, No. 8, April 1987, pp. 18–19.

sistance to help to remedy the situation. Pollution of drinking water does not gain nearly as much attention as some massive ecological incidents because the effects are not spectacular and may be drawn out over a period of many months or even years.

Provision of drinking water has not been given the priority it should despite the fact that one third of all cities in the Soviet Union have difficulty in providing drinking water of even reasonable quality. The biological methods used to clean water extract only up to 40 per cent of non-organic compounds. This means that 60 per cent of nitrate, 70 per cent phosphate and 80 per cent potassium are left in the water.[2] To make this water safe for human consumption it needs to be diluted at least ten times over, but there is not enough clean water to do so. Consequently, much of the water does not meet WHO standards.

In addition, more and more pesticides are used in agriculture and, perhaps not surprisingly, a number of these are finding their way into drinking water. In the Syr Darya River of the Aral region, for example, the levels of DDT exceed by 50 times the recommended safe level of WHO.[3] This is just one example of what a Soviet writer has called 'the monstrous indifference of the Soviet economic system to nature'.[4]

An illustration of the expansion in pesticide use is that in 1982, 29 kinds of pesticides were employed, but by 1989 this figure had increased to 104. Not only surface water, but also the deep ground waters, important for future use, are affected. For example, recent tests on an underground stream in the Ukraine revealed high levels of pesticides and other chemicals. Even much cherished deep-water sources, including those of the health spas of Kislovodsk and Pyatigorsk (see Table 8.3) are now regularly contaminated.[5] The situation with regard to the many artesian wells in the country

Table 8.3   Percentage of 'natural products' not meeting quality standards owing
to environmental contamination in 1988

Mineral water (in total)	*0.3 km³*
Kislovodsk area	28%
Pyatigorsk area	29%
Therapeutic muds (in total)	*0.4 km³*
Saki area (Crimea)	42%
Kirov area	99.3%

Source: Sbornik statisticheskikh materialov 1989 (Moscow, Finansy i statistika,
1990).

is in doubt because of the lack of monitoring, but extensive pollution of
such sources would not be surprising.

An example of the problems of environmental managements in the Soviet Union is a case which has hardly been noticed by the press. In 1980 a
highly ambitious Party Secretary of the Krasnodar Region promised Moscow hierarchy a million tonne crop of rice. Rice had not been a traditional
crop in the region and to ensure a good harvest pesticides were used
indiscriminately. Attempts to allay public concern were enterprising, if not
particularly convincing. For example, the Party official responsible for
agricultural policy put a tablespoonful of the pesticides concerned in his
fish tank and showed that the fish did not die. This approach just demonstrates toxicological naivity in that, first, it assumes that death is the only
adverse effect of pesticides and, secondly, that man is like a fish. The Party
Secretary was Mikhail Gorbachov.

But politicians usually do not carry out experiments on themselves,
neither do they tend to live on the flight path of helicopters spraying
pesticides – a practice still widely used in the Krasnodar Region in 1989.

There have been many claims of ill health through use or misuse of
pesticides and fertilisers. In the last five years in the Krasnodar Region the
incidence of cancer has grown by 50 per cent among adults. Children's
asthma has trebled and there is a steady increase of alopecia (hair loss)
among children. Limited analysis of the food supply in August 1989 revealed 0.064 mg/kg of the herbicide propanid in Krasnodar rice.[6] In Moldavia
there are claims of stunted growth of children and increases in infant
mortality and morbidity. In Turkmenia the Ministry of Health has reported
that pesticides are causing increases in many diseases of the liver and
pancreas.[7]

Every year around 25,000 new chemical compounds are introduced commercially into the Soviet Union. Some 150,000 chemicals are now considered to be possible environmental pollutants, and many have been found in rivers and lakes. In most cases their toxic properties are unknown as is their potential to produce additive or even synergistic effects. To establish and improve environmental quality it is necessary to have enforceable standards for each chemical/class of chemicals based on health criteria. As in most other parts of the world, of the chemicals which might be expected to contribute to pollution or indeed have been found to do so only a relatively small number has an official standard. The reason for this is that such standards can only be set if there is enough data together with a suitable analytical method. In most cases neither exists. As a consequence, in the Rostov Region agricultural use of chemicals in 1986 involved 128 brand names, 60 per cent of which did not have an official standard.

Even where standards are established, they are often not adhered to. Nitrate is a particular problem because of its massive and widespread use as a fertiliser. There are many claims of ill health from exposure to nitrate, including increased incidence of high blood pressure, allergies, cancer and mental disorders, though the role of nitrate in their causation is not established.

Agriculture in the Soviet Union is not only responsible for pollution by pesticides but for many other water quality problems. The disposal of untreated farm sludge into rivers and lakes still remains a common practice. There appears to be total indifference to this type of pollution; this is not surprising because there is little commitment by the authorities to preventing it. For example, a large meat producing farm might have an income of between 9 and 11 million roubles a year, but the maximum fine for river pollution, if it is imposed at all, is 10 roubles.[8] Materials like farm sludge are not necessarily particularly toxic *per se*. However, they can produce serious damage by encouraging the growth of algae and bacteria, which may starve the rivers and lakes of oxygen and encourage the production of toxins.

The extensive use of nitrate fertilisers has led to similar effects in many lakes and seas. In contrast to the situation in many Western countries the production of such fertilisers is expected to double in the next ten years, which can only exacerbate the nitrate pollution of both drinking and recreational waters.

The Black Sea, a favourite area with holidaymakers, now has signs on its beaches forbidding swimming because of serious contamination with algae, bacteria and chemical pollution. Hydrogen sulphide (a microbiological product) can now be found at a depth of 75 metres, which is 125 metres nearer to the surface than was the case at the beginning of the century. It is predicted that the Black Sea will be entirely devoid of life within thirty or forty years.

In spite of such prophecies there are few signs of serious attempts to reverse the trend. Thus, the total amount of effluent discharged into the sea in 1988 in the Soviet Union as a whole was estimated to be 99 million cubic metres, of which 5 million cubic metres was untreated.

High content of chloro-organic pesticides is found not only in sea water but also in fish (see Table 8.4). Caspian sturgeon, a vital export, is becoming extinct. Oil pollution, which exceeds the average level in the sea by 10 to 20 times is considered to be a contributory factor to the six fold decrease in fish catch in the last thirty years, although the other forms of pollutants described above are also important. The economic loss from this industry alone is estimated at 25 million roubles a year.

Table 8.4   Reported number of incidents resulting in mass death of fish because of pollution

1965–1980	1,348
1981–1985	1,000
1986–1987	498

Sources: V. Luklyanenko, 'O generalnoi kontseptsii okhrany vodoyomov ot zagryaznenii', *Vestnik Akademii Nauk SSSR*, No. 4, 1990.

In addition to the above-mentioned examples, where there is continued contamination of the drinking water supply by the overuse or misuse of chemicals or poor effluent controls, the Soviet Union also has its share of major acute releases of chemicals into the water supply as a result of fires, explosions, pipe or valve failures, etc. This was at its most dramatic at Chernobyl, but much smaller-scale events appear to be commonplace. Bearing in mind the ageing nature of much of its chemical industry and the inadequacy of accident preventive and containment procedures and facilities, this state of affairs is hardly surprising.

A very recent vivid illustration of such an effect was in the city of Ufa (in the Urals) in early spring 1990 when a very large release of phenol occurred from a factory. This release affected the entire city's drinking water supply and the adverse effects on the population were so widespread that WHO was asked urgently to provide experts to help in handling the situation.

The future in respect of water quality in the Soviet Union remains fraught with problems. Population growth will continue to place increased demands on industry and agriculture. Increasingly, as is now the case in many

Western countries, this will need to be reconciled with the growing 'green awareness' of the public. As a recent study on attitudes of the public to Chernobyl and other environmental issues has shown, the green awareness is already an important political force. In order to meet these growing public demands legislation will have to be introduced along the following lines:

(a) Waste water should not be allowed into lakes, rivers and seas without proper treatment.
(b) Water has to be regarded as a precious resource, therefore industry, agriculture, household use and misuse of water must be monitored and where necessary sanctions taken against offenders.
(c) The philosophy of minimisation of pollution at source needs to be introduced. This can only be achieved by strong public pressure and the education of industry and others in implementing the relevant technique.
(d) Extensive monitoring and strong enforcement of water quality standards with heavy penalties for offenders needs to be introduced.

There are signs that public pressure is already having an effect in many parts of the Soviet Union. There has very recently been established both a USSR Ecological Fund and a State Ecological Safety Service to monitor the work of all industries in the country. The USSR State Committee on Nature Conservation has also been newly founded to work out the country's ecological strategy and secure complete ecological glasnost.

Some local authorities now require payment for the use of recreational grounds along rivers and around lakes.[9] There is also a much more aggressive enforcement policy. In the Russian Federation alone the sum for which various firms were sued for polluting water in 1989 reached 150 million roubles.

Although these are encouraging signs of some preparedness for action to limit pollution, the Soviet Union is not yet even getting to grips with containing the growth of pollution, let alone reducing it.[10] In 1989 it has been estimated, for example, that the amount of untreated waste water passing into lakes and seas increased by 3.8 million cubic metres.

The scale of providing an adequate water supply for the entire population of the Soviet Union is also a very daunting one. It is estimated that only one out of ten people in the country has ready access to relatively clean water at present.

It is apparent that if the Soviet Union is to meet the required environmental and water supply goals, a massive commitment in both human and financial terms will be necessary. Since pollution knows no national boundaries this must be regarded as an international problem.

Children's Disaster Zone*
Olga Litvinenko

Children are not to blame. They did not ask to come into the world in a maternity home that infected them with disease. It isn't their fault their parents' houses are being knocked down. It's not their fault they have to breathe radioactive air. We have 83 million children in the Soviet Union, about a third of the entire population. Every year 6,000 die of cancer. It isn't their fault. Some 20 per cent of the Soviet population now lives in ecological disaster zones, between 35 and 40 per cent in ecology 'unfavourable' conditions. Every tenth schoolchild suffers from allergy ailments, every tenth has high blood pressure.

It isn't their fault.

Of every thousand children born in the USSR, as many as 24 die before their first birthday. The comparative (1988) figures show the UK as 9, France as 8 and Japan as 5.

Some 4.5 million Soviet schoolchildren are studying in buildings that are either condemned or in need of major repairs. It isn't their fault. More than 200 of our children are already infected with AIDS. It isn't their fault.

More than 300,000 children live in areas that have a pollution level of between 5 and 15 curies per square kilometre, 64,400 in areas with over 15 curies. It isn't their fault.

That is why children of the Land of the Soviets – that very country which proclaimed one of the world's falsest slogans 'All that is best for children!' – have no need of our advice, our talk, our wrangling. They need protection. Whatever their age they are little citizens of our homeland, citizens in need of help.

The 'Greens' Earn Public Trust†
Vladimir Lupandin and Gennady Denisovsky

A joint survey carried out in Moscow and the Moscow Region by the USSR Institute of Sociology and the American University of Houston shows that

* From *Sobesednik*, No. 22, May 1990, p. 3.
† From *Moscow News*, No. 27, 1990, p. 7.

Table 8.5 Level of public trust in various organisations*

	Fully trust	Trust %	Partly trust	No trust %
The church	17.5	46.8	24.1	4.8
The 'green movement'	12.9	41.6	16.3	8.5
The armed forces	12.3	44.1	33.9	8.0
The judiciary	2.0	18.3	52.1	20.7
The government	4.0	24.3	42.1	22.5
The Communist Party	5.4	33.4	37.0	17.3
The Komsomol	2.8	23.5	38.0	28.4
Trade Unions	3.8	33.4	39.4	18.7
The militia	3.0	19.9	53.3	20.5

*The 'don't knows' were counted, but not included in the table published.

the Soviet ecology movement is second only to the church in enjoying public trust.

Respondents to the survey described the 'greens' as a non-governmental movement concerned with public initiatives and campaigns against the building of projects detrimental to the environment. Examples given were the campaign to save Lake Baikal, to stop projects to divert the flow of Siberian rivers, to prevent the building of nuclear power plants, the Volga–Chograi Canal and the Katun Hydroelectric Power Station, to halt further expansion of the Astrakhan Gas Condensate Plant, and to stop construction of plants for producing protein-vitamin animal feeds. The public also want objective information on the true scale of the Chernobyl disaster and the aftermath of nuclear tests in the Semipalatinsk and Novaya Zemlya testing ranges.

The findings of the survey (shown in Table 8.5 as a percentage of a total number of those polled) show the level of public trust in various organisations.

One of the poll's findings is the prominence given by all respondents to environmental problems. As is evidence from Table 8.6, over 98 per cent of those polled are more concerned about such problems than they are about the growth in crime, food shortages, the AIDS threat and inter-ethnic conflicts.

When comparing the ratings of problems in terms of how they concerned 'myself personally' and 'the state', it was clear that the greatest threat to the state was perceived to come from inter-ethnic conflicts, but the greatest threat to people personally from environmental pollution.

Table 8.6   Levels of public concern on various issues

	Very important %	Important %	Partly important %	Not important %
Food shortages	69.4	25.0	4.4	1.2
Shortages of necessities	63.2	30.2	5.8	0.2
Consumer durables shortages	41.0	45.1	12.5	1.0
Environmental pollution	74.4	23.7	1.4	0.4
Rising crime	71.8	22.9	3.6	1.2
AIDS threat	60.8	23.5	7.2	7.2
Inter-ethnic conflicts	58.8	27.2	6.8	5.0
Drunkenness	43.3	28.0	43.3	10.9
Anti-semitism	21.3	20.3	25.4	0.2

It was also found that 79 per cent of those polled were willing to help ecological movements with donations, and that 76.6 per cent would not tolerate environmental pollution for the sake of economic development.

It would seem from the survey that circumstances favour the establishment and growth of a 'green' party, which could count on considerable public support. On the other hand, the movement is so heterogeneous, with such a diversity of public and political 'green' organisations, that it might be difficult to forge enduring unity. The extensive moral support and willingness to provide funds to solve acute ecological problems could well be dissipated in a disunited movement.

Grim Aftermath of Chernobyl for Belorussia*

Vyacheslav Khodosovsky

In the republic worst affected by the disaster at the Chernobyl nuclear power station, local health authorities have proved unequal to the challenge of coping with Chernobyl's aftermath. One reason is the sheer scale of the catastrophe. Although Chernobyl is actually in the Ukrainian Republic,

*From *Soviet Weekly*, 24 May 1990, pp. 8–9.

some 70 per cent of the contaminated area lies in neighbouring Belorussia because it had the misfortune to lie directly upwind of the reactor that exploded on 26 April 1986.

One fifth of Belorussia, in an area where 2.2 million people live, is contaminated by radioactive isotopes, particularly caesium-137, strontium-90 and plutonium-239 and 240. A quarter of these people are children under 14, and they were the first to feel the effects of the disaster. When I visited the children's haematology centre in Minsk recently, I found 60 children receiving treatment for leukaemia. All needed bone marrow transplants. They cannot have them in Belorussia because of the lack of specialists and equipment. Even painkillers to relieve their suffering are in short supply.

New cases of children with blood disorders have tripled in two years. Some of the patients even come from the Minsk Region which suffered the smallest radiation dose. The incidence of congenital leukosis, once rare, has increased ten times, and the death rate has trebled.

I was told by Olga Aleinikova, the Centre's Director, that only 15 per cent of the leukosis patients survive, whereas the USA and Germany had 75 per cent survival rates. Sadly, not a single child has been sent abroad for treatment because neither the Republic's Health Ministry, nor the parents have hard currency to pay for foreign treatment.

Other diseases and ailments have increased: anaemia, respiratory, gastroenteric and endocrinal disorders, mental breakdown and pregnancy problems; the immunity system has broken down in many patients; serious congenital deformities have occurred; and thyroid disorders are particularly common.

The long-term effects of lengthy exposure to even small doses of radiation are yet to be seen; no one can guarantee there will not be an aftershock of cancer and genetic diseases.

Journalists writing about Chernobyl know how hard it was to gather objective data and information about the actual state of affairs in the affected area, and how much pressure was brought to bear on them. Reporters accused of 'stirring up emotions' and 'creating panic' were abused by angry government and Communist Party officials.

A chart of caesium-137 contamination in Belorussia was only published three years after the disaster. A year on, the chart has been changed, but it is still not detailed enough to show the real scale of the disaster. Charts of other types of radioactive contamination have still not seen light of day, and local people in the affected area are still allowed to pick mushrooms and berries, and grow fruit and vegetables in their gardens, oblivious of the dangers.

Most people in the affected areas have 'hot particles' – microscopic pieces of unburnt nuclear fuel – embedded in their lungs. Professor Yevgeny Petriayev discovered that 70 out of the 100 people he examined had as many as between 15,000 and 20,000 hot particles in their lungs, showing up as tiny luminous lumps coated in a membrane of melted lung tissue.

The Republic is very short of radiation meters. Their manufacture has only just begun four years after the disaster! The cause is the usual one: bureaucratic reluctance to face facts. Public ignorance ensures immunity for those whose duty it is to save the population, yet are too slow to do anything effective.

Chernobyl remains a zone of 'restricted openness'. The forest in the vicinity of the Chernobyl power plant recently caught fire again, the soot and smoke lifting radioactive particles to places where the wind could carry them much farther afield. But no warnings were given.

The Belorussian capital Minsk recently had a massive protest demonstration. As bells tolled, the marchers walked along the main street carrying black flags and placards bearing the names of hundreds of populated areas where it is dangerous to live. They were demanding government action to deal with the effects of the disaster.

Neither Belorussian government leaders, nor Belorussian Party officials had dared stray from the Moscow line. They had even brushed aside repeated warnings from the Belorussian Academy of Sciences on the consequences of Chernobyl. Local authorities took their orders from above and made no special plea for help. Health Ministry officials made out that nothing serious had happened.

Perhaps that is why the money which poured into the Chernobyl fund was spent on covering losses suffered by the Nuclear Power Ministry instead of on medical aid or radiation meters. Only the consistent stand taken by the Belorussian Academy of Sciences and a powerful public lobby forced the local authorities to review their position and take action.

It cannot be denied that the work done in the years following the disaster is enormous. Over 25,000 people have been evacuated from the zone immediately bordering on the stricken plant; 170 new villages have been built for the evacuees; the public has been health screened and extensive clean-up work has been done.

Much of that work, however, has been futile. It is hard to believe, but many of the new villages have been built in regions where radiation levels are still dangerously high. Until last year Belorussia had been receiving unadjusted farming plans on contaminated land, thereby perpetuating the spread of radioactive nuclides. Worst of all is the plight of people living in areas where the radiation level has reached a frightening 100 curies per square kilometre.

Fortunately things are changing. Last October the government launched a five-year disaster programme based on proposals made by Belorussian scientists, medical researchers and economists. As many as 120,000 people from more than 520 areas in the south and south-east of the Republic will gradually be moved to clean regions.

It would be encouraging, four years on, to think that common sense has finally triumphed and proper steps are being taken. But Belorussia lacks the means to deal properly with the Chernobyl consequences. Some Belorussians are calling for the Republican government to stop money going into the federal budget. With separatist passions rising, such calls are likely to increase, and the authorities may yet have to pay a heavy price for their past inertia and their ignoring of both common sense and the plight of the Belorussian people.

Four Years After Chernobyl*
Ivan Chernyak

The Chernobyl accident was an extreme ecological phenomenon in scale and consequences at both national and international levels; for the Belorussian people it was a huge disaster.

Some 70 per cent of the area affected by radioactive fall-out is in Belorussia; 27 towns and 2,697 villages containing 2.2 million – a fifth of Belorussia's entire population – come within the contaminated zone. Belorussia has lost 20 per cent of its total farmland, that is 1.6 million hectares. About a million hectares of the overall 6.3 million hectares of forest have suffered serious radiation fall-out.

The government has taken a number of urgent measures: resettling people from the worst affected areas, providing them with medical examination, treatment and rehabilitation where necessary, launching improvement schemes for communities, supplying uncontaminated foodstuffs. It has designated areas as those under 'strict supervision' (exceeding 15 curies per square kilometre) and 'permanent supervision' (between 5 and 15 curies); all people living in these areas have to be regularly tested.

Despite such measures, more than 100,000 people are still living in areas with caesium-137 contamination densities in excess of 15 curies per square

*From *Anglo-Soviet Journal*, No. 2, 1990, pp. 8–10.

kilometre. The 1990–95 government programme adopted in October 1989 envisages a stage-by-stage resettlement of people from areas where radio-active contamination of the environment and food can result in the accumu-lation of radionuclides in the body. At least 118,000 people from 526 towns and villages are scheduled for resettlement. In the first stage 17,000 people from 112 communities are to move; 4,700 from 62 communities will be transferred in the second stage (1991–92); and 96,500 from 352 communi-ties will be shifted in the third stage (by 1995).

Chernobyl: Russia's Gaping Wound*
Yuri Lodkin

The 'Russian zone of Chernobyl' was kept top secret for three years. From the very start the authorities told residents in the south-western areas of the Bryansk Region that 'radioactive fall-out had slightly increased but did not pose any threat to public health'. It was only last April that Moscow papers carried the first articles on the wide-scale consequences of the Chernobyl threat to Bryansk Region. And then in June the USSR Meteorological Centre made known tables of radioactive caesium fall-out in populated areas.

As many as 700 towns and villages of the Bryansk area were on this gloomy register. According to the Centre's average data several dozen populated areas were located within the zone of dense pollution of over 40 curies per square kilometre. Such average statistics conceal much more worrying figures. For example, 68.18 curies per square kilometre were measured in the village of Zaborie in Krasnogorsk district. I happened to take part in the tests and I can vouch that some garden allotments of Zaborie showed a reading of between 180 and 220 curies. At the time the readings were pooh-poohed by scientists at the Leningrad Radiation Institute. Today, however, we have precise data provided by the Met Centre, and they show an average pollution in Zaborie of 111 curies, and the maximum pollution density has soared beyond 311 curies – greater than in many of the most dangerous parts of the Chernobyl 30-kilometre zone. Today the Centre's register includes 1,500 populated areas.

It is now accepted that over 110,000 Russians live in areas which should be no-go zones on international standards.

*From *Argumenty i fakty*, No.25, 1990, pp. 4–5.

Children provide the most tragic cases. No provision has been made in the last four years for pre-school children to take a summer convalescence outside the radioactive zone, and only a few schoolchildren have spent part of their holidays in Pioneer camps in non-contaminated regions. Children are being deprived of the elementary joys of life: they cannot play or do any sport in the open air, they cannot work on school allotments or in school farm brigades, and they are strictly forbidden to swim or to walk in the woods. Doctors have noted a sharp deterioration in the immunity of both children and adults, causing a rise in the number of somatic diseases.

The measures being taken on Russian land to eliminate the consequences of the Chernobyl catastrophe can only be labelled as 'papering over the cracks'. The unsystematic nature of the half-measures taken, the red tape that bedevils the Russian government and the criminal indifference of Russian ministries and departments all led to Bryansk people receiving a greater radiation dose since 1986 than those living in similar supervised zones in the Ukraine and Belorussia.

It is perfectly evident today that all we can do to ensure maximum safety conditions is to move people to 'clean' areas. The experts say this would be economically less onerous than funding a clean-up project in the contaminated region.

It is planned to resettle over 5,000 'Bryansk Chernobylers' from 40 of the most polluted villages to new homes in the next two years. Given the current construction rate, however, the plans may never see light of day. In line with republican government legislation, the construction organisations of Russia's 15 regions are to help Bryansk people move to brand new villages; but they are dragging their feet. Three regions have refused outright to give a hand, and the local regional authorities are unable to budge the 'refuseniks'. That is why it is absolutely essential to set up in Bryansk a coordinated committee of the Russian Council of Ministers empowered to get things moving. We can only meet the planned schedules for house building by strict supervision from such a committee.

Our prime priority must be to look after the children. We should do everything possible to get them out of the polluted zone during summertime. I believe that this can be done with the help of enterprises in European Russian with their own Pioneer camps, rest homes and sanatoria. At the same time, we must provide the children with really clean produce, especially fresh fruit and vegetables.

The starting point for further planned work to minimise the consequences of the Chernobyl catastrophe must be the thorough testing for radiation of all danger zones. We have got to know the truth about pollution levels both for caesium and for the entire 'isotope family'. Knowing how things stand will enable us to plan and implement the necessary safety measures.

No More Chernobyls*
Andrei Illesh

More than 250 of those who worked at Chernobyl, during and after the century's worst accident, are already dead. Causes of death vary. But one thing is clear: we are paying dearly for Chernobyl, and nobody knows what the final death toll will be.

The Chernobyl Society is a charity recently established to help the victims and to campaign for safety in the nuclear power industry. The 'liquidators', those who helped in the aftermath of the tragedy and suffered radiation, were the first to run into official bureaucracy. Their stories give the lie to the government's reassuring statistics. But the voices of individuals are often not heard in the corridors of power. It is not so easy to ignore a public movement. Hence the need for the Chernobyl Society.

It is campaigning to bring the nuclear power industry (the design, construction and operation of nuclear plants) under effective public control. The Society is already exercising control over radiation levels at all atomic power plants. But it is concerned with more than technical matters. It is well aware that people who lived in contaminated areas and were victims of Chernobyl need skilled medical and material assistance and legal protection. The Society is compiling a data bank of all radiation victims. Its electronic card index will help it defend the interests of all radiation sufferers, including people employed at all nuclear plants, service personnel and other people exposed to radiation at or near nuclear test sites.

The Society's aim is to abolish 'radiation illiteracy' in the country and to purchase foreign testing equipment and medicines. It has already arranged for severely ill patients to travel abroad for treatment and for child victims to spend their summer holidays at health resorts at home and abroad.

The Society can be contacted at PO Box 17, Moscow 129010.

Ecological Disaster Zone†
S. Amirizde and A. Samokhin

Current ecological and socio-economic processes underway in the Aral Sea area make it an ecological catastrophe zone.

---

* From *Moscow News*, No. 46, 1989, p. 2
† From *Argumenty i fakty*, No. 51, 1989, pp. 4–5.

Up to 3 million people live on land encompassed by the ecological disaster. Without going into too detailed an economic analysis, let us state just the major consequence of past profligate attitudes to the Sea's wealth. The Aral Sea level has fallen by 14 metres, the area of water has shrunk by 40 per cent and the water volume by 65 per cent.

The Sea's dried-up bed has resulted in extensive salt accumulation and salt-dust storms. The unrestrained impregnation of the soil with mineral fertiliser has led to arable land becoming poisoned and a source of environmental poisoning. The waters of the Amu Darya and Syr Darya rivers are polluted by poisonous chemicals and high concentrations of harmful components from heavy metals, cancerogenous substances and harmful bacteria. Through lack of other sources many people in the Karakalpak Autonomous Republic and the Kyzyl-Ord and Chimkent regions continue to use polluted water. Yet even that water is not enough for their needs! Its use is 5–6 times less than the norm for the region.

The Aral is terminally ill. People are sick from drinking its pesticide-polluted water. Over the last 20 years the morbidity rate of the population in the Aral area has doubled, the child mortality rate has increased from 44.7 per thousand born in 1965 to 71.5 born in 1986; in some places it is even up to 80–90. The death rate of women in giving birth is 1.3 for the Kyzyl-Ord Region, which is 4.3 times higher than the country's average. The Karakalpak Autonomous Republic, once leader of the nation in its birth rate, is now the leader in its death rate; over 80 per cent of its women of child-bearing age suffer from anaemia (cf. the country's average of 27.3 per cent). As many as 87 per cent of the women have various chronic diseases, while 90 per cent of all hospitalised children between one and two months have been found to possess an alarming amount of salt in their urine.

In the last 15 years alone the Kyzyl-Ord Region of Kazakhstan has had 36 serious outbreaks of infectious epidemics having a water source. Throughout the Aral Sea area there has been a 30-fold increase in typhoid fever, a sevenfold increase in viral hepatitis, and large increases in the percentage of tubercular and oncological diseases (15 times higher than the country's average).

The Aral tragedy is not new. Both 'formal' and informal organisations, as well as the general public, have made constant representations to the authorities, and resolutions have been passed . . . But the measures taken are woefully inadequate.

The recently convened expanded presidium of the Red Cross and Red Crescent societies recognised the Aral area as a human disaster zone and called upon the Ecological Committee of the USSR Supreme Soviet to declare the region a disaster zone.

The Soviet Red Cross has outlined specific measures to alleviate the hardship: rendering aid to the region in supplying drinking water, acquiring and distributing children's food to large families, especially in the rural areas of the Aral region, organising effective medical and hygiene education programmes.

The Red Cross and USSR Trade Ministry have already assigned an extra 16 tonnes of Finnish children's food and 25,000 disposable syringes to the area. Negotiations are underway with the International League of Red Cross and Red Crescent societies and UNICEF to obtain foreign equipment for cleaning the water.

The Red Cross is appealing to all Soviet people, individuals and office and factory personnel to make contributions to help Aral area inhabitants, sending their contributions to any local organisation of the Red Cross or Red Crescent.

NOTES

1.	*Ogonyok*, No. 50, December 1989, p. 3.
2.	V. Lukyanenko, 'O generalnoi kontsepsii *okhrany* vodoymov ot zagryaznenii', *Vestnik Akademii Nauk SSSR*, No. 4, 1990, pp. 74–81.
3.	M. Shakhanov, 'Gorkaya sol Arala', *Sovetskie profsoyuzy*, No. 8, April, pp. 18–19.
4.	A. Kovalchuk, 'Pod ugrozoi polnotsennost budushchikh pokolenii', *Ekologiya: problemy i programmy*, No. 1, 1990, pp. 3–4.
5.	V. Poltaranov, 'Kurorty v opasnosti', *Sovetskie profsoyuzy*, No. 2, January 1989, pp. 24–25.
6.	M. Podgorodnikov, 'Pod ugrozoi – deti', *Literaturnaya gazeta*, No. 34, August 1989, p. 12.
7.	Z. Wolfson, 'Nitrates – a new problem for the Soviet consumer', *Report on the USSR*, 1989, pp. 6–8.
8.	V. Tabolsky, 'Igra zhdot dobra', *Sovetskie profsoyuzy*, No. 19, September 1989, pp. 20–1.
9.	G. Shipitko 'Vvedeno ogranichenie', *Izvestiya*, No. 87, March 1990.
10.	N. Moissev, 'Problemy planetarnovo masshtaba', *Adygeiskaya pravda*, August 1989.

Part Five
Deviance

9 Prostitution
Elizabeth Waters

In a letter to a Soviet journal a reader speculated recently that if the communists had known in 1917 that seventy years on prostitution would still be a problem they would not have made the revolution.[1] Though this seems unlikely, it is true, nevertheless, that the persistence of prostitution in the 1920s, along with private enterprise, gambling and high-living, was seen as a defeat by many Bolsheviks who had hoped that their victory over the landlords and capitalists would put an end to all traces of decadent bourgeois culture. In the early 1930s, as the Stalinist system consolidated, prostitutes, who still walked the central streets in considerable numbers, were rounded up and sent to camps; prostitution was said to have been 'liquidated', along with unemployment and inequality, and discussion on the topic ceased. Even during the Khrushchovian Thaw, when the ideals of the post-revolutionary period made a partial come-back, and even in the 1970s, when Soviet sociology emerged from the twilight, prostitution remained a taboo subject. Over the past six years the situation has changed. Prostitution has made headlines; it has provided material for documentaries and for public debate, for literature and the theatre. Initially, the press took the lead with descriptions of the lives and times of the modern prostitute, and commentary on prostitution's moral and political economy. Gradually the 'experts' – the academics and professionals – were drawn into the debate, reporting on their research and putting their views, both in the popular press and in the specialist literature. As the authorship and location of debate diversified, the treatment of the issue shifted considerably. At first, the prostitute was counted among the anti-social elements of society, alongside the drug addicts and alcoholics, and the dealers and speculators of the 'second economy', whose spiritual bankruptcy and refusal of honest work threatened the smooth progress of reforms; as perestroika took firmer hold and the problems that confronted society were discovered to be deep-rooted and recalcitrant, she was recast in the role of disadvantaged citizen in search of survival, of representative of a fledgling enterprise culture, and even of protestor against the constraints of social convention.[2]

In the summer of 1987, the trade union newspaper *Trud* published an article entitled, 'What price love?' It told the story of two young Soviet girls who had suffered serious injuries, the one at the hand of her mother, the other at the hand of her boyfriend, both for engaging in prostitution. The

133

mother and boyfriend had taken it upon themselves to pass sentence because the law did not recognise prostitution as a crime. Women can be
caught by the militia working in a brothel, the journalist revealed, and they
will be let go to carry on with their lives as if nothing has happened.
Prostitution is not an isolated phenomenon in the Soviet Union, he told *Trud*
readers: there are organised dens of vice in provincial cities, and pimps
work the Black Sea resorts. District militia precincts keep registers of
prostitutes, not because they have committed an offence, but because they
invariably have connections with the criminal world of petty thieves and
crooks. Prostitutes are also linked with the world of bribery and the black
market, since it is men from this milieu who form their clientele. With their
huge earnings, fine clothes and life of pleasure, he continued, prostitutes
bear no resemblance to their pre-revolutionary predecessors; far from
being unfortunate victims of society, they despise us ordinary people with
our small wages. These in themselves he regarded as weighty enough
reasons for the introduction of harsh legal penalties for prostitution, but he
added two others – the world AIDS epidemic, and the danger that prostitutes pose to the 'spiritual health of society'. A tough campaign against
prostitution, he concluded, must be an integral part of the battle for
perestroika.

We have set out to cleanse our society from every form of foulness –
from greedy hands, to which unearned income clings, from drunkenness
and alcoholism, from drug abuse and the misfortunes that accompany it.
Prostitution has ceased to be a rarity due to the passivity of the law, but
it should, of course, have no place in our life.[3]

The article was typical of the dozens that were published during 1986 and
1987 in central and republican newspapers, in papers devoted to young
people and in papers devoted to satire: it dwelt on the wealth and privilege
enjoyed by prostitutes, on their connections with the second economy, and
their spiritual degeneration. It set out to be sensational, it registered right-
eous indignation and it advocated retribution.

Journalists turned their attention in the main to the elite of the profession,
to the prostitutes who made large sums of money, most of them through
their dealings with foreigners and whose lives were far removed from the
drab humdrum existence of the average citizen. *Moskovskie novosti* disclosed that the annual income of a foreign-currency prostitute (*valyutnaya
prostitutka*, or colloquially *putanka*) was 30,000 roubles, well over ten
times the national average.[4] *Komsomolskaya pravda* followed a young
woman into a hotel for foreign tourists, a highly desirable location:

'A fashionably dressed young woman passes through the half-open door. Coquettish fair fringe, large grey eyes, skilfully painted, jacket decorated with an unimaginable number of pockets, zips, buttons. In a word, stylish and, let's be objective, rather striking.

She settles comfortably into a deep armchair near the entrance to the late-night bar and reaches in her bag for a packet of American cigarettes. But she doesn't hurry to light up. She yawns with fatigue, raising her hand to cover her mouth.[5]

Descriptions of the prostitutes' life-styles were long and lingering, but indignation was never far from the surface. One journalist noted that prostitutes both fascinated and repelled at one and the same time; like the dissection of a frog, he said, the spectacle is 'disgusting', but impossible not to watch.[6] The spectacle was disgusting, partly because, as the press constantly pointed out, the prostitutes had not earned their wealth honestly, they were associated with the 'second economy', the world of illegal business, which in the first years of the Gorbachov era was the target of a fierce government campaign. Their position on the margins of society and of legality did indeed draw them into a complex web of dubious relationships: there were the pay-offs to hotel staff, to doormen and waiters, there were arrangements with the taxi drivers, doctors and shop managers who provided transport, medical check-ups, smoked sausage and imported knee-high boots; and most incriminating of all, there were dealings with black marketeers to convert foreign currency into roubles. Prostitutes were often unemployed or if they had jobs it was often to avoid the charge of 'parasitism' and they paid someone else to do the work for them.

Their sexual transgressions were the other reason for the disgust they were said to inspire. The moral health of society, a matter of discussion and anxiety, was said by the press to be basically sound; the elimination and re-education of the few anti-social elements would clear the way for a complete recovery. In this context prostitutes were a dangerous aberration, a cancer in an otherwise healthy body, a shameful blot on an otherwise flawless landscape. 'The people', wrote Yevgen Dodolev, 'have always known how dangerous the overt existence of such women is for the moral health of society.'[7] Society had to wash away the dirt, to cleanse itself. It had to 'find a vaccine' that would conquer its sickness.[8] Metaphors of pollution and purification, of disease and cure, were constantly employed. *Komsomolskaya pravda* urged the militia and the comsomol to 'rid the face of our society' of the filth of prostitution.[9] Other papers wrote also of mire and purification, of swamp and marsh, of slime and muck, of ooze and quagmire, a veritable thesaurus of variation on a single theme. The well-known journalist, Vitaly Vitaliev, took these turns of phrase at their face value; he admitted that during his trip to research an article on prostitution, 'I wanted to wash all the time, I took three showers a day and scrubbed my hands with pumice stone; I risked scraping them to the bone, but I couldn't get rid of the feeling that I was dirty.'[10] L. Goiko recorded a similar reaction: reading files on prostitution was an unpleasant business: 'It was as though I was touching something filthy.'[11]

The press coverage of prostitution also had a political dimension. It provided opportunity for the expression of thinly-veiled racism. Attention was drawn to the involvement in prostitution of the foreign student community, which is predominantly third world. One journalist, describing a black marketeer who had contact with a group of prostitutes, noted that he was 'from a southern country' and 'for some reason was called Paul although his name was really Mohamed'.[12] *Sovetskaya Belorussiya* told the story of a young man who persuaded his friend, a fellow drug addict, to prostitute herself to finance their habit, and, in the absence of a suitable foreign tourist, arranged a deal with a black African student, Nsatunkaszi. 'Foreign students', the paper commented, '(not all, of course, but far too many) behave in a very free and easy manner as if the laws were not meant for them.'[13]

Foreigners played other and more sinister roles. Western security agencies, it was claimed, sent their people into the USSR to marry prostitutes.[14] Why the agencies should want to pay money to bring Soviet *putanki* to the West (where the husbands, it was said, promptly deserted them), and how by doing this they 'discredited socialism', was not clearly explained. The link between sexual and economic misdemeanours on the one hand, and crimes of a political nature on the other, was, perhaps, seen as self-evident. Elsewhere, this connection was formulated explicitly: a woman who sells her body is capable of selling her country; prostitutes 'sullied' our 'honour'; they speculated in spiritual values, an action 'close to treachery'.[15]

The early press coverage presented the prostitute in a totally unsympathetic light – she was materialistic, immoral and politically suspect – and the press demanded that she be punished. Government agencies were exhorted to greater efforts in the fight to clean up society. Since prior to the revelations of perestroika prostitutes were taken into custody to be 'liquidated', there could not logically be laws against them, and there were none. One journalist remarked that prostitutes nevertheless often got what they deserved – when they were stripped naked and thrown out into the cold by drunken clients, when they wanted children and found they could not have them, when their children were taken from them by the court or when they were imprisoned for other offences.[16] The press hankered, though, for more reliable justice and was loud and united in its call for an end to this 'absurd situation'.[17] Current legal measures against prostitution were criticised for their 'imperfections', and for failing to provide real 'control'.[18] Speaking on Latvian radio, Janis Laukroe, Chairman of a People's Court in Riga, said: 'We need an appropriate law against prostitution . . . against women of easy virtue who have lost their human face and put to shame the noble name of the Soviet citizen. Such is the view on this matter of all workers in law enforcement establishments.'[19] In mid-1987, the Presidium of the USSR Supreme Soviet went some way towards meeting the demands; it established a fine of 100 roubles for a first offence and of 200 roubles for a second offence falling within a twelve month period. This measure was widely held as a step in the right direction, but an inadequate one. The reaction of *Trud* was typical: the new legislation was 'a ray of hope', but 'can you really stop these brazen representatives of "the oldest profession" with a 100-rouble fine?'[20]

In the West, prostitution, for the most part, is treated as a matter of welfare, or of health and hygiene, and only a small minority calls for moral censure and criminal sentences.[21] The reliance of Soviet journalists on the militia and the security organisations for interviews and information was, perhaps, one reason for the widespread support for tough measures.[22] Although prostitution was not talked of publicly before the late 1980s, it had for over twenty years been recognised as a growing urban problem by the militia, who kept unofficial files on prostitutes and did its utmost to contain their activities.[23] In Russia (as elsewhere) the guardians of law and order, both before and after the revolution, have consistently favoured policies of repression against prostitution. Under the tsarist regime, from 1843, a system of regulation obliged prostitutes to register with the police and report regularly for medical examinations. After the revolution, the militia canvassed a return to regulation (abolished in 1917 by the Provisional Government), in the early 1920s it promoted a plan for a Moral Militia, and in the late 1920s – this time with more success – it pushed for harsher measures against prostitution. The evidence suggests that in more recent times, too, the militia has used all its legal powers (and some extra-legal ones, too) to make life as difficult as possible for prostitutes.[24] In Moscow, in 1986, 726 women were held for trying to stay overnight in the homes of foreigners.[25] By 1988, Tashkent and Sochi had 'combined action plans' against prostitution[26] and in 53 cities the Ministry for Internal Affairs was operating special task forces. The same year the press reported a Moral Militia operating unofficially in Riga.[27]

Militia officials were sought out and cited frequently by the journalists, partly because they were well-informed on the subject of prostitution, but undoubtedly also because their opinions fitted the climate of the times. Soviet ideology taught that the USSR was by and large socialist, and that socialist societies provided conditions for the good life; deviant behaviour resulted, it followed, from individual pathologies and perversities, and the individual, not the system, must shoulder the blame and pay the penalties. These were the premises that over the years have informed Soviet attitudes on a wide variety of 'deviance', and were at hand in the early years of perestroika to be applied to 'new' social problems, including prostitution.

These premises were not simply imposed from above by the authorities on an unwilling public; they found response and reinforcement in popular prejudice. To peoples buffeted by a precipitous and harrowing modernisation, the ideal of the close-knit and clean-living family was something to hold on to. In a world alarmingly prone to flux, a moral code that set strict rules of behaviour and ostracised those who did not keep to them had enormous appeal.

There was thus no shortage of readers' letters to the press expressing outrage at the doings of the *putanki*. *Pravda Ukrainy* published a selection from its post-bag on prostitution:

> 'While we carry on these heated discussions about this and that, all this muck will take deep root, camouflage itself and find other forms for its depraved activities.'

> 'It's time for us all to deal with [the prostitutes] in such a way that not a trace of this vileness remains.' [Prison] sentences will serve . . . to bring an end to the stench of prostitution.'

> [Tough measures] are probably the inevitable costs [for eliminating prostitution. It's no good complaining. Cleansing the body of foulness, cutting out the abscesses from the healthy body is a painful process.'

The paper was in total agreement with these sentiments and commented contentedly: 'Though the authors of the letters are of various ages, professions, and social position, their attitude to the "Josephines" is one and the same – "pluck the weeds from the fields".'[28] Letters sent to *Krokodil*, the satirical magazine, and *Trud* were in much the same vein. Prostitutes should be 'exiled to the North Pole', sent to 'do forced labour', 'shot on the spot'.[29] A. Podgorny of Ivanovo District thought it immoral and impermissible to make peace with prostitution; N. Alekseeva of Krasnoyarsk 'utterly approved of an addition to the existing [legal] code'; K. Zamaisky of Moscow District considered that prostitutes brought out the worst in a person, they raised 'the foul dregs from the depths'.[30]

Though both the press reports and the readers' letters exhibited considerable consistency in their approach to prostitution, even in 1987 when moral indignation reached its apogee, there were a few dissenting voices. An article in *Sovetskaya Estoniya* by a local lawyer, arguing that women ought not to go to restaurants alone in case they were mistaken for prostitutes, provoked an ironic reply from Y. Bogacheva:

'Absolutely right! Comrade Yanovich's article . . . has got it, undoubtedly, absolutely right. Women must not be allowed out alone to restaurants at night without men. Nor should they be let out alone in the daytime. After all, there's no guarantee that an early-rising foreigner will not be abroad at this hour. It would be best for women to go out only when wearing a veil. If a woman has any self-respect at all she will gladly accept this small inconvenience.'

Three women engineers also wrote in defending their right to go out without men and to mix with foreigners if they chose. 'What kind of mutual understanding can there be if we are patently frightened to make contact with foreigners?'[31] One correspondent, from the popular weekly *Nedelya*, reporting an interview with a 19-year-old girl who made her living in the sex industry, registered bewilderment rather than condemnation. '[H]ow I pity this young girl, this prodigal soul', he wrote.[32]

Some journalists were accused of paying lip-service only to moral indignation, while painting in such detail the lives of luxurious idleness led by prostitutes that their writing was in effect an advertisement for the profession. According to the head of the Ministry of Internal Affairs administration, the press had 'popularised prostitution' so effectively that fourteen- and fifteen-year-old provincial girls were flocking to the cities to try their luck.[33] The younger generation was certainly, it became clear, less inclined than the press to condemn prostitution. A survey organised by the literary weekly *Literaturnaya gazeta* and the main sociological journal *Sotsiologicheskie issledovaniya* found that young people, particularly young girls, regarded the profession without censure and were impressed by its high earnings. Students at ten Moscow secondary schools, asked to rate a list of top-paid jobs, placed prostitution joint ninth, alongside more conventional employment such as director and shop assistant, and above diplomat, taxi-driver and butcher.[34]

The arts were accused along with journalism – and with more obvious reasons – of encouraging young people to adopt a tolerant attitude towards prostitution. *Stars in the Morning Sky*, a play by Aleksandr Galin, portrayed sympathetically a group of prostitutes exiled from Moscow during the

Olympic Games in 1980.[35] Vladimir Kunin's story *Interdevochka*, published in the Leningrad literary journal *Avrora* in 1988, told the story of a *putanka* whose dream of marrying a foreigner comes true. All does not end happily, however, for, bored and frustrated by her life as the wife of a Swedish businessman, she successfully courts death on a rainy highway. Within the confines of this conventional moral fable, the author writes with sensitivity of the lives of the Leningrad prostitutes, who come across as wittier, stronger and more complex than his other characters.

Fiction has traditionally, in the Soviet Union as in pre-revoluntionary Russia before it, served as a vehicle for the social criticism that could not find direct expression. In the more relaxed atmosphere of perestroika, issues such as prostitution have been addressed directly. A documentary *Gruppa riska*, premiered in 1988, took as its starting point a letter from sixteen medical students demanding that prostitutes, along with homosexuals and drug addicts, be eliminated. The aim was, the scriptwriter explained, to show people as they are without making moral judgements. But its stance was not neutral: by offering explanations for the behaviour of the 'risk group', the documentary encouraged viewers to condone it. The journal, *Ogonyok*, published excerpts of interviews with thirteen members of one of the audiences, some of whom expressed agreement with the film's philosophy (Yelena Gudkova, a 45-year-old architect, said it was not for her either to justify or to judge; Eldar Razroev, an engineer, made the same point – 'we don't have the right to defend or to accuse. They could equally accuse us. They are members of our society, the same as we are'[37]); others shared the attitudes of the medical students. *Ogonyok's* non-partisan approach, its offer of a range of opinions, was, however, more apparent than real, for its commentary inclined towards broad-mindedness. Moreover, the extremism of the film's critics and their social profile served to discredit narrow-mindedness. A Komsomol functionary, Vadim Samolyotov, disapproved of the documentary on the grounds that it showed prostitution in an attractive light; to understand, he argued, was not to forgive. 'I'm a person of old-fashioned views and my opinion is that all prostitutes should be 'put down',' Grigory Vasilenko, a militiaman, was quoted as saying. '[W]hat sort of punishment is a 50 rouble fine? Ten years in prison with compulsory treatment – that's more like it.' Komsomol functionaries and the militia are not among perestroika's heroes.

Some members of the legal profession expressed themselves unhappy at the widespread demand for the criminalisation of prostitution. I. Galperin in May 1987 asked the readers of *Literaturnaya gazeta* to picture the prostitute in the dock while her client, a 'respectable rascal', stood in the witness box: 'It would be hard, surely, to think up a more effective way to discredit [our policy of] equality of the sexes, the prestige of our system.' On a more practical level, he pointed to the problem of definition – was accepting an expensive meal from a chance acquaintance on a summer holiday prostitution or not? – and to the heavy expenses (investigations, interrogations and house searches) that the criminalisation of prostitution would necessarily incur.[38]

His more liberal approach to prostitution, at that time espoused by a minority, began over the next eighteen months to gain ground. The spirit of glasnost and reform that in 1986 and 1987 had first brought prostitution to public attention gathered momentum, creating a climate increasingly unfavourable to the advocacy of repressive measures against social deviants. As the arrests and executions of the Stalinist period and the economic mismanagements and failures of a more recent era came under the spotlight, as corruption was shown to have been endemic and inhumanity the norm, old ideological and patriotic certainties crumbled. It became more difficult to accuse prostitutes of moral turpitude and to demand their punishment.

The increasing participation in the debate of the academics and professionals also on the whole bolstered the more liberal outlook. A survey carried out to establish the views of the 'experts' on prostitution found that the vast majority was strongly opposed to repressive policies. Over 90 per cent rejected criminalisation ('God forbid' and 'I'm absolutely against it' were typical responses) on the grounds that prostitution did not present sufficient danger to society to warrant legal regulation, society was partly to blame for its existence, and criminalisation was ineffective and open to abuse.[39] It is unclear from the survey whether the sample included academics from across the country or from Moscow and Leningrad only. Respondents were asked their views on the causes of prostitution, on its consequences, and on appropriate measures for combating it. They connected prostitution to social inequalities, the erosion of moral norms and inadequate socialisation; they were almost evenly divided on the question of whether prostitution inevitably led to crime, twenty (47.6 per cent) believing that it did, and twenty-two (52 per cent) believing that it did not; they proposed to reduce prostitution by an increase in living standards (twelve (28.5 percent)), and an improvement in the status of the family (four (9.5 per cent)) and in cultural (seventeen (40 per cent)) and educational levels (seven (16.7 per cent)); an undisclosed number wanted to cleanse the moral atmosphere, in part by banning films that promoted sexual anarchy and depravity.

Other evidence suggests that scholars in the provinces and in the republics of the Caucasus and Central Asia are less likely to adopt a liberal approach to prostitution than their colleagues in the capitals and in the industralised and Westernised republics. A. Kirsta and K. Speransky, respectively deputy of the administrative department of the Krasnodarsk Communist Party Regional (*krai*) Committee and reader at Kuban State University, writing in one of the main legal journals of 1988, expressed unequivocal support for the criminalisation of prostitution: for prison sentences, heavy fines of up to 1,000 roubles and terms of corrective labour. They insisted that measures of legal control were essential in the fight against social problems, and they mentioned approvingly the Stalinist educationalist Anton Makarenko, a disciplinarian and believer in the therapy of labour. They characterised foreigners as 'bearers of bourgeois morality', and they defended with passion the 'socialist way of life', writing:

As an anti-social phenomenon prostitution possesses great social danger from the point of view of communist morality, the protection of the health of the population and the law. Moral and sexual corruption (especially of underage persons and of youth), and the education in a private-property psychology are incompatible with the socialist way of life, and with the principle of social justice.[40]

Scholars in the Baltic republics spoke with a more modern voice. The Estonian legal journal, *Sovetskoe pravo*, which has pioneered a whole range of previously forbidden topics, published a brief history of prostitution which argued that repression does not work.[41] The same case was put in the same journal by Y. Gilinsky, a legal specialist by training, currently President of the Section on the Sociology of Deviant Behaviour at the Leningrad Branch of the USSR Sociological Association. In his view, contemporary prostitution was a product of the 'era of stagnation', reflecting 'as in a drop of water' the perversions of socialism perpetrated under the rule of Stalin and Brezhnev. 'Only our extraordinary disregard of history and of logic and of learning', he concluded, 'can explain our sacred faith in the force of prohibition, repression and moralising.' Though prostitution is immoral, in his view, it is no more so than the prostitution practised by some writers and politicians. 'What are the grounds for punishing the sale of the body more harshly than the sale of the spirit (the intellect)?'[42]

Some sociologists also connected prostitution with the 'era of stagnation', specifically with the consumer mentality that was said to have developed during the Brezhnev years. According to A. A. Gabiani and M. A. Manuilsky, prostitutes interviewed in Tbilisi in the mid-1980s had taken to the streets not because they were in desperate need but because they wanted to better their living standards. The stark contrast between the modest means of most young women and the price of approximating to the ideal woman of the television and cinema screen created, in their view, favourable conditions for the growth of prostitution. The results of their survey, published in 1987, upset many of the stereotypes and clichés that were circulating in the press at the time: prostitutes, they found, were of average education and from ordinary backgrounds; most of them worked or had in the past worked; few made large sums of money or spent their earnings on luxury items; and their clients were native men not foreigners.[43] If the information the authors offered was, in the context of the Soviet discussion, revolutionary, their conclusions were more conventional. They evidently accepted the necessity for legal measures against prostitution, though emphasising that these were insufficient and had to be complemented by a range of educational and other programmes to change attitudes. The authors were hopeful that once 'stagnation' had been overcome there would 'undoubtedly be a reduction in prostitution'.

The second study of prostitution to appear in *Sotsiologicheskie issledovaniya* took a rather different perspective.[44] Its author, S. I. Golod, shared the view that prostitution was social and transient rather than biological and eternal, but for him the 'era of stagnation', while not irrelevant, was of secondary importance. He placed prostitution in the wider social and historical context of the evolution of family forms and relationships between the sexes in the transition from patriarchal to modern society. Elsewhere he has referred approvingly to American sociologists who believe that the transformation of the family over the past half century or so has altered in particular the position of women.[45] Their emancipation and the decline of totalitarian and Christian morality have, he argues, promoted the emergence of a single moral standard for both sexes and increased the importance of love and affection in relationships between them.

But as romantic love has made its mark in the modern industrial world, so too has alienation. Thus, while prostitution has declined dramatically this century, it has by no means disappeared entirely, and in Western countries about 3–5 per cent of young men visit prostitutes. Surveys carried out in the Soviet Union indicate, Golod reports, that the habits of young Soviet men are not dissimilar. In other words, the USSR is experiencing processes that are not unique, but on the contrary are common to all industrialised nations: as levels of urbanisation and education rise, tolerance of extra-marital sexual relations increases and the attitudes of men and women towards personal relationships tend to converge. While these developments have contributed to the reduction of prostitution, countervailing circumstances – the increasing size of towns, the weakening of traditional family and community ties, the bureaucratic and detached nature of much social intercourse, the imperfections of education and welfare policies – have produced new demands for commercial sex and a new supply of women prepared to make their living on the streets. Viewed in this way, prostitution is inevitable and comprehensible, and the panic about spiritual bankruptcy and moral degeneration misplaced. Golod, for one, has made clear that the greater freedom of choice in private life which modern society offers is something to be welcomed; prostitution is not something to be fought with fines and prison sentences but with culture and love.[46]

Belief in the benefits of freedom and choice was not confined to sociological circles. Over the course of 1988 and 1989 the press began to criticise party and government control of political and economic life. On social problems the efficacy of repressive measures was challenged; enthusiasm for fining and imprisoning prostitutes waned. A liberal perspective on the issue was certainly not unanimously adopted, but by 1990 it found wide acceptance. Militia officials were no longer the only source of information on prostitution and were not always accorded the same deference as in the past. A journalist from *Sovetskaya kultura*, interviewing an important official from the Ministry for Internal Affairs, cast doubts on the militia's competence (their campaigns against prostitution are ineffective), picked him up on his inconsistencies (if prostitution were not, as he said, fuelled by social reasons, why bother to fight it?), and challenged the notion of state regulation and control (surely it is up to the woman to chose whether she trades her body or not?).[48]

As the idea of the market grew more acceptable, the fire went out of the campaign against the 'second economy'. The prostitute was no longer made scapegoat for the world of unearned incomes and decadent living. On the contrary, she was transformed by some into a symbol of resistance to the old conventions, to the straightjacket of the stagnant society. Yelena Yakovleva, the actress who played the heroine in the film of Kunin's *Interdevochka*, put the view that 'often prostitution was a form of protest against the demagogy, the lies and injustice, with which [the prostitutes] came into contact'. She also insisted that most prostitutes were ordinary girls who got tired of making do and making ends meet.[49] Poverty has been a common theme in recent press discussion on prostitution – wages are so low, prices so high, life so hard, no wonder young girls do not want to repeat the cheerless drudgery of their mothers. This economic interpretation of prostitution is given a distinctly feminist twist by Tatyana Suvorova, a Tass correspondent. She shows every sympathy for 'Olga', who left her job as a nurse to become a prostitute, accepting this as her way of attempting to achieve social equality and bridge the gap between those who were 'chauffeured to school exams' and those who had to walk. The mother, at first upset by her daughter's decision, is eventually persuaded of its wisdom, we are told. 'Olga's' view that her profession is a way of making money just like any other is given the seal of approval by a reference (tongue in cheek one supposes) to Friedrich Engels, who in his *Origin of the Family* is alleged to have written that 'prostitution was a social institution like any other'.[50] Moving from the particular to the general, Tatyana Suvorova launches into an angry paragraph about the poorly paid jobs women do, their unbearable living conditions, and the inadequate response to their tribulations of the Committee of Soviet Women. She warns that the economic reforms may push women out of production unless appropriate measures are taken, and she argues that to secure the financial and spiritual future of women, more money and better welfare are essential.[51] In similar critical vein another journalist observes:

> In these times of relative prosperity women still have the same double burden – at work and in the kitchen – the same difficulties in achieving beauty and elegance without exhausting themselves in their scramble round the shops and the endless queueing. And on top of all that, the constant struggle with the male part of the population for the right to be really equal, for the opportunity for self-affirmation.[52]

Presentation in the context of the debate about living standards and equality, desensationalises the topic, and pragmatic acceptance of prostitution as a strategy of survival deflects the critique of the moral crusaders.

The feminists have tended to share the moralists' certainty that prostitutes can make considerable fortunes, but instead of deploring this situation, they apparently derive satisfaction from the knowledge that prostitution offers a solution to the economic woes of at least some Soviet women. Others insist that prostitution does not pay. Leonid Zhukovitsky has argued that prostitutes even in their heyday are rarely able to save much, so great are their overheads, so short are their careers. He does not imply that poverty, illness and an unhappy end are their just desserts; rather he paints his grim picture in the name of truth, so that young girls can, as it were, make rational decisions about their future in full possession of all the facts. He also suggests, subversively, that prostitution serves a useful purpose, otherwise it would not have survived for so long; he points to the plight of sailors and soldiers unable to fulfil their sexual needs in the conventional way.[53] Others who share the view that sexual like other bodily needs should be recognised as natural and catered for without fuss and anxiety have proposed the legalisation of prostitution and the establishment of organised brothels.[54] The opportunities for franker consideration of sex and sexuality have also suggested an equation between the prostitute and the erotic. Early press reports described the physical attributes of prostitutes in a manner designed to titillate; these ends can now be pursued more openly, and articles on prostitution are frequently accompanied by drawings or photographs of women in costumes and poses that are explicitly sexual.[55] Representing sexuality in this way would seem antithetical to the feminist approach, but both projects have common roots in a determination to oppose the restrictions of the old political system, to challenge albeit in different ways gender stereotypes and conventional morality.[56] These new themes and interpretations in the debate on prostitution – economic and feminist, functionalist and erotic – have been introduced gradually since 1988, some papers taking them up earlier and more consistently than others.

Sobesednik, the supplement to the youth paper, *Komsomolskaya pravda*, and a pioneer of the 'new thinking' on prostitution as on other social issues, interpreted the demand for the criminalisation of prostitution, which it opposed unequivocally, as part of the legacy of Stalinism and its obsession with bans and threats and punishments. It refused to see the existence of prostitution in the Soviet Union as cause for panic: the French don't see their prostitutes are bringing shame on the nation, so why should the Soviets?[57] The popular magazine, *Ogonyok*, which in the second half of the 1980s, under the editorship of Vitaly Korotich, had won itself a solid reputation for openness, extended its liberal politics to prostitution. After a rather shaky start – a first article understood glasnost to mean the tracking down and punishing of prostitutes – changed tack, and added prostitutes to its list of social categories to be championed against the depredations of the administrative-command system. As well as its feature on the documentary, *Gruppa riska*, it published a humorous (fictional) story of a bungling apparatchik's attempt to organise a state brothel system (under the auspices of a 'Ministry of Frivolity'). By focusing on the incompetence and hypocrisy of officialdom, the author discredited its censorious attitudes and punitive policies.[58]

Other publications have also moved with the times, making a dramatic leap from support of repression to advocacy of non-intervention. *Krokodil*, initially labelled prostitution a 'shameful and dangerous phenomenon', and outlined with approval the various security initiatives designed to stamp it out.[59] Early cartoons on the subject – and there have been dozens over recent years[60] – drew attention to the absence of a law punishing prostitutes. In one from 1987 a militiaman is excusing himself for having let go a prostitute (a scantily dressed and generously made-up young woman seen in the background leaving the office). 'What could I do?' he is saying. 'It's not against the law.'[61] Another published in 1988 shows a drunk being bundled into a militia van while a prostitute meanwhile accepts an invitation from a bow-tied gallant to take a ride in a large limousine.[62] In subsequent years the desire to promote repression was less in evidence. One cartoon reflecting the new philosophy of tolerance features a duffel-coated man standing outside a factory and contemplating the 'situations vacant' board to which, below the familiar list of turners and milling machine operators has been added *putany*. His glasses are popping off his nose in surprise, and his deer-stalker hat has risen several inches above his head. A rain-coated felt-hatted bureaucrat at his side, briefcase in hand, remarks with equanimity: 'What is to be done? The factory needs foreign currency.'[63]

This sort of joke was not universally appreciated. A senior official of the Ministry for Internal Affairs, A. I. Gurov, while accepting that criminalisation might not be a panacea, considered heavy fines to be acceptable and effective.[64] In other respects A. I. Gurov's views are an indication of the ideological distances that have been covered since perestroika began. As proof that prostitution is not rooted in social conditions, he pointed to its existence in the West where, he says, 'women are not exploited'; the foreign clients of the *putanki* are described not as 'carriers of bourgeois culture', but instead as the true appreciators of the inferior quality of Russian prostitutes. 'By the way,' he says, 'the foreigners' assessment of our prostitutes – and let them hear this – is very unflattering. They don't see them as feminine, the way they do the Parisian prostitutes. Our women are animals in bed and that's the only reason they are of interest.'

Y. Chaikovsky, the Head of the Group for Combating Prostitution has argued that the police should have the right to fine women on the spot.[65] I. Karpets, formerly head of criminal investigation, presently Director of the All-Union Institute for Strengthening Law and Order, told a correspondent from *Argumenty i fakty* in 1987 that he disapproved of contemporary society's tolerant attitude towards prostitution, and proposed that such offences as disturbance of the peace, contravention of passport regulations and maintenance of a parasitic life-style be used against prostitutes.[66] The following year, in a second interview with the same paper, he came out even more strongly in favour of measures of force in the fight against prostitution, and floated the idea of the forcible detention of prostitutes for a period of one or two years in order to re-educate them and teach them work.[67] Though there have been no legal changes made since the introduction of administrative charges, there have been attempts to improve the already-existing mechanisms of control. An official register of prostitutes was begun in 1987;[68] during the same period many cities set up special task forces to close brothels and tighten security round hotels.[69] Something akin to the pre-revoluntionary system of regulation has in fact emerged: women detained by the militia are given two warnings. On the third detention they are officially booked and their papers processed by the local authorities; their names can then be entered on to the register and the women obliged to undergo medical examinations. Changes in the press coverage have not apparently influenced the attitudes and activities of the law enforcement agencies.

Pravda has suggested that on social issues the media is in fact out of step with public opinion, and too 'trusting of academics', citing a television programme whose panel had been unanimously against capital punishment, but whose audience had been 80 per cent in favour.[70] Readers' letters published in the newspapers have continued from time to time to express support for repressive legislation. A 38-year-old woman, identified in *Molodoi kommunist* merely as S. T., complained that 'prostitutes have been hanging round our necks and taking the mickey out of us for far too long and should be made to work'. More enlightened views, though, have definitely predominated. V. Ivanenko from Khmelnitsky warned in the same journal that criminalisation was likely to produce a witch hunt; Vladimir Tishchenko, an engineer from Voroshilovgrad, contributed a long and spirited defence of women in general and of prostitutes in particular.[71] Three young men, waiting to see the film, *Interdevochka* (the queues were long, even by Soviet standards), were reported as saying that people have the right to do what they want with their own bodies, and that banning prostitution would be 'undemocratic'. An elderly ex-philosophy teacher, also in the line for tickets, referred understandingly to the pressures on low-paid women to earn extra cash by whatever means.

Readers' letters, of course, can and often are selected to suit the journalist or newspaper in question. Public opinion surveys have not as yet directly tackled attitudes to prostitution.[72] Public organisations, however, or at least some of them, have taken the view that personal life is a private matter: a writers' organisation, informed by the militia that one of its members had been picked up for prostitution, wrote back that she carried out her literary duties competently and what she did in her free time was her own affair.[73] Many educational establishments, notified that the extra-curricular activities of certain female students included prostitution, do not even bother to reply.[74] Local authorities, who are responsible for imposing the administrative fines established in 1987, have proved anything but zealous. In Moscow, 133 cases passed on to them by the militia during the first months of 1988 led to the imposition of a mere twelve fines, totalling 800 roubles.[75]

Starting as an *ad hoc* set of programmes designed to improve the economy, perestroika has developed into a fundamental critique of Soviet society, of its past and its present, of its political, economic and social systems. The debate on prostitution over the past few years reflects very clearly this transformation. Initially, the press focused on the elite of the profession, the foreign currency prostitutes, who made for sensational revelations of extravagant living. Their wealth was held up for condemnation as well as for envious contemplation. The censors first permitted discussion of prostitution in 1986 and 1987, a time when the government was engaged in a war against corruption, and so almost inevitably much was made of the links between the prostitutes and the black marketeers, whose shady economic activities were said to block the path to socialist efficiency and plenty. Prostitutes made a most convenient scapegoat because their earnings were immoral in sexual as well as economic terms. They trampled on traditional family values, they exemplified the spiritual emptiness, the disregard of proper feelings and behaviour that had been diagnosed as a disturbing characteristic of contemporary society, particularly of its younger generation. At this stage the Party and the government believed in the capacity of administrative methods to cure the country's ills: a hard line on corruption would bring the economy back on course; better policing would eradicate prostitution and help the Soviet Union back to sound moral health.

By 1988 and 1989 the journalists and their readers had moved on. The prostitute no longer attracted the same attention either as sybarite or as figure of the underworld. The new economic order, in which private enterprise had a legitimate if still tightly circumscribed role, was providing justification for social inequalities. The endorsement of market mechanisms cast a new light on the prostitute's determined pursuit of economic gain. Alterations in currency regulations removed the taint of illegality from her profession. At the same time her wealth (if indeed it did exist, and it was questioned by some) no longer appeared fantastic. The profits of the *putanki* were not in the same league as those of the successful cooperative businessmen. These nouveaux riches, who are more conspicuous and more stylish in their consumption than the old Party bureaucracy, have provided a wide range of subjects for escapist fantasy; in comparison with more respectable competitors, the prostitute has lost lustre as a role model for vicarious living. The prostitute remains a subject for discourse on sexuality, though changed beyond recognition. There is far less mileage to be had from condemnation of the prostitute's quest for fine clothes and cosmetics when the Soviet press has printed earnestly approving articles on the charms of Soviet beauty queens, far less mileage to be had from condemnation of her moral failings when *Playboy* has carried a provocative photo of a Soviet film star taken with her government's full approval and presumably to its financial advantage. In line with the Party espousal of 'universal human values' and of a gentler, more caring society, the moral crusading has subsided. The repressive measures previously adopted by the government to solve social problems have been discredited. Just as the anti-alcohol campaign has been widely condemned, so force in the fight against prostitution has come in for increasing criticism.

Over the past two or three years sociologists have begun, along with other scholars, to take part in the debate on prostitution. Initially the press showed much scepticism about their willingness to meet the challenge. 'Sociologists are unfortunately as of old indifferent to this theme,' wrote one journalist in 1987.[76] Another remarked that, 'a blue moon' was more likely than 'interest in the question of prostitution from sociologists'.[77] Others were less critical, but nevertheless pressed for more information, arguing that rational ways of dealing with the problem could not be formulated until more was known about it.[78] The profession has done something to meet these demands. The survey of prostitutes in Tbilisi has been followed by others in Moscow and elsewhere; the publication of statistics is promised.[79]

The results to have appeared so far have shown Soviet prostitutes to be for the most part ordinary Soviet women, but living like other ordinary women under extraordinary pressures. They may not be as poor as their prerevolutionary predecessors, but in the relatively more industrialised Soviet context they count among the disadvantaged – their education is poor, their cultural level is low, their housing cramped, their incomes small. The acute political and social upheavals through which the Soviet Union is presently passing are hitting women particularly – as workers with jobs to lose, as housekeepers with homes to organise and as mothers with children to feed – and in consequence the economic imperatives to prostitution are likely to increase. In the autumn of 1990 a woman wrote to *Argumenty i fakty* explaining how circumstances were forcing her into prostitution: her children were sick and could not be sent to a nursery; she had to look after them and could not go out to work.

> 'I don't have any income other than my husband's 170 roubles. And I can't make ends meet with that. The children need fresh food but the money only lasts for the first fortnight. I've sold everything that I owned and now there's nothing left for sale.'[80]

She confessed she did not know how to go about becoming a prostitute and sought the paper's advice.

NOTES

1. 'V otvet na povest Vladimira Kunina "Interdevochka",' *Avrora*, No. 8, 1988, p. 104. The letterwriter was Viktoria Petrovna Dukk, a 76-year-old pensioner from Leningrad.
2. Western writings on contemporary Soviet prostitution include a calculation of its contribution to the 'second economy' and two analyses of the debates in the press and professional literature: R. Ahlberg, 'Prostitution in der Sowjetunion', *Osteuropa*, No. 6, 1989, pp. 513–28; E. Waters, 'Restructuring the "woman question": perestroika and prostitution', *Feminist Review*, No. 33, pp. 3–19.
3. M. Gurtovoi, 'Pochom lyubov?', *Trud*, 31 July 1987.
4. V. Loshak, 'Zakulisnye milliardy', *Moskovskie novosti*, No. 15, 1989, p. 12.
5. D. Mysyakov and P. Yakubovich, '"Dama" s podachkoi', *Komsomolskaya pravda*, 9 October 1986.
6. V. Yurlov, '"Putany" iz "kirgizstana"', *Sovetskaya Kirgiziya*, 16 May 1987.
7. Y. Dodolev, 'Oprokinuty mir', *Smena*, No. 5, 1987, p. 30.
8. G. Kurov, 'Ispoved "nochnoi babochki"', *Sovetskaya kultura*, 19 March 1987.
9. D. Mysyakov and P. Yakubovich, op. cit.
10. V. Vitaliev, '"chuma lyubvi" – blesk i nishcheta sovremennykh kurtizanok', *Krokodil*, No. 9, 1987, pp. 4–5.
11. L. Goiko, 'Po klichke Murka', *Pravda Ukrainy*, 6 may 1987.
12. D. Mysyakov and P. Yakubovich, op. cit.
13. P. Yakubovich, 'Nevolniki udovolstvii', *Sovetskaya Belorussiya*, 23 July 1988.
14. An unnamed *Daily Mirror* article is cited as the source of this information. See 'Prodavshiesya', *Sovetskaya Belorussiya*; reprinted in *Argumenty i fakty*, No. 32, 1986, p. 7.
15. V. Yurlov, *Sovetskaya Kirgiziya*; 'Prodavshiesya', *Argumenty i fakty*. See also A. Palchevsky, 'Barer nesovmestimosti', *Sovetskaya Belorussiya*, 18 July 1986, and I. Inovel, 'Tyazhkoe bremya lyogkovo povedeniya', *Zarya Vostoka*, 25 September 1987.
16. V. Dubkovsky, 'Devochki s prigorka', *Leningradskaya pravda*, 7 June 1987.
17. Ibid.
18. B. Muratov and S. Sergeev, 'Krakh "zhrits lyubov"', *Kazakhstanskaya pravda*, 18 September 1988; D. Mysyakov and P. Yakubovich, op. cit.
19. 'Prostitution in Latvia: "Cuckoo Mothers"', broadcast from Riga in Latvian, 22 May 1987, SU./85741B/10.
20. M. Gurtovoi, op. cit.
21. The television programme *Verdict*, broadcast on Channel 4 in July 1990, found that only two of its twelve jury, made up of 'ordinary' people, thought prostitution immoral.
22. See L. Kislanskaya's interview with Lt Col Y. Chaikovsky of the Moscow Criminal Investigation Department, '"Lyogkoe povedenie" na vesakh pravosudiya', *Sovetskaya Rossiya*, 12 March 1987.

   V. Dubkovsky, in his article, 'Girls from the hill', wrote that since it was impossible to survey the problem of prostitution in its entirety from the 'hill' he had 'turned to the lawkeeping authorities'.

23. V. Konovalov, 'SSSR i prostitusiya i borba s nei', *Novoe russkoe slovo*, 17 September 1987.
24. Ibid.
25. Ibid.
26. S. Taranov, '200 faktorov riska', *Izvestiya*, 30 August 1988.
27. L. Nikitinsky, 'Nochnye babochki v sachke "militsii nravov"', *Krokodil*, 22 August, 1988, p. 11. See also A. Anosov, 'Dno', *Sovetskaya torgovlya*, 15 July 1989; L. Kislinskaya, 'Chevo my zhdom?', *Trud*, 14 August 1988; Y. Glants, 'Nochnye "gastroli"', *Trud*, 4 May 1988.
28. V. Sharov, 'I my – parazity', *Pravda Ukrainy*, 15 May 1987.
29. 'Lekarstvo ot "chumy lyubvi": sushchestvuet li ono?', *Krokodil*, No. 20, 1987, pp. 4–5.
30. M. Gurtovoi, 'Tyazhkaya rasplata za "lyokuyu zhizn"', *Trud*, 7 February 1988.
31. The original article was: K. Yanovich, 'Pochom lyubov'?', *Sovetskaya Estoniya*, 16 October 1987. For the replies, see 'Rezonans. Pochom lyubov'?', *Sovetskaya Estoniya*, 29 December 1987.
32. V. Stepanov, 'Bez linii zhizni', *Nedelya*, No. 21, 1987, p. 19.
33. N. Maidanskaya, 'Proza "sladkoi zhizni"', *Sovetskaya kultura*, 24 March 1990. See also 'Gruppa riska. Trinadtsat mneniy', *Ogonyok*, No. 49, 1988, pp. 20–1.
34. 'Laboratoriya molodyozhnykh problem povodit itogi issledovaniya "Podrostki i dengi"', *Literaturnaya gazeta*, No. 36. 1987.
35. A. Galin, 'Stars in the morning sky', in M. Glenny (ed.) *Stars in the Morning Sky* (London: Nick Hern Books, 1983), pp. 1–59.
36. Vladimir Kunin, 'Interdevochka', *Avrora*, 1988, No. 2, pp. 87–139; 1988, No. 3, pp. 89–125.
37. 'Gruppa riska. Trinadtsat mneniy', *Ogonyok*, No. 49, 1988.
38. I. Galperin, 'Krainyaya neobkhodimost', *Literaturnaya gazeta*, 13 May, 1987.
39. A. P. Dyachenko and N. A. Averina, 'Ekspertnye otsenki problem prostitutsii v SSSR', in B.M. Levin and S.G. Klimova (eds), *Problemy borby s deviantnym povedeniem* (Moscow, 1989), pp. 88–99.
40. A. Kirsta and K. Speransky, 'Nuzhna li ugolovnaya otvetstvennost za prostitutsiya?', *Sovetskaya yustitsiya*, No. 16, 1988, pp. 19–20.
41. K. Gustavson, 'Iz istorii prostitusii', *Sovetskoe pravo*, 1988, No. 2, pp. 135–7.
42. Y. Gilinksy, 'O prostitutsii, ili kak v kaple vody', *Sovetskoe pravo*, 1989, No. 1, pp. 24–27.
43. A. A. Gabiani and M. A. Manuilsky, 'Tsena "lyubvi" (Obsledovanie prostitutok v Gruzii)', *Sotsialisticheskie issledovaniya*, No. 6, 1987, pp. 61–8.
44. S. I. Golod, 'Prostitutsiya v kontekste izmeneniya polovoi morali', *Sotsiologicheskie issledovaniya*, No. 2, 1988, pp. 65–70. A book by S.I. Golod, *Prostitutsiya v kontekste izmenenii seksualnoi morali*, is forthcoming.
45. A. Sobolevsky, 'Revolutsiya lyubvi i evolyutsiya semi', *Ekho*, No. 8 (182) 1989, pp. 143–51.
46. O. Serdobolsky, 'Ne pervaya i ne drevneishaya', *Ekho planety*, 1989, No. 33, pp. 26–37.
47. See, for example, S. Kuzin, 'Blesk i slyozy', *Pravda Ukrainy*, 13 April 1988;

Y. Glants, *Trud*, S. Taranov, *Izvestiya*, L. Nikitinsky, *Krokodil*, L. Kislinskaya, *Trud*.

48. N. Maidanskaya, op. cit.
49. V. Zhilyaeva, 'Gruppa riska', *Sovetskaya Rossiya*, 25 October 1988.
50. F. Engels did not write anything of the kind, though he might not have disagreed with the proposition. In *Die Frau und der Sozialismus*, August Bebel wrote that prostitution was 'a necessary institution of the bourgeois world'. See A. Bebel, *Woman in the Past, Present and Future* (London: Zwan Publications, 1988), p. 91.
51. T. Suvorova, '"Interdevochka" v zerkale politekonomii', *Molodyozh Estonii*, 8 July 1989.
52. T. Chernyshkova, 'Khau du yu du, interdevochka', *Sobesednik*, No. 35, 1989, p. 6.
53. L. Zhukovitsky, 'I dvadtsat sem kopeek v karmane', *Molodoi kommunist*, No. 6, 1988, p. 62. T. Chernyshkova in *Sobesednik* also argued that prostitutes perform a social service.
54. G. Bartkevicha, 'Legalizuem prostitutsiyu', *Femida*, No. 1, 1990, pp. 29–31.
55. Ibid., p. 30.
56. For a more detailed discussion of this point see my, 'Sex and semiotic confusion: report from Moscow', *Australian Feminist Studies*, No. 12, 1990, pp. 1–14.
57. T. Chernyshkova, op. cit.
58. Mikhail Uspensky, 'Ministerstvo lyogkovo povedeniya', *Ogonyok*, No. 42, 1988, p. 32.
59. L. Nikitinsky, op. cit.
60. Cartoons on the subject of prostitution to appear during 1989 included: No. 20, p. 11; No. 21, p. 9; No. 32, p. 5; No. 33, pp. 8–9.
61. *Krokodil*, No. 20, 1987, p. 5.
62. *Krokodil*, No. 17, 1988, p. 2.
63. *Krokodil*, No. 1, 1990, p. 5.
64. N. Maidanskaya, op. cit.
65. S. Taranov, '200 faktorov riska', *Izvestiya*, 30 August 1988.
66. I. Karpets, 'Znat, shtoby borotsya', *Argumenty i fakty*, No. 5, 1987.
67. I. Karpets, 'Sotsialnoe nasledovanie ili priobretonnye poroki?', *Argumenty i fakty*, No. 12, 1988.
68. V. Zhilyaeva, *Sovetskaya Rossiya*, 25 October 1988.
69. A Paris-Match journalist was told by a 'contact' that shortly after a hardhitting article by Yevgeny Dodolev in *Moskovsky komsomolets*, security at the foreign tourist hotel in Moscow 'Kosmos' was tightened and only those with passes were permitted entry. See V. Ginzburg, 'Prostitutsiya v SSSR', *Novoe russkoe slovo*, 3 April 1987, p. 11.
70. A. Vartanov, 'Analiz ili konstatanya', *Pravda*, 24 November 1989.
71. See letters appended to the article on prostitution by S. Makhonina, '"Zhristsy svobodnoi lyubvi" togda i teper', *Molodoi kommunist*, 1989, No. 8, pp. 69–78.
72. L. Zhukovitsky maintained that no one he talked to 'seethed with indignation', that indignation 'seethed' only in the pages of the newspapers, *Molodoi kommunist*, No. 6, 1988, p. 63.
73. L. Kislinskaya, 'Chevo my zhdom', *Trud*, 14 August 1988.

74. S. Samoilis, '"Sladkaya" zhizn v odinochestve', *Leningradskaya pravda*, 17 November 1987.
75. S. Taranov, op. cit.
76. I. Osinsky, Y. Popov, 'Grekhopadenie', *Sovetskaya Belorussiya*, 13 November 1987.
77. A. Melnik, 'Eleonora khochet poznakomitsya', *Pravda Ukrainy*, 18 October 1987.
78. See L. Zhukovitsky, op. cit.' S. Makhonina, ibid.
79. F. Ivanov, 'O prestupnosti – glasno', *Izvestiya*, 10 September 1988.
80. 'Prostite', *Argumenty i fakty*, No. 35, 1990.

10 Changing Attitudes to Delinquency

Victoria Semyonova

The theory of lack of a social basis for conflict between generations in socialist society implied that young people did their parents' bidding, followed the common good (social altruism) and imitated the adult way of life:

> Soviet scholars study the social outlook of young people, their orientations, interests and requirements. And the results invariably testify that contemporary Soviet youth possesses the remarkable qualities of being true to communist ideals, dedicated to the interests of socialist society, and shows an ever mounting social activity.[1]

On that principle youth deviant behaviour was dealt with extremely widely – as any deviation from the norm and pattern of conduct in society. Such deviance contained, first, its own criminal youth behaviour (theft, acts of aggression, hooliganism) i.e. 'negative' social conduct that comes within the purview of criminal law and at the same time is present in all social groups.

Second, it embraced youth subculture (from hedonistic values and life styles to extravagant external appearance). Public opinion consistently waged a battle with new youth fashions (narrow or wide trousers, various hair styles), norms of behaviour and values initially associated with jazz culture, and then the hippy and rock culture.

Scholarly literature rejected the existence of the very concept of youth culture as a subculture or counter-culture in regard to official culture. The only consistent proponent of the subculture concept was Igor Kon.[2]

The natural desire for youth subculture as criticism of or protest against the cultural traditions of the older generation was regarded as an attack on the political foundation of society and only existed clandestinely. This led to an underground youth market, an orientation on patterns of Western youth culture (for its debased condition) and a distorted emulation of the attributes of that culture. There arose the notion of 'underground' youth culture in the circumstances of stagnation.

Deviant behaviour, thirdly, also contained the mass initiative youth actions and movements that arose outside the framework of the single young organisation – the Komsomol (Young Communist League). For a long time bans existed even on amateur song clubs, youth housing cooperatives, youth interest groups, not to mention political groupings of the 1960s such as the Youth Associations in Voronezh and the Young Communard society in Tula. In their place we had youth initiatives inspired from without, like Komsomol construction sites, the conquest of the virgin lands, and so on, where youth was used as cheap labour.

All these forms of youth action were persecuted both by moral pressure (exclusion from the Komsomol and education institutions) and by criminal prosecution.

Youth deviance from adult behaviour norms was punished fairly severely. In 1980 as many as 78 per cent of those found guilty of criminal responsibility between the ages of 14 and 29 were sentenced to deprivation of freedom (the figure in 1989, for comparison, was a mere 55 per cent).[3]

These facts from recent youth history illustrate the role played by young people in Soviet society in the 1960s, 1970s and 1980s: they were reduced to being a transmission belt of social experience. And any deviation from the norm was regarded as a betrayal and a breakdown in ideological training by adult society. Lack of social freedom deprived young people of any chance of expressing their uniqueness, their individuality; everything original in the generation was regarded as unnecessary ballast. The ban on individuality levelled out particular personalities and deprived young people as a social group of the ability to influence or correct social development. This was one way of affirming the processes of stagnation in society generally.

It is therefore hardly surprising that one observer should remark that the country actually had no youth, just little old people. Perhaps that is exactly as it was – the typically youthful qualities of adventure, protest, extravagance and bohemian life styles, and therefore dynamism and mobility, were reduced to naught in such conditions.

From the standpoint of contemporary social youth theory, the deviant behaviour of each fresh generation, understood in the broad sense as nontraditional, is the only and necessary source of normal social development. Deviant youth behaviour is more likely to be criticised for the lack of such deviance in which young people demonstrate their uniqueness and innovatory potential.

Accordingly, the basic function of youth as a stage of human development consists in forming society's new social experience by transmitting and transforming the social experience of the previous generations.

Theories in structural functionalism give priority in the process to the first component – adaptation of generations to the norms and values passed on by previous generations. Such theories have their beginnings in the works of Talcott Parsons and S. N. Eisenstadt.

According to Eisenstadt, youth is a transitional phase between the world of childhood and that of adulthood. Youth culture is a moment in the distintegration of society.[4] For Parsons, it is an aspiration to escape from social control and pressure from adult society into diversionary time-consumption, and it is thereby a deviation, a dysfunction in social existence.[5]

Theories in psycho-dynamics prefer the second component (transformation) of social experience, explaining it as the human organism's propensity to an intensive intellectual and emotional development at a given age – as the take-off from childhood to young adulthood.[6]

In our view, however, the best sociological approach is that where the formation of a generation's social experience is regarded more as a dialectical balance between transmission and transformation, where the specific correlation between components depends on the overall context of socialisation of the generation. The sources of these theories go back to Mannheim who felt that a generation's own collective experience at certain historical moments is shaped more intensively. This corresponds to periods of radical social change: the more intensive the change, the greater the gap between the outlook of the generations.[7]

Today, the situation is changing radically. We see in society the mounting need for new people, bearers of dynamism, political leaders, original thinkers, active statesmen and stateswomen capable of making a dynamic contribution to the social situation.

Naturally this focuses on young people and their ability for innovation. We are talking about the formation of an intellectual elite, of young enterprising personalities. The idea of the growing politicisation of Soviet youth is broadly popular, including among some Western scholars. There are forecasts about the historic role of the present generation of young people and its future contribution to rapid and radical social change.[8]

The concept of deviant behaviour has undergone a certain deformation. We have removed the ban on many aspects of youthful activity. Researchers are now seriously studying various facets of juvenile delinquency, rejecting the notion of primordial criminology of youth. Youth subcultural manifestations have become objects of analysis. I. Andreyeva and L. Novikova are looking at 'youth subculture not as a mass deviation' in the behaviour of an entire generation, but as a phenomenon of the cultural-historical process arising in a society that swiftly attains material abundance, yet has not yet worked out appropriate mechanisms of social homeostasis.[9]

Attempts are being made to remove legal restrains on many aspects of youth activity: we are debating laws on public organisations, on a social policy towards young people, and so on.

It is natural to assume that young people at a time of any radical restructuring of economic, political and social relations should belong to historic generations; this is bound to lead to a radical reassessment of their values and the mores of older generations, the shaping of self-awareness and political organisations, a more progressive set of values. The most remarkable aspect of the political youth movements in the West in the 1960s was precisely renunciation of the values of the parents' generation, and acute criticism of them, which became the basis for forming the youth movement.

The present-day younger generation would therefore be expected to have a clearly expressed tendency towards deviance (in both a negative and a positive sense) – i.e. it should possess a social uniqueness.

Within the bounds of this approach we have tried to analyse the position of the Soviet younger generation in regard to social change. We were interested particularly in the measure of participation in social change, thereby reproducing and developing new social relations through the medium of that generation.

We chose the generation of 22–24-year-olds who are currently at a stage of active entry into social life: initial adaptation within the structure of adult society through work or study in higher educational institutions, development of their own families, emergence of the generation's political and social experience.

One characteristic of this generation is that its schooling fell within the so-called stagnation years, which was bound to affect its values and patterns of behaviour taken from the society of that period. The period of active entry into 'adult' life was at a time of the break-up of old traditional structures and the genesis of new ones. The younger generation is restructuring social relations outside the framework of its specific existence. It is thereby more an object than a subject of social change, experiencing the impact of both stable traditional and dynamic non-traditional social relations.

We studied the generation's position in regard to social change according to the following criteria:

(a) participation in socio-political movements;
(b) attitudes towards topical political problems;
(c) orientation on certain values.

We carried out the study in the latter part of 1989 in the Tula Region within the *Paths of a Generation* longitudinal investigation. As many as a thousand persons were questioned in a quota sample, proportionally representing the generation with secondary schooling of the region. In qualifying the data we also took into consideration research carried out by other methods in other areas, which enabled us to support the argumentation of our findings and to broaden the scope of the conclusions.

Our findings are presented in the rest of this paper.

YOUTH PARTICIPATION IN A SOCIO-POLITICAL INFORMAL MOVEMENT

Our research revealed that only 5 per cent of those surveyed put themselves in any informal group, including only 0.1 per cent in a socio-political informal movement. By socio-political movement we mean philosophical, political or ecological groupings or groups that reflect the interests of the local community. This shows young people who have set up informal associations have passed over their most socially meaningful forms to adults. They themselves overwhelmingly prefer subcultural forms of activity.

What is more, even verbal orientations on setting up an alternative youth organisation show that three-quarters of young people in various regions do not associate themselves with any political organisation; they prefer an organisation of a cultural-recreational or legal-defensive nature.

Few young people take part in 'adult' informal political associations. For example, even in such a mass political organisation as the Lithuanian National Front (Sajudis), which embraces some 180,000 people, the share of young people up to 30 is just a few per cent.

The first published catalogue of informal associations, containing some 1,000 titles, has a mere 7 per cent as the share of young people's own associations (according to orientation or composition of participants). To demonstrate the wide variety of youth associations, we cite the names of just some, the most important, of them: the Moscow Union of Democratic Youth, the Union of Students (Moscow), the 'System' hippy movement, the Union of Young Christians (Leningrad), the Russian Union of Young Democrats, Green-Heap (Kiev), the Democratic Youth League (Riga), Young Lithuania (Vilnius), Interbrigades (Moscow), Chain Reaction (heavy metal fans) (Nizhny Tagil).

The youth associations are extremely diverse: some are of a subcultural nature – e.g. the 'System', a mass movement of Soviet hippies; others espouse social initiative and come close to being an ecological movement – like Green-Heap in Kiev. There is a national-cultural strain in independence movements: Young Lithuania, the Column of Independent Youth No. 1

(Vyru in Estonia). Despite their diverse names and orientations, however, most tend to exist in the form of clubs rather than as political movements. They arose mainly during 1989 and 1990 and embrace no more than between 100 and 150 people on average.

In spite of the broad spectrum of youth organisations, the small and parochial character of the majority shows that no real mass youth movement exists today. None of the groups can pretend to reflect or defend the interests of a substantial group of young people and they cannot offer a serious alternative to the Young Communist League.

This may be due to the following. For a long time youth was in a state of social anaemia; it was unable to display any initiative, so that it actually lost the habit of trying to organise itself. Even now, when society is changing, it is removing itself from participation in any social movement.

The absence of mass youth organisations is all the more paradoxical in that the problems of the social status of youth, the economic position on the labour market and in the consumption sphere are such crucial issues and are bound to worsen in the impending crisis years – i.e. we are faced with the social need for a youth movement for its own legal defence and protection. For the moment the younger generation is unable to meet that need.

SUBJECTIVE POLITICAL POSITION TOWARDS PRESSING POLITICAL PROBLEMS

We investigated the younger generation's opinion on major political problems, using conservative–progressive criteria; we used responses to key questions by which we divided opinion into conservative and progressive. They included questions on attitudes to the cooperative movement, the multi-party principle, nationalist movements and decentralisation of power.

Our hypothesis was that the unique nature of the generation, if it does exist, should manifest itself either in (a) a bias towards progressive views, or (b) a position of political extremism, which is more typical of youth consciousness, or (c) a more radical position of students by contrast with young workers (in so far as students are more consistent bearers of youth consciousness), or (d) a more radical position compared with older age groups.

In the course of our investigation, however, we found that these criteria were not sustained. First, according to responses to all four questions, 53 per cent may be classed as conservatively inclined and 30 per cent progressively inclined (17 per cent took an indefinite position – finding it hard to answer). Consequently, youth opinion tended more towards conservative than progressive attitudes.

Second, while it is true that people with radical (extremist) views among young people in the survey were more numerous than those with moderate views (the answers were analysed on a four-point scale: radical conservatives, moderate conservatives, moderate progressives and radical progressives) – 55 per cent against 30 per cent – the radical conservatives were double the radical progressives – 29 per cent against 14 per cent. So, almost a third of the respondents held rigid conservative positions: categorically opposing the cooperative movement and the multi-party system, considering national concerns a manifestation of nationalism and lack of gratitude to Russia, and in favour of tightening up control and centralised planning in resolving economic problems.

Third, the politics of students was somewhat more to the left than that of young workers. What this meant, however was that they contained fewer radial conservatives and more moderate conservatives. In other words, the largest group among workers was the radical conservatives – 37 per cent, while it was moderate conservatives – 30 per cent – among students.

The findings of largely conservative orientations in the Tula Region generally coincide with those collected in other parts of the country. Thus, a survey of various youth categories held in five areas of the country (Lithuania, the Ukraine, the Altai, Tadzhikistan and Tataria) in April 1990, shows somewhat different quantitative results and a considerable scattering among the regions, yet the basic trends and conclusions are the same. Generally speaking the bulk of youth respondents displayed a moderate conservatism. Young people did not show any particular radicalism: only 27 per cent were in favour of radical progressive changes, 23 per cent were for conservative change.[10]

We did not look at comparisons between the political orientations of young people and those of older age groups. But the findings obtained by other researchers (a sample survey of 12,000 people carried out by the Social Sciences Academy in 1989) showed that there was no essential difference in the political orientations of youth and older people in regard to political protest – the difference between the groups does not exceed 3–5 per cent on various calculations.[11] The findings of the Central Public Opinion Survey Institute from various population categories on the cooperative movement also do no contain substantial differences between people by age.[12]

Thus the younger generation is not yet able to elaborate its own opinions, remaining captive to childhood-ingrained views.

YOUTH VALUE ORIENTATIONS

Four years ago, when investigating the younger generation as it started out
on life (in the last year at secondary school), we singled out two traditional
major orientation types:

(a) The first was a fairly clear-cut orientation on material well-being, a
    quiet life and desire to be among close friends and relatives. We may
    call this material well-being.
(b) The second type was oriented on the public good – a social altruism
    and one that was based on a socially approved stereotype of
    behaviour.

An important conclusion from the research was that, despite differences
in territory, residence and climate, variations were minimal between the
regions in this particular orientation. Such minimal differences consist only
in the degree of expression of those types of orientation in groups of areas
inclining towards various religious-cultural traditions: Islam (Tadzhikistan),
Russian Orthodox (regions of the Russian Federation and Belorussia),
Protestantism and Catholicism (Baltic Republics). Consequently, the
orientations are fairly universal over the entire country.

Youth oriented on material well-being comprised a third of those we
surveyed. Mainly it represented graduates of technical colleges and, consequently, it was mainly made up of future semi-skilled workers in various
sectors of industry.

The orientation on material well-being as a vital objective is a natural and
necessary part of each social system, although in the Soviet Union it was for
many years regarded as on the decline and somewhat shameful.

It is natural to suppose that as social maturity grows, the share of young
people oriented on this set of values will increase with the need to establish
one's own family and household. The findings of a follow-up investigation
carried out four years after the respondents had left school confirm that the
orientation on setting up a family, bringing up children and living with
one's chosen partner – i.e. orientation on a 'private' life-style – markedly
grew. Of all the spheres of human activity the family is recognised as the
most important – ten times more frequently than other factors, like a
specialist job, social work and studies. Objective findings on the leisure
time budget of this age group – 20–24 years of age – show that between 40
and 50 per cent of leisure time on days off is given over to domestic
concerns within the family. With rural youth this indicator grows to 80–85
per cent. As social maturity increases from 16 to 29, so the share of
'domestic' leisure grows by 7–10 per cent on average.

So, at the present time the share among 22–24-year-olds of those oriented on traditional values of a 'private' life-style has substantially increased. There are no grounds to believe that these young people will take an active part in the democratic transformation of society.

The priority orientation of young people on reproducing authoritarian relations within the family to the detriment of the democratic is confirmation enough of this. The respondents who already have children intend largely to construct their relations with them on the basis of control and subordination (vertically) and much less on the basis of partnership (horizontally).

The educational strategy of parents will therefore help to reproduce in the coming generation a traditional authoritarian and not a democratic type of personality.

The increasing trend to a private life-style is also due to a reduction in the number of those oriented after school on the second type of orientation – the common good.

At the time of the survey, a third of the group nominated that value after leaving school (at 17–18). However, one may assume that the size of the category will dwindle with age. This is due, first, to the age specifics of young people entering marriage age and, second, to numerous disappointments awaiting this group as they grow older: of those who intend to continue their studies after school, only half can realistically do so – only 29 per cent out of 60 per cent.

Of those who went out to work, two-thirds are not following their specialism obtained at school. Most say their work expectations have not been justified; a third say they were justified only partially and a third say they were utterly unjustified (findings in Estonia).

The statistics testify to disillusionment over job expectations. From year to year the share is growing of those not following their trade owing to lack of vacancies – they make up today a third of all 20–24-year-olds at work. The proportion is also growing of those who neither work nor study. Since 1985 the number of those who after studies have no work or study had grown on average throughout the country by 12,600, including by 1,800 in Russia.[13]

It is therefore logical that orientation on social altruism is inevitably going to founder because of, on the one hand, the increasing proportion of young people oriented on traditional family values and incapable of social innovation and, on the other, the increasing proportion of marginal youth. This latter group is the most fertile soil for purely negative deviance, i.e. criminal behaviour.

SUMMARY

To sum up, we may note that the long-held social policy oriented on banning any youth deviation from the norms and patterns of behaviour of the older generations has borne fruit. The chickens are coming home to roost. Today's younger generation is not at all oriented on social innovation; by inertia it adheres to the principles and norms of the prohibition policy acquired in school during the stagnation years.

Despite the changing social situation and the removal of bans from most forms of youth activity, young people seem to hold to traditional patterns and are in no hurry to manifest themselves as a generation on the historical stage. We need supplementary social efforts to unlock the innovatory potential of the younger generation. Otherwise it will be yet another lost generation, and not one that is in any way historic.

NOTES

1. N. M. Blinov, 'Sotsiologiya molodyozhi: dostizheniya i problemy', *Sotsiologicheskie issledovaniya*, No. 2, 1982, p. 9.
2. Igor Kon, *Psikhologiya starsheklassnikov* (Moscow: Molodaya gvardia, 1980), pp. 87–103.
3. See *Molodyozh SSSR. Statistichesky sbornik* (Moscow: Finansy i statistika, 1989), pp. 236–7.
4. S.N. Eisenstadt, *From Generation to Generation* (Chicago: Free Press, 1956).
5. Talcott Parsons, 'Age and sex in the social structure of the United States,' in *Essays in Sociological Theory* (Chicago: Free Press, 1954).
6. K. Erikson, *Wayward Puritans: A Study in the Sociology of Knowledge* (New York: John Wiley, 1966).
7. H. Mannheim, *Essays on the Sociology of Knowledge* (London: Hutchinson, 1952).
8. M. Brake, *Sociology of Youth Culture and Youth Subcultures: Sex and Drugs and Rock'n'Roll* (London: Boston and Henley, 1980); J. Riordan, 'Soviet youth: pioneers of change', *Soviet Studies*, Vol. XL, No. 4, October 1988, pp. 556–72.
9. I. Andreyeva and L. Novikova, *Neformalnye obyedineniya molodyozhi: vchera, sevodnya, zavtra* (Moscow: Pedagogika, 1988), p. 26.
10. *Analiticheskaya zapiska po rezultatam express-oprosa molodyozhi nakanune XXI syezda VLKSM* (Moscow: Molodaya gvardia, 1990).
11. See *Neformalnaya volna* (Moscow: Vysshaya komsomolskaya shkola, 1990), p. 80.
12. See *Argumenty i fakty*, No. 35, 1989.
13. *Molodyozh SSSR* (Moscow: Finansy i statistika, 1989).

Part Six
Leisure

11 Playing to New Rules: Soviet Sport and Perestroika

Jim Riordan

During the 1980s radical changes began to appear in communist sport, thereby breaking the mould of its functionalised and bureaucratic (plan-fulfilment) structure. Until then not only had the Soviet-pioneered, state-controlled, utilitarian system hampered a true appraisal of realities that lay beneath the 'universal' statistics and 'idealised' veneer, it had prevented concessions to particular groups in the population – the 'we know what's good for you' syndrome by which men tell women what sports they should play; the fit tell the disabled that sport is not for them; the old tell the young they can only play on their (old) terms, in their clubs, using their facilities; the political leadership, mindful of the nation's and ideology's international reputation, decides that competitive Olympic (i.e. European) sports are the only civilised forms of culture.

It has to be said that not only has this system helped to make several communist states (the USSR, GDR, Cuba, Hungary) forces to be reckoned with in world sport, but its orientation to social change through sport (for purposes of improving defence, health and hygiene, integration, productivity and international prestige) has also found ready imitators in many developing states.

In the early 1980s, however, China began increasingly to orient its sports policy to the West, particularly the USA, opening up the country to commercial sport for leisure and recreation – from golf to baseball,[1] from boxing (which had been banned for several years) to women's soccer, snooker, bodybuilding and weightlifting.[2] At the same time, it started to pay more attention to hitherto neglected groups and sports – e.g. the disabled and the folk games of national minorities.[3]

Such processes in China prompted a reappraisal of sport in the Soviet Union after March 1985, and this, in turn, had repercussions throughout Eastern Europe. This chapter will survey what seem to be the major trends in Soviet sport in the latter part of the 1980s and early 1990s.

SPORT FOR ALL

The Soviet leadership has always maintained in public that *massovost* takes precedence over *masterstvo*, and down the years it has produced regiments of statistics to prove the case: that millions are regular, active participants in sport; that the vast majority of school and college students gain a *GTO* (*Gotov k trudu i oborone* – 'Prepared for Labour and Defence', initially based on Baden-Powell's Boy Scout athletics badges) in the national fitness programme;[4] that rising millions (a third of the population) take part in the quadrennial spartakiads;[5] and that the bulk of workers do their daily dozen – 'production gymnastics' – at the workplace.

We now learn in this 'honesty is the best policy' era that these figures were fraudulent and a show to impress people above and below and to meet pre-set targets (each school, region, factory and farm received a sports quota and incurred penalties and criticism if they fell short). It is now admitted that only 8 per cent of men and 2 per cent of women engage in sport regularly.[6] It is also admitted that when put to the test a mere 41 out of 700 Moscow schoolchildren taking part in the city sports tournament could meet all the *GTO* requirements, and only 0.5 per cent of the capital's 11-year-olds met *GTO* standards.[7] Even among men doing their national service as many as a third could not meet the norms.[8]

Although swimming is an obligatory element in the *GTO* programme, we now learn that only 11 per cent of schoolchildren can swim and fewer than 5 per cent pass the *GTO* swimming norm.[9] In Moscow, 70 per cent of schoolchildren cannot swim.[10] Even in a Republic with a Californian climate, Armenia, most youngsters cannot swim.[11] All college and university students must attend two sessions a week of sport and physical exercise during their first academic year, yet a survey at Moscow State University discovered that only 17 per cent of students were physically fit. The conclusion drawn from the survey was that compulsion results in resistance and anti-sport sentiments.[12]

For most people, sport remains out of reach: some two-thirds of workers do not belong to sports organisations and their physical fitness evidently 'makes only a tiny contribution to higher productivity, a lower sickness rate and resolution of social and economic problems'.[13]

Significantly, the 1991 Spartakiad passed off in a low-key fashion with several sports cancelled, participation and duration severely limited for lack of funds. There are also signs that the *GTO* programme is being quietly abandoned, partly out of a desire to break with the past 'fiddling of the books' and partly from its increasing unpopularity with teachers and young people.

A serious move to involve more young people in casual sport and recreation activities was made back in 1981 when the government decreed that sports schools (i.e. clubs) should not be confined only to gifted athletes:[14] henceforth roughly half the 7,500 sports schools (those run by local councils and education authorities) would be open to all.[15] Yet subsequent reports frequently complained of sports centre managers and coaches trying to keep ordinary enthusiasts out.

The next step was to depart from the hallowed principle of completely free sport by introducing charges for use of pool, gym, court and stadium; that, at least, it was thought, might induce amenity owners to open their doors. Further, with official permission given in 1987 for cooperative ventures to start up, a number of cooperative health, fitness and sports clubs began to appear. A health club opened in Moscow in mid-1988, for example, charging three roubles as entrance fee and a scale of charges for various treatments and activities.[16] In Leningrad, the Juventus Health and Sports Club had come into existence a few months earlier with activities ranging from Aikido wrestling, skateboarding and break-dancing to tennis, swimming and weight-watching exercises. A month's membership cost about ten roubles; the club had a regular membership of 600 within months of opening, and had another 800 on its waiting list.[17] A cooperative group in the town of Podolsk, some 50 km south of Moscow, had the bright idea of hiring out municipal sports facilities during 'fallow' time – evenings and weekends; it charged 1.30 roubles an hour for swimming, just under a rouble for an hour's use of sports grounds and 2.20 roubles for a two-hour sauna session.[18] At the same time, in Georgia, the former tennis player Alex Metreveli opened a string of tennis clubs along the Black Sea coast and in Tbilisi.[19]

A major change has also come over the trade union sports societies: in mid-1987 the eight leading societies amalgamated to form a single sports organisation in an attempt to improve facilities and service to the public as well as to 'democratise the work of the sports clubs'. They also declared their intention of reducing top-level leagues and competitions so as to divert more funds to sport for all and to cater for a diversity of interest groups and health clubs.[20]

At school the physical education curriculum has been adjusted to make some form of recreation a daily feature for all children and to provide a choice of activity.[21] And in higher education, students can now choose the times at which they engage in their compulsory sports activity, and they have a wider choice of recreation activity.

INDEPENDENT CLUBS

Young people have not sat around awaiting government resolutions. In fact, a major cause of official action is that young people have been turning their backs on official organisations, like the Young Pioneers and the Young Communist League (Komsomol) – which has lost 20 million members in the past five years[22] – and officially recommended and sponsored activities, and have been forming their own groups and clubs. Although initially illegal, since only officially sanctioned groups have been permitted in the USSR, the authorities seemed unable or unwilling to suppress them. Finally, in May 1986, they set the official seal on their existence by changing the law.[23]

In the field of sport, the clubs range from soccer fan clubs to groups for sports in which the authorities have been slow to provide facilities – aerobics, yoga, body building, jogging, karate and other combat sports. One of the first independent groups was made up of soccer fans in the late 1970s and early 1980s, especially of Moscow Spartak, with their own distinctive red and white home-knitted scarves and hats. They were followed, understandably, by combat sports clubs for both defence and offence in the spreading street and soccer gang clashes. One of the more sinister groups, the Lyubery, tends to be obsessed with martial arts and body building, constructing their own gyms in the (central heating) basements of blocks of flats.[24]

The forced acceptance of such independent clubs is a radical departure for the authorities; after all, no youth groups free of Party tutelage had been tolerated since the 1920s.

WOMEN AND SPORT

Up and down the USSR women have long ignored the pontification of male leaders about their participation in 'harmful' sports – soccer, body building, ice hockey, judo, weightlifting, water polo and long distance running. As recently as 1973 the USSR Sports Committee issued a resolution discouraging women from participating in sports which were allegedly harmful to the female organism and encourage male voyeurism. Women's soccer, for example, was said to be 'injurious to a woman's organism . . . Physical stress typical of playing soccer can cause harm to sexual functions, varicose veins, thrombophlebitis and so on'.[25] What the resolution did not explain was why playing soccer was harmless for men, or why those ailments did not result from approved (Olympic) sports like basketball and field hockey.

Within the space of a few years, however, Soviet women have held four national judo championships and a world judo championship, and as many as 15,000 women are registered in judo clubs.[26] The first women's national soccer championship was held in August 1987, sponsored by the campaigning youth weekly *Sobesednik* (eight teams took part in the first year, 20 in 1988, and 50 from virtually every part of the country in 1989) and the first international (v. Czechoslovakia) took place in 1988.[27] Moscow State University formed its first women's water polo team back in 1982; the women's sport has now spread to several other cities and the Soviet women's team played its first international fixture (v. Hungary) in 1987.[28] Weightlifting and body building are developing apace: the first women's body building championship was held in Tyumen in 1988, and women have been members of body building clubs in the Baltic Republics at least since 1986.[29] Women's ice hockey has reappeared for the first time since the 1920s, and women are doing the marathon, pole vault, triple jump and hammer throwing.[30] These changes have all come about thanks to a few women who were prepared to defy official sanction, ridicule and even persecution in order to establish their right to pursue the sport of their choice. But commerce is also evident: women's boxing and wrestling tournaments have appeared since 1990.

SPORT AND THE DISABLED

Another disadvantaged group to benefit from the wind of change is the physically and mentally handicapped, long neglected by the Soviet sports establishment. It is now admitted that 'for a long time we pretended the problem did not exist. We thought: the state looks after the handicapped, social security provides living and working conditions for them. What else do they want?'[31]

Before 1988 the USSR had never held domestic championships at any level for any category of handicapped person. Two years after China had staged its first nationwide games for the handicapped and in the year of the Seoul Paralympics, the newly formed Disabled Sports Federation held its inaugural championship in the Estonian capital of Tallinn. This was the culmination of long years of campaigning by pressure groups, recently joined by the many thousands of maimed young ex-Afghanistan veterans. While, again, it is the Baltic Republics that are in the forefront of providing facilities for the handicapped, elsewhere conditions are plainly woeful. Even 'Moscow has no equipment, coach, doctor or sports facilities for the disabled' (1987).[32]

After a number of well publicised complaints that 'sport for the disabled has been developing around the world with virtually no participation from the Soviet Union',[33] a team of invalid athletes (13 blind men) was sent to the Olympics for the very first time, at Seoul in 1988. Unlike its able-bodied compatriots in the Olympic Games, who won a quarter of all Olympic medals, the Soviet disabled team won no medals at all. But at least a start has been made. Furthermore, as well as movement towards caring more for minorities, the Soviet government is also showing signs of encouraging folk game festivals, especially among non-Russian groups in the population.[34]

CHANGING THE IMAGE OF SOVIET SPORT

The sudden spate of honesty and the broaching of previously unmentionable (censored) subjects have revealed the dark side of Soviet sport and stirred up considerable debate. Journalists now talk frankly about match fixing in major spectator sports, bribery of referees, drug taking and other nefarious activities hitherto only mentioned in the context of capitalist sport. They have also raised questions about the very fundamentals of communist sport: its ethics and ethos.

In an article entitled 'It is people who lose' and supported by a full-page caricature of two muscle-bound colossuses carrying a winner's podium over the heads of a host of casual athletes, a journalist from *Ogonyok* derided the 'win at all costs' mentality and the privileges for the elite. He recalled the pentathlete Boris Onishchenko, caught cheating at the Montreal Olympics in 1976: 'Did his coach really know nothing? Did the sports leadership subject him to public ostracism?'[35] He went on to mention two Soviet weightlifters caught selling anabolic steroids in Canada (taken *out of* the USSR). The problem of drugs has also been raised in the press and on an unscripted TV programme by two respected ex-athletes and prominent sports officials: the weightlifter Yuri Vlasov and the long jumper Igor Ter-Ovanesyan.

During a live TV debate on Soviet sport in late 1986, Vlasov, the Chairman of the USSR Weightlifting Federation, broke the silence on drug taking; he declared that immense damage had been done to Soviet sport, and weightlifting in particular, by the 'coach pharmacologist' who worked alongside the sports coach. Not only did Vlasov accuse Soviet athletes of using anabolics 'for several decades', but he named names – specifically that of ex-Olympic weightlifter, coach and top sports official Arkady Vorobyov, 'who was one of the first to distribute anabolic steroids to members of our national team'.[36] Vlasov then revealed in a newspaper interview that, following his accusations, Soviet officials had stopped him travelling abroad.[37]

A year after Vlasov's TV revelations, the daily sports paper *Sovetsky sport* claimed that Oleg Solovyov, coach to Novosibirsk's top swimmers, had encouraged the use of anabolic steroids in training sessions.[38] Subsequently, following the Seoul Olympics and the Ben Johnson drug scandal, Ter-Ovanesyan, now the senior Soviet track and field coach, launched a well publicised campaign against drug taking in Soviet sport. Admitting that 'many of our athletes' take drugs, he mentioned that even several school athletes had been detected taking steroids: 'I think that society needs proper legislation to combat this evil, seriously punishing both doctors and athletes, coaches and drug suppliers.'[39]

The most sensational revelation on drugs came in mid-1989, with *Leninskoe znamya* admitting that some 290 athletes and coaches had been punished for using forbidden drugs in the three years prior to the Seoul 1988 Olympics.[40] Certainly no other country in the world has had anything like that number of positive drug tests registered; it is also probably the world's highest per capita figure.

Another stone overturned by investigative journalists is that of 'amateur' status. As the top Soviet swimmer, Vladimir Salnikov, revealed in *Argumenty i fakty* early in 1989, 'We have rid ourselves of hypocritical declarations about so-called amateurism and sporting achievements. Professionalism has been recognised and athletes no longer have to compromise themselves.'[41] It has to be said in parenthesis that the Soviet leadership (Stalin) only introduced 'state amateur status' into Soviet sport in the early 1950s, under pressure from the International Olympic Committee, as a ploy to join the Olympic movement (the USSR was admitted in May 1951). From then on the appearance had to be given that performers received no remuneration from their sports performance, nor did they devote themselves full-time to sport. The public, of course, knew differently, but it was part of the doublethink of the 1950–85 period never to mention it in public. Glasnost is drawing aside the veil. As a letter to the youth monthly *Yunost* has put it, 'We got used to living a double life because many of our idols did the same. We condemned professional sport in the West and were proud that our champions were amateurs. We took it for granted that they trained for six or seven hours each day after work or study. But everyone knew that most athletes never went to work or college, and that they only met their workmates or fellow students on pay day.'[42]

It is now officially admitted that top soccer players, for example, receive between 200 and 300 roubles a month for playing soccer and spend as many as 250 days annually in training.[43] Journalists have also broached other once censored topics, like the security service sponsorship of Dinamo and army officer sinecures for athletes sponsored by the armed forces.[44]

Under pressure, the sports establishment has talked of taking steps to make sports, especially soccer, clubs self-financing and officially to give all players of Master of Sport ranking and over what they have always had unofficially: professional status. This naturally follows the amendment to Olympic regulations that permits professional performers in the Games. By mid-1991, however, no firm decision on the latter issue had been taken, although several soccer clubs have become self-financing and openly professional. The first, Dnepr, not only became Soviet league champions in 1988, but made a handsome profit into the bargain. In the 1989 soccer season, three top clubs, Dinamo Kiev, Dinamo Tbilisi and Shakhtyor Donetsk, followed suit.[45] In cycling, a 14-strong team signed a contract in late 1988 with the San Marino aluminium firm Alfa Lum to form the first-ever professional Soviet cycling team under contract to a foreign company (with the USSR Sports Committee taking a third of their earnings).[46] Perhaps the greatest *volte face* in sporting principles is the entry of Soviet boxers and wrestlers into the professional ranks. The USSR Boxing Federation has signed a contract with North American promoters that will take 24 Soviet boxers to North American.[47] Similarly, eight heavyweight wrestlers are currently performing in Japanese professional rings.[48]

Fears are being voiced, nonetheless, that the encouragement of open professionalism might spoil the 'stars' even more than at present. It is nostalgically recalled that once upon a time Soviet athletes would go through fire to gain medals and glory for their country: 'That was before good mother Adidas fed them from her bountiful bosom, spoiled them with life on the foreign circuit or even overseas training. Today's athletes, however, are "scientifically programmed", rigged out in the latest fashions and packed full of home-produced "vitamins"; as a result, we have produced capricious idols and we don't know what to do with them.'[49]

In 1991 over a hundred Soviet soccer players were earning a living abroad.

MORALITY OF PROFESSIONAL SPORT

A logical extension of the debate on the future of Soviet sport is seriously to question the morality of top-class sport today. A number of articles in the press have 'only recently started to mention out loud the major problem (in sport) – deception, the rust that begins to corrode a child's innocent mind from that moment when the first mischievous thought clouds the pure joy of playing – that besides enjoying himself he can make something out of it.'[50]

This brings us to a basic question that was raised frequently in the 1920s, yet has rarely been aired since: what price is society prepared to pay for talent? Such fundamental (to a socialist society) questions are certainly being asked now. How wide should the gap in privileges be between the stars and the masses? Should a communist society encourage the formation of an elite based on the luck of nature's draw and thereby perpetuate original inequalities rather than properly compensating for the lottery of birth? Or as Yury Vlasov has put it, 'Who needs big-time sport? What is it that makes hundreds and thousands of healthy young people cast aside their studies and work? Why do state institutions spend such vast sums of money on top sport? Who needs those medals and records?'[51]

The following extract from *Ogonyok* also faces squarely up to the problem:

> From a youngster's first steps in sport he is accustomed to being a parasite, clandestinely assigned to miners, oilers or builders who generously repay his artless 'feints' with worldly goods of which miners, oilers or builders can only dream. City apartments, cars, overseas trips, a free and easy life by the seaside – how all that caresses youthful vanity, lifts him above the grey mass of those who have been waiting years for housing, phones and cars, and who have to pay for the seaside and the foreign trips out of their own pocket.[52]

Besides criticising perverted morality that such privileges engender, a number of Soviet writers have called into question the exploitation of children for the sake of sporting glory. A sports monthly has written of the 'strict regimentation and deprivation of many of childhood's joys, the numerous trips, lengthy training camps, hotel stays, separations from family and school . . . all this leads to moral impairment.'[53]

Yet when Vlasov complained of the 'inhuman forms of professionalism' involving 12- and 13-year old youngsters, especially in gymnastics and swimming, he was accused by Soviet coaches of 'undermining Soviet sport'. Disillusioned, he resigned his post as Chairman of the Weightlifting Federation and returned to writing fiction (and subsequently has become an outspoken MP).[54]

All the same, more and more critics are taking up the cudgels against early specialisation and intensive training of children at the age of five, six or seven, particularly after the publication of a study of children's sports schools in Kazan, showing that 'there was practically no difference between beginners and top athletes when it came to the number of intensive training sessions'.[55]

The mood of glasnost appears more to favour sport for all than special privileges for the gifted.

CONVERGENCE IN SPORT

Yet another consequence of the 'new thinking' seems to be the bringing closer of some facets of Soviet sport to those in the West; it is nonetheless a contradictory process that may have popular acclaim, yet at the same time lead Soviet sport further away from the new morality it seeks.

For a start, commercial sports (in a professional, commodity sense) like golf, baseball, Grand Prix, motor racing, even American football, have arrived in the USSR. Moscow had its first golf course (nine holes) in 1988, partly designed for the foreign diplomatic corps and partly intended to prepare Soviet challengers for international golf tournaments (60 teenagers are registered at the club's golf school).[56] The American billionaire Armand Hammer was planning a second golf course at Nakhabino, some 30 km from the centre of Moscow.[57] With an eye to the inclusion of baseball in the Olympic Games, the sports establishment has 'created' Soviet baseball clubs (just as it 'created' field hockey teams by fiat, in the early 1970s expressly for Olympic participation – again without any grassroots tradition); the first baseball league came into being in 1988, a year after the first national championship. By late 1988 there were 30 baseball clubs in the country and a special children's baseball school in Tashkent.

Following the holding of the first Grand Prix Formula 1 race in a communist country, Hungary, in 1988, the Soviet Union is now designing a world-class track. Even such a culture-specific sport as rugby league is being implanted into the country, with the first league championship launched with eight teams in 1991. The sport was already being taught in two dozen Moscow schools.[59] It was even planned to stage bullfighting in Moscow's Lenin Stadium, but public protest forced the organisers (the Komsomol) to cancel the show.[60]

The USSR Sports Committee and an American corporation agreed to stage a Dallas Cowboys v. Washington Redskins football game on 2 September 1989 'for the Glasnost Cup' (!), in order to promote the game in the USSR. The US sponsors were intending to fly in as many as 6,000 fans for the match.

To cap it all, the first dog (borzoi) races were held at Moscow's Ippodrom

Racecourse in the autumn of 1987. Largely as a concession to the public, horse racing in all forms (trotting, hurdling, steeplechasing and racing on the flat – with gambling on the state totalisator) has existed for most of the Soviet period, although up till now 'no mention of it had been made in the press, simply because it was not accepted practice'; nor has it ever featured on TV, despite the country's 3,000 racehorses and 17 annual race meetings.[62]

Other 'imports' and the resurfacing of old sports include snooker, darts, billiards (it is said that there are as many as 5,000 players[63]), the Chinese sport of wushu (martial arts) (52 cities are said to have wushu clubs with over 30,000 members[64]) and body building – the first international body building contest, watched by 16,000 spectators, was held in Moscow in late 1988, jointly sponsored by West Germany's Armstrong Company and the USSR Sports Service;[65] Soviet body buildings made their international debut at the world championship in spring 1989.[66]

Sponsorship, both foreign and domestic, has become a common feature in a range of sports, with soccer teams sporting the Dorna or the Ocrim Spa logo since the 1987–88 season.[67] So intense is the interest in gaining foreign sponsorship that 'the National Olympic Committee has set up a federation of sponsors to coordinate commercial activity in the interests of Soviet sport and of strengthening ties abroad.'[68]

Another innovation in Soviet sport, bringing it into line with Western (capitalist) practices, is to sell leading Soviet players to Western teams. Initially, in 1987, these were players of 30 or over, but the lure of dollars and the will of individual 'stars' seem to have reduced the age limit considerably, particularly in the major spectator sports like soccer, ice hockey and basketball. By mid-1989 as many as 27 leading ice hockey players were signed up for the North American NHL.[69] As an example of such a deal (in soccer), the national goalkeeper Renat Dasaev signed a $2 million contract for two years with the Spanish club Sevilla: the USSR Sports Commitee took 55 per cent of the proceeds, Dasaev's club Spartak took 40 per cent, and the Italian agents Dorna, which set up the deal, took 5 per cent.[70] The striker Zavarov, however, was sold to Juventus of Italy for $5 million and his former club Dinamo Kiev 'was able to become self-financing [i.e. openly professional] on the $2 million it gained from the transaction.'[71]

The thorny question of remuneration, especially when foreign currency is involved, has caused acrimonious debate. On one side, state officials claim that Soviet-trained 'stars' have a civic duty to devote the bulk of their foreign earnings to the benefit of Soviet sport generally.[72] On the other, as the top male tennis player, Andrei Chesnokov, has put it, he earns lucrative foreign currency on the world tennis circuit, yet is permitted only $25 *per diem* – 'not enough even to feed myself'.[73] In early 1989 Chesnokov's female partner Natalia Zvereva took the unprecedented step of retaining her prize money, refusing to compensate the USSR Sports Committee.

Some critics, including Zvereva and Chesnokov, accuse officials of wasting huge sums of money 'on trips abroad for Sports Committee bosses and their retinue, on officials who needlessly accompany teams and on translators who in most cases are not needed'[74] (but who in the past were often used to 'keep an eye' on athletes abroad and to report back to the KGB on returning home).

The Sports Committee is also accused of going 'on a hard currency spending spree when it badly wants the USSR to win'; at the Calgary Winter Olympics in 1988, for example, each Soviet gold medal winner 'received $5,000 no matter how strong the rivals were'.[75] For a gold medal at the Seoul Olympics in the same year, the Soviet Sports Minister admitted that Soviet recipients would gain 12,000 roubles (6,000 for silver and 4,000 for bronze medals); since the Soviet team won 55 gold medals and 132 medals overall, it cost the Sports Committee about a million roubles (part paid in dollars) in bonuses alone.[76]

In view of the admittance of some of the top professional basketball players to the Olympics, Soviet basketball teams have begun to play against top US professionals, and Soviet players have been sold to US teams. Furthermore, discussions were underway in early 1989 for a Soviet ice-hockey team to compete in the North American Ice Hockey League (for the Stanley Cup). Negotiations were also being held with a Canadian sponsor for Soviet boxers (24 were candidates) to box professionally in Western rings.

It may well be that the spirit of openness will soon persuade the sports leadership to accept open competition in all sporting contests, including the Olympics, and to declare all Soviet top-level athletes as practising professionals. It is now admitted that today some 90,000 Soviet athletes are full-time professionals.[77] Professionalisation may signify an end to bureaucratic interference in sport; it may also contribute to the independence and dignity of athletes, coaches, sports organisers and journalists (who no longer have to pretend professionals are amateurs). However, as the history of Western sport has shown, professionalism in sport represents a set of practices that can be every bit as pernicious and unhealthy as they may be liberating and healthy. In the Soviet Union today, no one – fans, officials, players, or journalists – wishes to see the Soviet domestic leagues become merely a farm system for the wealthiest clubs in Western Europe and North America.

Not everyone is happy at what they see as a race for irrational glory, as the cultivation of irrational loyalties, as unreasonable prominences given to the winning of sports victories, the setting of records and the collection of trophies – a fetishisation in sport. In fact, a feature of popular antipathy to the pre-Gorbachov 'stagnation' period is precisely reaction against the tub-thumping, flag-waving obsession with international sports success. As a writer in *Sobesednik* put it before the Seoul Olympics:

> International prestige may be important, but what is far more important is sport for all at home, the number of people the Olympic victories attract into sport and how we accommodate them. So don't let us spend too much time celebrating, we must look down from the Olympic heights upon the realities of the world around us.[78]

A political commentator in *Moscow News* suggested the Soviet press publish two tables: alongside that of Olympic medals should be a table showing the per capita provision of sports amenities for each nation. If that were done, 'we would be in a very different position'. He cited the example of artificial skating rinks: Canada had 10,000, the USA 1,500, Sweden 343 and the USSR just 102.[79] The swimmer Salnikov has contrasted the US total of a million swimming pools with the Soviet figure of 2,500.[80] As the *Moscow News* commentator concluded, 'Not long ago statistics were so "cleverly" compiled that it seemed the entire population went in for sport . . . Can't we see for ourselves that much more emphasis is being put on professional sport, on training record-breakers, champions, medal-winners than on sport for all?'[81] It is a contentious issue and one not unknown in other countries.

CONCLUSIONS

Today the inheritors of the sports system evolved during the Stalin, Khrushchev and Brezhnev years find themselves in a quandary: to what extent should they break with the past? How sharply and through what new forms should change be brought about? In the field of culture, and specifically of physical culture, how should they dismantle the various by now well entrenched fetishised institutions and values?

Today, in the disintegrating USSR, the old sports structure of army and KGB sponsorship, of state control and support (e.g. through the 40 sports boarding schools), of trade union grassroots and league organisation, is giving way to a new structure based on commercial, independent club and patronage principles. Further, the various ethnic groups are preferring their own independent teams to combined effort and success.

It is possible that Soviet and communist sport generally will become a hybrid of the worst of both worlds, retaining the bureaucracy, instrumentalism and authoritarianism of the old ways and adding only the exploitation and corruption of some forms of Western sport. The final result will not inspire admiration. Much the same could be said of the larger reform processes now under way in the Soviet Union and elsewhere in Eastern Europe. Sport may not play a key role in determining the fate of the reforms, but its ultimate shape should tell us much about the success and failure of the socialist experiment and the post-Soviet and post-socialist structure.

NOTES

1. See Ma Yihua, 'Friendship through golf', *China Sports*, 1988, No. 10, pp. 17–21; Z. Wubin, 'A rising sport in China', *China Sports*, 1985, No. 9, pp. 5–7.
2. See Xu Qi, 'Women's sports in China', *China Sports*, 1989, No. 3, pp. 2–15.
3. See Zhao Chongqi, 'Minority people's sports meet', *China Sports*, 1986, No. 3, pp. 33–5: China staged its first Minority People's Folk Games in Beijing from 8 September to 20 October 1985; it attracted some 3,000 participants from 30 ethnic groups.
4. For details of the 1985 *GTO* programme see J. Riordan, 'School Physical Education in the Soviet Union', *Physical Education Review*, 9, No. 2 (1986), pp. 100–7; for details of the influence of Scout athletics norms on the first *BGTO* (Budgotov k trudu i oborone – 'Be Prepared for Labour and Defence' – note the 'Be Prepared'), see J. Riordan, 'The Russian Boy Scouts', *History Today*, 38 (October 1988), pp. 48–52.
5. For a history of the Spartakiads see J. Riordan, *Sport in Soviet Society* (Cambridge: Cambridge University Press, 1977), pp. 248–53.
6. O. Dmitrieva, 'Bokal protiv detstvu', *Komsomolskaya pravda*, 8 June 1985, p. 2.
7. M. Kondratieva, 'Na uroke i v zhizni', *Molodoi kommunist*, 1986, No. 12, p. 74.
8. K. S. Kemirchyan, 'O zadachakh respublikanskoi partiinoi organizatsii', *Kommunist*, 25 September 1984, p. 2.
9. S. Belits-Gelman, 'Lipa ne tonet', *Ogonyok*, 1987, No. 4, p. 27.
10. See *Pravda*, 1 February 1988, p. 8.
11. Demirchyan, p. 2.
12. B. Novikov, 'Ne zabudut li oni kak khodit'?' *Sport v SSSR*, 1988, No. 3, p. 39.
13. Vladimir Balashov, 'Proizvodstvennaya gimnastika i proizvoditel'nost', *Sport v SSSR*, 1988, No. 7, p. 15.
14. 'Postanovlenie TsK KPSS i Soveta ministrov SSSR "O dalneishem podyome massovosti fizicheskoi kultury i sporta"', *Sovetsky sport*, 24 September 1981, p. 1.

15. The remainder of sports schools, roughly 3,400, are run by the Dinamo and armed forces sports clubs.
16. 'Novi kooperativnyi klub zdorovya', *Moskovskie novosti*, 1988, No. 7, p. 14.
17. New sports coop for Leningrad', *Soviet Weekly*, 7 May 1988, p. 14.
18. 'Public gets coop sport dividend', *Soviet Weekly*, 18 June 1988, p. 18.
19. 'Metreveli and co. open new tennis centres', *Soviet Weekly*, 22 October 1988, p. 16.
20. Balashov, p. 14.
21. Riordan, 'School physical education . . .'.
22. Alexander Anufriev, 'Pochemu ya ushol iz komsomola', *Sobesednik*, 1989, No. 17, p. 3.
23. For more details, see J. Riordan, 'Soviet youth: pioneers of change', *Soviet Studies*, XL, No. 4 (October 1988), p. 560.
24. Ibid., pp. 564–566.
25. R. Davletshina, 'Futbol i zhenshchiny', *Teoriya i praktika fizicheskoi kultury*, 1973, No. 10, p. 62.
26. V. Merkulov, 'Pressing on regardless', *Soviet Weekly*, 17 October 1987, p. 16.
27. 'Vosem, dvadtsat, pyatdesyat', *Sobesednik*, 1989, No. 7, p. 2.
28. V. Tsirlin, 'Vodnoe polo dlya zhenshchin', *Sport v SSSR*, 1986, No. 8, p. 45.
29. 'Krasavitsa vilnyanka-88', *Sobesednik*, 1988, No. 18, p. 6.
30. Merkulov.
31. V. Ponomareva, 'Yeshcho odna pobeda', *Sobesednik*, 1987, No. 37 (September), p. 12.
32. Ibid.
33. S. Shenkman, 'Disabled Sport: An End to Bleeding Hearts', *Soviet Weekly*, 11 June 1988, p. 16. See also *Sport v SSSR*, 1988, No. 5, pp. 50–2.
34. For example, a Russian troika championship was held in Krasnodar in 1986, and new emphasis has been given to the folk games of Siberian peoples in the annual Sports Festival of Peoples of the Far North (see *Soviet Weekly*, 6 September 1986, p. 11 and 1 November 1986, p. 14).
35. S. Tokarev, 'Ne proigral by chelovek', *Ogonyok*, 1987, No. 9, p. 20.
36. A. Klaz, 'Rekordy po retseptu?', *Smena*, 4 May 1988, p. 3. See also Yury Vlasov, 'Drugs and cruelty', *Moscow News*, 1988, No. 37, p. 15.
37. Vlasov.
38. Klaz.
39. Igor Ter-Ovanesyan, 'I declare war on anabolics!', *Moscow News*, 1988.
40. Vasilii Gromyko, 'Nash styd', *Leninskoe znamya*, 28 March 1989, p. 2.
41. Vladimir Salnikov, 'Vremya nadozhd', *Argumenty i fakty*, 1989, No. 1, p. 3.
42. A. Novikov, 'Pismo redaktsii', *Yunost*, 1988, No. 6, p. 9.
43. 'Skolko poluchaet futbolist?' *Moskovskie novosti*, 1988, No. 10, p. 15.
44. O. Petrichenko, 'Ne sotvori sebe kumira', *Ogonyok*, March 1987, No. 12, p. 15. In all countries with Dinamo clubs (from Albania to Yugoslavia, the GDR to the USSR) the governing body providing finance and ultimate control is the Ministry for Internal Affairs (several other countries – notably Poland, Hungary and Romania – give such clubs a 'domestic' name): see Riordan, *Sport in Soviet Society*, pp. 292–5.
45. Igor Oransky, 'Ne bogi gorshki obzhigayut . . .' *Moskovskii komsomolets*, 28 February 1989, p. 3.

46.   M. Shlaev, 'Pervaya sovetskaya professionalnaya komanda', *Moskovskie novosti*, 1988, No. 50, p. 15; W. Fotheringham, 'Russian pros ready for taste of the big time', *Cycling Weekly*, 2 February 1989, pp. 8–9.

47.   Mark Vodovozov, 'Borba na ringe', *Moskovskie novosti*, 15 January 1989, No. 3, p. 15.

48.   Oransky.

49.   Petrichenko.

50.   Petrichenko.

51.   See Timur Absalyamov, 'Komu on nuzhen, etot sport?', *Sobesednik*, 1989, No. 7 (February), p. 11.

52.   Petrichenko.

53.   L. Kedrov, 'Sport v vozraste 6 let: za i protiv', *Sport v SSSR*, 1987, No. 6, p. 27.

54.   Vlasov.

55.   Kedrov.

56.   'Golf i Tumba', *Nedelya*, 1987, No. 41 (18 September), p. 13; 'Moscow's first golf club gets into the swing of things', *Soviet Weekly*, 27 November 1988, p. 16.

57.   Ibid.

58.   A. Bezruchenko, 'Soviet baseball moves on from first base', *Soviet Weekly*, 30 April 1988, p. 14.

59.   Derek Kotz, 'Up-and-under running', *Soviet Weekly*, 7, March 1991, p. 15.

60.   'The corrida is coming to Moscow', *Soviet Weekly*, 6, June 1990, p. 16.

61.   Yelena Zubova, 'Amerikanskii "desant" na stadion "Dinamo"', *Moskovskii komsomolets*, 28 February 1989, p. 4.

62.   O. Dun, 'They're off!', *Soviet Weekly*, 30 April 1988, p. 14.

63.   Mikhail Shakhov, 'Shar – v luzhu!', *Moskovskie novosti*, 15 January 1989, No. 3, p. 15.

64.   Vladimir Kirilluk, 'Ushu', *Sobesednik*, 1988, No. 46 (November), p. 16.

65.   Oransky.

66.   'Sovetskii kulturizm', *Molodoi kommunist*, 1989, No. 4, p. 63.

67.   'Sweet smell of sports sponsorship', *Soviet Weekly*, 26 November 1988, p. 16.

68.   Ibid.

69.   'Khokkeisty zhdut razresheniya . . .', *Sovetskii sport*, 29 April 1989, p. 4.

70.   'Dasayev goes to Sevilla', *Soviet Weekly*, 5 November 1988, p. 16.

71.   Vladimir Kirilluk, 'Enter the new sports supporters', *Soviet Weekly*, 6 May 1989, p. 16.

72.   B. Geskin, 'Emotsii i banknoty', *Sovetsky sport*, 28 August 1988, p. 1.

73.   V. Dvortsov, 'Skolko nashi "zvyozdy" dolzhny poluchat?', *Moskovskie novosti*, May 1988, No. 19, p. 15.

74.   Geskin, p. 1.

75.   S. Petrov, 'Skolko stoit olimpiiskaya komanda', *Moskovskie novosti*, 1988, No. 39, p. 15.

76.   D. Rennick, 'Soviet Olympians compete for pre-set quota of medals', *The Korea Herald*, 27 September 1988, p. 9. The author (JR) heard the Sports Ministers' words at a news conference in Seoul just prior to the opening of the 1988 Summer Olympic Games.

77. 'Professional backup still required', *Soviet Weekly*, 30 September 1989, p. 16.
78. Anatoly Isaev, 'Lomtik olimpiiskovo piroga', *Sobesednik*, 1989, No. 2 (January), p. 12.
79. A. Druzenko, 'Olimpiiskaya slava', *Moskovskie novosti*, November 1988, p. 15.
80. Salnikov. Another author makes the point that the USSR has one swimming pool for 115,000 people, West Germany and Japan have one pool for 3–4,000 people, Hungary and Czechoslovakia have one for every 10–15,000 people. Alexander Churkin, 'Melko plavaem', *Moskovskie novosti*, 15 January 1989, No. 3, p. 15.
81. Druzenko.

12 The Changing Face of Soviet Sport

The Mafia and American Football*
Dmitri Radyshevsky

I recently noticed a newspaper report about a match between two teams formed to play American football – the Moscow Bruins and the Sverdlovsk Federals. I recalled that item when I found myself sitting by chance at the same cafe table as four 'Schwarzeneggers' from the Moscow Bruins. Out of professional curiosity I asked them about the game and was amazed at their responses.

'Why did we take up American football? Very simple. We knew some guys in Lubertsy who used to run a protection racket, taking extortion money from co-op owners; they decided to invest their cash in a money-making project. So they took us on, hired a coach in the USA and bought gear from West Germany. Then they rented a gym, swimming pool and cafeteria, and signed up two doctors.'

The football players admitted that some of them were former boxers, wrestlers and karate experts; the rest were ex-thieves. They claimed that the system had pushed them into crime, but that football gave them a chance to make honest money. I asked how much they were paid. One said 500 roubles a month. All of them laughed.

'Well, let's say six, seven hundred . . . Bonuses bring us up to about ten times the average earnings, with hard currency on top.'

I asked whether they made more money playing football than they would have done as protection 'heavies'.

'Ah, but they can't travel round the world. We've already played in the States, and we've been promised trips to Taiwan, Japan and France. Anyway, co-ops are here today, gone tomorrow. Football's here to stay.'

I asked about injury risk.

'You take your choice: break your back for 140 roubles a month or do the same for ten times that amount. Whatever you do involves risk – playing

*From *Moscow News*, No. 8, 20–26 July 1990, p. 5.

football or "leaning on" co-op owners. In any case, most of the players are ex-convicts.'

I wondered how many enthusiasts were willing to join them.

'Heaps. But most quit straightaway. We put them on the turf and rough them up a bit. When someone like me, 150 kilos, hits you, it takes a lot of nerve to stand your ground. You've got to be to tough to make it.'

The formal part of our conversation ended there. Enlivened by booze, the Bruins turned to other customers in the cafe, bending coins, juggling with weights. I was left with my thoughts.

First, our country is putting a new commodity on to the world market. As one of the Bruins put it: 'We're going to play in France. But if we don't get a contract we'll go back to the protection racket; there's plenty of work for thirty "heavies" like us.'

Second, we now know one way in which the mafia launders its money.

Third and most important, hard currency has succeeded in doing what 70 years of Soviet education has failed to do: make good guys out of bad. They've thrown away their brass knuckles and left the hippies and co-ops in peace, and now they've taken up American football. (I only hope it isn't ruined by becoming a mass sport!)

The American dream has come true in Lubertsy! I'm delighted for you guys, honest. I wish you luck. Play on. Break your bones if the fans are prepared to pay for the spectacle. Buy yourself a Mercedes in Toronto instead of at Moscow's used car mart.

And one last thing. Teach our politicians to launder their ill-gotten gains as profitably as you have. If they bring in some hard currency they'll finally have done the country some good. And until they drive you back into racketeering, enjoy life on the right side of the law.

The Blinding Gleam of Medals*
Ivan Isayev

The changes in the country have touched on all aspects of our life, including sport. But deep-going perestroika, as many respected coaches and athletes affirm, is slow to make headway. It is desperately hard to alter radically the entrenched schemes and instructions which prevent Soviet sport from normal development.

*From *Molodoi kommunist*, No. 5, 1989, pp. 72–7.

I well appreciate that such words will not be welcome to some of our sports leaders, especially now, after the dazzling team victories at the Calgary and Seoul Olympic Games. Yet that is just what makes the present so different from the not-so-distant past: even triumphant fanfares cannot silence coaches and athletes themselves from speaking out about the multi-fold problems or, rather, the long-existing deficiencies in our sport which we scarcely had courage to mention hitherto. There is certainly plenty to talk about.

An odd situation exists today when we beat the USA and East Germany in Olympic gold medals, yet lose hands down when it comes to sports halls, swimming pools, recreation centres. To mention just one figure: the USA has a thousand times more swimming pools per million inhabitants than the USSR!

When and why did such a colossal chasm open? How could it happen that even the young war-racked Soviet Republic of the 1920s and 1930s showed such enthusiasm for sport and building sports centres, whereas in the 1950s and 1960s when our economy was so much stronger and the country stood firmly on its feet our leaders began to pay less and less attention to mass sport so that, in the end, it is no exaggeration to say that the country is in a pitiful state?

It was in the 1950s and 1960s that the USSR made its wide-ranging international sporting debut. It was then that we were seduced by glittering and unequivocal sports victories into trying to demonstrate to the whole world the advantages of our socialist system. Here is what Andrei Karpov, Merited Coach of the USSR and Merited Master of Sport in skiing, has to say:

We had prepared a good team for the world championships in 1952. I was called into the Sports Committee and asked to give a guarantee we would win the championship. How on earth could I, especially when our skiers had never performed internationally? In any case, we all knew very well what might happen if we failed to honour a pledge – we realised where the demand for such invariable victories came from. So I said I could give no cast-iron guarantee. I was therefore told we would not go. It was as simple as that. So we never did get to the world championship.

We don't have to go back so far. Only recently our journalists and TV commentators would illumine any sports contest by scrupulously counting up the number of medals and points gained by representatives of the socialist and capitalist camps; and if the socialist countries managed to win more 'gold' the commentators immediately concluded that our sports system had the edge by its mass and democratic nature.

The dazzling victories of our 'stars' required more and more financial injections every year. Where was the USSR State Sports Committee to get the funds? It cut the budget for mass sport for which it never had to answer seriously to anyone. An Olympic 'gold' was there for all to see! The sports functionaries were prepared to fight for that to the bitter end, offering more and more victims up on the altar of big-time sport.

No one is surprised any more at the ridiculous picture of a factory with poor sports facilities supporting a greedy 'cuckoo' in its nest in the shape of a soccer or ice hockey team. Further, it was this 'cuckoo' that normally had first claim on even the modest sports resources that existed. Meanwhile the ordinary worker had nowhere to play, nowhere to swim . . . The funds assigned for promoting sport for all were diverted into maintaining such teams of 'masters'. And the law of redistribution worked like clockwork in the last two decades.

Mass or, as it is better known, amateur, sport in the West gets its funds separately from professional sport. For a modest payment, which even the most underprivileged sections of the public can afford, anyone can engage in a sport in advanced capitalist countries. (I exclude such exotic sports as flights into the stratosphere.) Sometimes money earned by professionals is used to promote mass sport; but the opposite is never the case. In other words, 'their' professional sport gets its money from advertising, sponsors, income from TV, ticket sales etc. If a sport is able to 'feed' itself – attract spectators and therefore sponsors, advertising and television – it exists and operates as a professional concern. If not, then no one will invest cash in a loss-making business. That is why the world has so few professional sports: soccer, ice hockey, chess, tennis, basketball, baseball, boxing, cycling, car racing, and some regional sports (like American football in the USA or sumo wrestling in Japan). As for skating or skiing, they are semi-professional sports. In the West a Graeco-Roman wrestler or weightlifter has first to find funding or gain a grant from the national team to be able to train full-time. Otherwise he'll have to earn his living and train in his spare time. That's why athletes from socialist states have dominated sports like rowing, weightlifting and wrestling, since they come up against true amateurs.

But it is time to cost out those victories.

It was not so long ago that we categorically refuted the principle of putting our sport on a self-financing basis. It was 'over there' that you could 'sell' players and turn athletes into 'bill boards'. We safeguarded the honour and dignity of our citizens; it was the state, or, rather, you and I, that financed sports development. However, it was the USSR Sports Committee that ran sports, and our health only interested it to a minimum extent (it was hardly worth expecting medals from you or me); it had no shame in dipping its hand into our pockets to gain its medals, thereby depriving us of sports centres and swimming pools, recreational facilities and gymnasiums.

But now the ice has begun to move, as the saying goes. We are signing contracts with foreign clubs (. . . by the way, have you noticed they are 'selling' and we are delicately 'signing contracts'. . .) using ads to earn roubles and dollars. And here we have the Sports Committee reporting that now Soviet sport is self-financing, it isn't taking a kopeck from state pockets; on the contrary, it is putting foreign earnings into the state budget. Marvellous, but why aren't these joyful reports bringing us more pools and gyms?

It would be naive to expect gyms and pools to appear overnight, but it would be nice to have a guarantee that they will be built in sufficient numbers tomorrow.

What has to be done? A perfectly logical answer would be once and for all to partition the financing of mass sport off from so-called high-attainment sport. Since you and I are paying for mass sport (in the form of income tax and various employee's contributions) we should get something back. Let 'elite' sport fund itself. Let us finally pay honest money to soccer players who entertain us and let them become professionals. And let the amateurs (archers, scullers, fencers) work like everyone else; if they want to do a sport they'll have to do so in their spare time. The sports movement has to be run on healthy economic lines. Then we shall be able to compete honestly and on equal terms with foreign athletes – with both professionals and amateurs.

What happens at the moment is that within top-class sport there is a very obvious process of transferring funds from one sport to another. Do you really think we pay due respect to the chess, soccer, ice hockey and tennis stars who provide a cash flow for the Sports Committee? Nothing of the sort! According to senior coaches of the Soviet hockey, soccer and tennis teams, Tikhonov, Lobanovsky and Tarnishchev, the material facilities for the sports are at stone age level! Although their players make a lot of money, the country woefully lacks ice rinks, soccer pitches and tennis courts. That is because the Sports Committee does what no one else in the world does: to even things up, it shifts money from the full to the empty pocket, thereby promoting some sports at the expense of others. You know the situation. That is how our industrial ministries maintain unprofitable plants at the expense of the profitable ones, killing off all the initiative and desire to work.

Perhaps someone will ask why the Sports Committee needs all this complicated machinery. It is all very simple. Just as with the industrial ministries where the chief indicator is the notorious output plan or percentage, so in sport the main indicator of the sports department's work is the plan, the percentage, the medals. And to win the medals we shamelessly plunder the really popular, and therefore profitable, sports and ruin mass sport. Nobody cares.

Last August the government, trade unions and Komsomol jointly adopted a resolution on improving the administration of soccer and other team games, and additional measures to supervise the maintenance of teams and athletes in the major sports. The resolution envisaged a USSR Soccer Union – the first association of professional athletes in the country. Vyacheslav Koloskov, chairman of the bureau for arranging the Union's founding conference and head of the Sports Committee's Soccer and Ice Hockey Board, said they would take account of the experience of British, German, Italian and French unions when establishing the new organisation. Then experts would prepare a draft constitution for the new union which would be published within two months of the founding meeting. Koloskov insisted that the union would operate independently.

True, 'interested parties' were sent the draft constitution which, after some minor amendments, could well have become the new soccer code. However, two and a half weeks before the conference met (instead of the promised two months for discussion), the daily *Soviet Sport* published a completely different draft which, in many people's view, was a step backwards by contrast with the first draft and even with the long-established charter of the USSR Soccer Federation. There was no mention of either the financial or organisational independence of the union; in any case there was no time to discuss the new, 'official' version. Koloskov and the Sports Committee had performed a crafty sleight of hand. And in times gone by they would probably have got away with it. They would have whispered in the corridors, diverted attention from the published draft – and adopted it. But times really are changing, and the reaction of conference delegates was quite unexpected.

Victor Lobanovsky, Senior Coach of Kiev Dinamo and ex-coach of the USSR soccer team:

The constitution is so vacuous that it isn't worth discussing. The Sports Committee-manufactured document leaves the soccer union no right to any uninhibited administrative or economic independence, which must be the principal condition for any normal operation. We cannot talk seriously on the basis of the draft before us.

Nikolai Starostin, Chief Officer of Moscow Spartak:

I read the draft that was published. Today I was given a draft made in Kiev. (NB the 'Lobanovsky team' had brought to Moscow a different version of the draft.) I believe that the draft rules from Kiev are more appropriate for a soccer union in that they ensure it a certain autonomy and, at the same time, will keep on the Federation for administering mass, school and college soccer.

Victor Artemiev, Chairman of the Moscow Soccer Federation:

Unfortunately the draft was drawn up by officials and bureaucrats. Logically, the soccer federation should take over from the Sports Committee all powers in running Soviet soccer. But what bureaucrats will voluntarily surrender power? They are asking us to change the label and keep the contents as before.

So there we have it. At last, they key word has emerged – 'power'. The Sports Committee has no intention of giving up soccer administration; soccer is the most popular and therefore most profitable sport. The Committee envisaged the soccer union being an association of professional coaches, players, referees and experts. But what it was trying to do was to substitute one draft for another at the last moment, so that there would be no time for public discussion, and it would deprive the future union of financial, legal and organisational independence, turning it into an appendage of the Sports Committee.

In the end, the conference agreed to set up a soccer union, but to reject the published rules and regulations as unsuitable even as a discussion document. It agreed to establish a commission headed by Victor Artemiev to draw up a new draft with account for the conference proposals.

Did we win the first round? Rather it ended in a draw, with soccer experts on one side of the barricades, and soccer administrators on the other.

I have gone into some detail on the soccer union because the case vividly demonstrates the position of the USSR Sports Committee. Sports administrators fully realise that if they permit soccer players to get together in an independent organisation they would set a precedent. Subsequently, tennis, chess, basketball and ice hockey players would all be agitating for their own autonomous unions . . . And the Sports Committee would lose its main source of finance; it would be left to run mass sport and the authentic amateur sports. It would forfeit the illusion of its being part of the public's favourite sports. Amateur sports just do not have the same kudos. The

Sports Committee would inevitably lose prestige and all that goes with it. It would have no choice but to look after mass sport, and that would mean bidding farewell to foreign trips and bathing in the world spotlight.

The Sports Committee is currently involved in signing more and more contracts with foreign soccer, basketball and other professional clubs. In itself this process is useful, but it tends to work in one direction and harbours the danger of us gradually becoming a sporting backwater, rather like South American soccer clubs that supply Europe with their stars. We all know that if Maradona, for example, had had the chance to earn millions in his homeland rather than in Italy he would probably have not left Argentina. It is no secret that our own stars are lured to Europe by the chance to make money. Perhaps the answer is that we have to learn to pay our stars ourselves.

Nowadays the main bone of contention, however, is who is to have power over Soviet sport: professional experts or the sports department with its huge staff of officials and its administrative-command system of running things. More and more we are talking of the need to set up professional sports unions: for chess, soccer and tennis players. Let us say openly and honestly: the establishment of such unions (as long as they become genuinely independent) impinges on the power of the Sports Committee to influence sports affairs. And let us admit just as candidly: the USSR Sports Committee will not concede power voluntarily – it makes no bones about that.

So we have a conflict. Probably the Sports Committee will become more flexible and start to manoeuvre, as it did over the soccer union. But we must be tough and consistent, and stick to our guns.

Index

192